Journalism/Communications Arts I

Mass Media

AND

Society

Study Guide/Workbook

FIFTH EDITION

J. Michael Reed
reedsmassmedia.wordpress.com

Saddleback College

Kendall Hunt publishing company

www.kendallhunt.com
Send all inquiries to:
4050 Westmark Drive
Dubuque, IA 52004-1840

Contents

Mass Media and Society
Study Guide and Workbook
Introduction

This book is meant to serve as a supplement to a mass media text. It emphasizes information that is deemed essential for transfer students to any four-year college or university as a communications/journalism major. However, much of the information has been deemed essential no matter what major a student might select. The content of this study guide is based on more than 30 years of college-level research, teaching experience, and feedback from students.

It is organized in a way that gives students the essentials for media debate and critique. The emphasis is on keeping the information relatively simple with an eye toward certain student learning outcomes. Sections on critical thinking skills and strategies along with an appendix with department goals and course term project assignments are included.

The book's uses student-transfer data and feedback to make sure that students leave the course actually "knowing" certain basic concepts, theories, history, court cases, and ethical issues and standards that will put them in the forefront of their four-year college or university classes.

Constant feedback from former students who have transferred to four-year institutions has been greatly facilitated by the "new media" i.e., Facebook, Twitter, Instagram. This fifth edition features the addition of outside resources like a mass media blog and several links to give students greater and faster access to important elements related to their general education.

Please enjoy!
J. Michael Reed

Chapter 1
Setting the Academic Agenda

This course should be one of the most interesting and fun courses you will take the first two years of college. Every day you live the content of this course. How many hours of television have you watched this week? How many hours have you watched to this point in your life? What impact do you feel television has had on your life? What impact do computers and the Internet have on your life? How have smart phones impacted your life and the lives of your friends? How much time do you spend reading, listening to music? Do you create or download your own music? What impact do the lyrics to songs have on your life? Have you seen a movie in the last couple of weeks? Do you listen to the radio in your car? How do all of these media influence the values and beliefs of Americans and, for that matter, world culture?

Really, you may know as much about the content of this course as your instructor. The instructor will introduce you to the language of media and encourage you to think about the impact of media in a more academic way. You will become students of the media and not just consumers.

Terms
Communication process:
Messages: source-message-receiver
encoders-channel-decoders
Receivers: Large groups, sometimes world-wide, anonymous, heterogeneous groups.

Blocks to the communication process:
Channel noise: The channel has been interrupted. This may include but not limited to static on radio, cable going out, typo or other errors in books, newspapers. Find other examples.
Semantic noise: language differences.
Feedback: In our economic system, most of the media is profit driven. Advertisers buy a stake in the messages sent out with the idea they will reap the economic benefits.
Let's think about some areas of media feedback that will help us in our discussion of the impact of media on society. Search your media outlets for Nielsen ratings each week. What books are on the NYTimes best seller list? Take note of the Billboard top hits, box office rating for movies, sales of cars, clothes, beer as a result of an advertising campaign. Check for hits on a blog or website. More…

More... List examples

All semester we will be using the terms demographics and psychographics in our discussion of the impact of media in our society.

Demographics: Readily measurable characteristics of audiences such as age, sex, race, income, and level of education.

Psychographics: Internal characteristics of audiences such as values, needs, beliefs, interests, and attitudes.

We can do a demographic survey of our class. Let's think about what we value. What about what we need? What do we believe and what influences our beliefs? What are our attitudes about certain issues? How do we establish attitudes? What influences the way we look at each other and the world? What is the impact of words and images in the media on our life?

Media Segmentation: The proliferation of newspapers, magazines, TV and cable stations, Internet, DVDs, CDs, and more give consumers many more choices and makes it hard for any one media to dominate the market.

Media Convergence: Large corporations that are content providers buy up more of the means to distribute and control that content. Large media mergers can give large corporations the ability to control content in a way never seen before.

PQ and CQ: Passion Quotient/Curiosity quotient.
Thomas L. Friedman, The World Is Flat 2.0, a **MUST** read for college students.

What will you do to make sure you are able to compete for a job with students around the globe? Many job seekers in other countries may be willing to work twice as hard for less pay.

High Tech/High Touch: The more technologically advanced we become, the more we yearn for the human touch. Example: Movie theaters vs. Home DVD or Netflix.

Models for your consideration

$—Power (education, knowledge)
Words—Images-Thought-Action
Power of the media

Study Guide Questions

How many hours a week do you read? (print media, magazines, newspapers, textbooks, etc.) Do you access news on your smart phone or other devices?
How many hours a week do you spend online?

     Reading news: (Online, via cell phone, TV)
     (Recommended online news source: AP (app)
     Associated Press for your smartphones or tablets.
     Gives news alerts to your home page.
     Facebook:
     Instagram
     Email:
     YouTube:
     Playing games:
     Doing research for classes:
     Other:

Have you or do you gamble online? Should online gambling be legal?

How much television do you watch on an average day?

What are your favorite programs and why?

How much time do you spend listening to a radio? Favorite programs or stations?

How much time do you spend on your smart phone each day?

How much time, on average, do you spend listening to MP3 player?

Do you watch TV programs on your MP3 player? If so which programs?

How many movies do you watch in a month? Favorite genre of movie?

List three things you value most:

List any strong beliefs:

List your main needs in life:

What are your main interests?

Do you think advertisers, movie producers, television producers, and other media gatekeepers are interested in the above items you listed? Why?

Student Notes

Chapter 2
Media Effects/Theory

The course title is Mass Media and Society, so it is important to include a general survey of a few of the theories about the impact of media on society. These theories include but are not limited to those listed here. Each will be briefly reviewed and discussed in class lecture. Please review your course text to prepare for discussion on these and other related theories.

Media theory deals with the process of media communication. Discussions will include why and how people receive and interpret these messages. How do people use these messages and what are the psychological, social, and cultural effects of these mass produced messages?

Media Functions: Inform, persuade, entertain, and transmit culture. Other terms used to describe functions that will be used in class: surveillance, interpretation, correlation, linkage, and more.

Process: Source (encoder)—message (channel)—receivers (decoder)

Terms

1. **Cognitive Needs:** Human needs to gain knowledge and understanding.
2. **Affective Needs:** Human needs for aesthetic, pleasurable, and emotional experiences.

Other needs discussed under the psychographic function of media could include our need to strengthen and evaluate values related to family, friends, our country, the world.

Through the entertainment function, needs related to escape, tension, release, and diversion may be addressed. Other functions will be discussed in later sections related to the theories and philosophies of Abraham Maslow and others.

Harold Lasswell, communication theorist, helped frame this issue:

"Who says what, to whom, through what channel, with what effect."

Direct Effects Theory (Bullet Theory): Propaganda and advertising campaigns can be very effective. Powerful messages in movie and television programming have strong impacts on society.

Individual Differences/Limited Effects Theory: Individual's values, needs, beliefs, and attitudes play a major role.

Social Learning Theory/Observed Learning and Modeling Theory: We learn from observing and modeling in the media and from direct experience as well.

Cultivation Theory: Television is partially responsible for shaping or "cultivating" a viewer's understanding of social reality.

Agenda Setting Theory: News influences our perception of the world.

> *FOX News*: Jan 18, 2006, 3:20 p.m.
> Setting the agenda for a U.S. attack on Iran that included maps of targets, weapons, and ordinance to be used. Brit Hume, "news" anchor or commentator? Magazines that set the agenda for debate on fashion, design, diet, and more.

Theories for further research and your consideration: Play theory, expectancy theories.

Topics for Discussion

Effects of advertising on children: What do you think?
Do ads for children's programs blur the line between program content and advertising?

Effects of violence in the media: Violence /conflict/human drama—Violence embodies conflict and conflict is the heart and soul of drama. There are many different levels of conflict. When does it rise to the level of violence? What do you think?

What is the impact of video game violence? Go to http://www.cbsnews.com/60-minutes/ and search for segments they have produced related to video game violence.

Desensitization: Repeated exposure to media violence causes a reduction in emotional response. How does this affect our feeling regarding news reports on war fronts?
Daily there are headlines in the media outlets about bombings and loss of life, not to mention the many maimed or injured in Iraq, Afghanistan, Syria, Libya, Egypt, and so on.
Fox News ALERT! ALERT! ALERT! Repeated for so many stories just to keep us on "Alert" and watching the network. The network had to come up with another word when something really terrible happens: Fox News URGENT. (Killings at the Virginia Naval Yard 2013)

Effects of sexually explicit materials on society: What do you think?
Online pornography may be affecting marital relationships.

Effects of underrepresentation or misrepresentation of minorities in the media:
What do you think?

Justice by television: Do you think people judge people by what is reported in the news rather than in the courts? Most of the morning talk shows host people involved in legal issues and then the networks have their own "legal experts", tell you how the case will evolve and be resolved. How does this information affect 6th Amendment rights?

Politics by television: Do you feel political ads should be more regulated?
Can you really believe what you are exposed to in most political ads or should you do some more research to get the facts?

The impact of Internet gambling on society: What do you think? Should gambling online be legal in the United States?

The impact of online pornography on society: What do you think the impact is and where would you draw the line? Go to 60 Mins.com and do a search for programs they have done on the impact of sexually explicit material on society.

The impact of smart phone technology on society:
Your class can write the results of this impact.

Polarization of America: What is the media's role?
Do the media love the "red" states and the "blue" states? Do the media like conflict? Do they like to frame issues as black and white? Does that make debate on important issues easier for most Americans to understand?
Young v Old
Minority v White
Secular v Religious
Liberal v Conservative
Urban v Rural

As you view "news" on the television networks, see how many times the news anchor asks during an interview, for a RESPONSE or a REACTION. Is there a difference?

Define acculturation:

Chapter 3
Yes! The Very Basics

We, the people of the United States, in order to form a more perfect union, establish justice, insure domestic tranquility, provide for the common defense, promote the general welfare, and secure the blessings of liberty to ourselves and our posterity, do ordain and establish this Constitution of the United States of America.

The Constitution established three estates of power.

Legislative

Legislates. Makes the laws under which *WE THE PEOPLE* live.

U.S. Congress:
- House of Representatives
- Senate

Executive

Executes the laws. President of the United States and his or her staff.

The oath to be taken by the president upon first entering office is specified in Article II, Section 1 of the U.S. Constitution:

*"I do solemnly swear (or affirm) that I will faithfully execute the office of President of the United States, and will to the best of my ability, preserve, protect, and defend the **Constitution** of the United States."*

Judicial

Determines if the laws are in keeping with our National Constitution.

Estates of Power: Legislative, executive, judicial, press, lobbyists.

First Amendment to the U.S. Constitution

CONGRESS SHALL MAKE NO LAW respecting an establishment of religion, or prohibiting the free exercise thereof; or abridging the freedom of speech, or of the press; or the right of the people peaceably to assemble, and to petition the government for a redress of grievances.

There were four basic freedoms that the former colonists wanted guaranteed before they would sign on to this new federal government. A fifth implicit freedom guaranteed here was "the public's right to know."

Many citizens feel that the First Amendment to the Constitution established a fourth power block: the **media.**

A case can be made that lobbyists now represent another major power block in our government, a potential fifth estate if you will.

The media, empowered by the First Amendment, acts as a check and balance for all the other power blocks.

Resource: *Miracle at Philadelphia* by Catherine Drinker Bowen.
From a meeting at the Pennsylvania State House in 1787 to the ratification of the document, the making of the U.S. Constitution was a true "miracle" of history. Among the 55 delegates to the constitutional convention were: George Washington, James Madison, Alexander Hamilton, Ben Franklin and Patrick Henry. Twelve delegates stayed in Philadelphia through that first summer.

Fourth Amendment to the U.S. Constitution

The right of the people to be secure in their persons, houses, papers, and effects, against unreasonable searches and seizures, shall not be violated, and no warrants shall issue, but upon probable cause, supported by Oath or affirmation, and particularly describing the place to be searched, and the persons or things to be seized.

Sixth Amendment to the U.S. Constitution

In all criminal prosecutions, the accused shall enjoy the right to a speedy and public trial, by an IMPARTIAL (emphasis author's) jury of the state and district wherein the crime shall have been committed, which district shall have been previously ascertained by law, and to be informed of the nature and cause of the accusation; to be confronted with the witnesses against him; to have compulsory process for obtaining witnesses in his favor, and to have the assistance of counsel for his defense.

Fourteenth Amendment to the U.S. Constitution
(Ratified July 9, 1868)

Section 1 of 5. All persons born or naturalized in the United States and subject to the jurisdiction thereof are citizens of the United States and of the state wherein they reside.

No State shall make or enforce any law which shall abridge the privileges or immunities of citizens of the United States; nor shall any state deprive any person of life, liberty, or property, without due process of law; nor deny to any person within its jurisdiction the equal protection of the laws.

Four Theories of the Press

How shall information be disseminated in a society?

Authoritarian: Private ownership of the means to disseminate. Government uses techniques such as licensing and taxation to monitor and control the media.
Plato (c. 427–347 B.C.E) said that even an enlightened society must be supervised by the wisest and strongest, i.e., rule by the educated, rich, and powerful. Niccoló Machiavelli's *The Prince* (1513) argues that the ends justify the means.
1712, The Stamp Act

Sedition: Criticism of the state

Totalitarian: The government owns the presses.

Libertarian: John Stuart Mill, *On Liberty* (1859), "right of mature individuals to think and act as they please so long as they do not hurt someone else." Introduced the idea of *utilitarianism* or the greatest happiness for the greatest number of people.

John Milton (1644), "Let all with something to say be free to express themselves. Let truth and falsehood grapple; whoever knew truth to be worse in a free and open encounter…though all the winds of doctrine were let loose to play upon the earth, so truth be in the field, we do injuriously by licensing and prohibiting, to misdoubt her strength," from a speech "Appeal for the Liberty of Unlicensed Printing." (*Areopagitica*)

President Thomas Jefferson:

> *"The basis of our government being the opinion of the people, the very first object should be to keep that right; and were it left to me to decide whether we should have a government without newspapers, or newspapers without a government, I should not hesitate a moment to prefer the latter."*

Social Responsibility: 1940s Commission on Freedom of the Press, a socially responsible press seeks to protect free expression of individuals in all manners of mass communication and requires the media to represent all points of view on the social spectrum. It promotes media ethics and responsibility.

The 1942 Hutchins Commission named after University of Chicago Chancellor Robert M. Hutchings, who was the chair of the commission. The commission was funded by Henry Luce (Time/Life) and the *Encyclopedia Britannica*.

Three fundamental positions:
1. Whoever enjoys freedom has certain obligations to society.
2. Society's welfare becomes the most overriding concern. An individual's rights to speak out are balanced by group rights to be free from invasion of privacy or libel; personal rights to free expression are described in terms of public access to the media, or the "public's right to know."
3. Media, as a matter of policy, carry views contrary to their own.

Do an online search for:

Jodi Arias trial (spring, summer 2013)
Trial of Michael Jackson's doctor
Trial of George Zimmerman (Florida 2013)
Amada Knox
Rodney King
O.J. Simpson

List cases the news media are covering now, that give information that may influence a defendant's right to an impartial jury.

What can judges do to insure that a defendant's Sixth Amendment rights are protected?

What rights to police officers have when it comes to searches and seizures?

What rights do you have?

The courts are reviewing cases related to officers taking your smart phone after a traffic stop and searching for information that may lead to other charges.

Study Guide Questions

Possible essay question:

What is the conflict between the First and Sixth Amendments to the U.S. Constitution? In your answer include the freedoms quarantined by each amendment and then discuss the inherent conflict. (Think public's right to know vs. fair and speedy trial by an IMPARTIAL jury.)

List at least five of the many functions specific to the legislature branch listed in the U.S. Constitution.

List five functions given specifically to the executive branch by the U.S. Constitution.

List the nine Supreme Court Justices today.

Give two examples pointing out the conflict between the "public's right to know" and the right of a citizen to a fair and speedy trial by an impartial jury.

Do you feel the media is too invasive of public figures' lives? Give an example to support your point of view.

Why do you think Thomas Jefferson thought the citizens of this country would be better off in a system with newspapers?

Do police have the right to conduct warrantless searches of data on a smart phone during a traffic stop?

Chapter 4
Prior Restraint

Even though our First Amendment is viewed as very libertarian in nature, our government has determined that it is not absolute under all circumstances.

Schenck v United States 1919

Schenck was an important case placing limits on the First Amendment right to freedom of expression.

The first five words of the First Amendment to the Constitution: Congress shall make NO (emphasis author's) law…restricting freedom of speech…

The United States' decision to enter World War I presented some interesting challenges to citizens' First Amendment rights.

We the People passed the **Espionage Act** (1917) two months after America declared war on Germany. The Act was amended in May 1918. The Act said that…"whoever, for the purpose of obtaining information respecting the national defense with intent or reason to believe that the information to be obtained is to be used to the injury of the United States or within the exclusive jurisdiction of the United States or any place in which any vessel, aircraft, arms, munitions, or other materials or instruments for use in time of war are being made, prepared, repaired. Whoever, being entrusted with or having lawful possession or control of any document or information, are in violation of trust, or to be listed, stolen, abstracted, or destroyed shall be punished by a fine of not more the $10,000 or by imprisonment for not more than two years or both."

The **Sedition Act** of 1918: Whoever, when the United States is at war, shall willfully make or convey false reports or false statements with intent to interfere with the operation or success of the military or naval forces of the United States or to promote the success of its enemies, or shall willfully make or convey false reports or false statements or say or do anything except by way of bona fide and not disloyal advice to an investor or investors…

*"Shall willfully cause or attempt to cause, or incite or attempt to incite, insubordination, disloyalty, mutiny, or refusal of duty, in the military or naval forces of the United States and whoever, when the United States is at war, shall **willfully utter, print, write or publish** any disloyal, profane, scurrilous, or abusive language about the form of government of the United States or the Constitution of the United States, or the military or naval forces of the United States, or the flag of the United States, or the uniform of the Army or Navy of the United States into contempt, scorn, contumely, or disrepute…and whoever shall by word or act support or favor the cause of any country with which the United*

States is at war or by word or act oppose the cause of the United States shall be punished by a fine of not more than $10,000...”

About 900 Americans were imprisoned in the months after the Act was passed by Congress. Eugene V. Debs was sentenced to ten years for a speech in Canton, Ohio, on June 16, 1918 attacking the Espionage Act.

Many citizens were opposed to the United States' involvement in WW I. Among them was Charles Schenck, General Secretary of the Socialist Party. He and his staff produced and distributed 15,000 leaflets urging young men not to register for the newly enacted draft, saying that the draft was a violation of their 13th Amendment rights. His offices were raided by the federal government and he was arrested, charged and convicted with violating the Espionage and Sedition Acts. Schenck's attorney appealed the case to the Supreme Court on the basis that the laws were overly restrictive of citizens' First Amendment rights and thus unconstitutional.

Chief Justice Edward Douglas White asked Justice Oliver Wendell Holmes to write the majority opinion in *Schenck v United States* (emphasis added):

*"We admit that in many places and in **ordinary** times (Schenck) in saying all that was said in the circular would have been within (his) constitutional rights. But the character of every act depends upon the **circumstances** in which it is done. The most stringent protection of free speech would not protect a man in **falsely shouting fire in a theatre**, and causing a panic. It does not even protect a man from injunction (order to stop) against uttering words that may have all the effect of force. The question in every case is whether the words used are used in such circumstances and are of such a nature **as to create a clear and present danger** that they will bring about the substantive evils that Congress has a right to prevent. It is a question of proximity and degree."*

"When a nation is at war many things that might be said in time of peace are such a hindrance to its effort that their utterance will not be endured so long as men fight and that no court could regard them as protected by any constitutional right."

Many authoritarian governments have attempted to restrict the flow of information. England's Henry VIII initiated methods such as licensing printing presses. In 1765, the British imposed the Stamp Act on the colonists. Under the British system, sedition or any criticism of the government was illegal.

Near v Minnesota 1931 (U.S. Supreme Court)

In 1925, the Minnesota state legislature passed a law that allowed government authorities to halt publication of any obscene, lewd, and lascivious...or malicious, scandalous, and defamatory newspaper, magazine, or other periodical as a public nuisance.

Jay Near and Howard Guilford used their newspaper, the *Saturday Press*, to accuse government officials of ignoring widespread racketeering, bootlegging, and illegal gambling. The newspaper was accused of being sensational and anti-Semitic in its hard-hitting articles. The county attorney filed a criminal complaint against the paper and a judge found Near and Guilford in violation of the state statute and ordered them to stop publication of the *Saturday Press* and enjoined them from starting up any like newspaper.

The Minnesota Supreme Court upheld the lower court conviction and the case went to the U.S. Supreme Court who reversed the conviction holding that the state law was overly restrictive of citizens' First Amendment rights. This case was also significant because the justices held that the First Amendment right is not absolute and that there were still circumstances that might justify a government prior restraint.

Pentagon Papers 1971

The executive branch of the government commissioned the Rand Corporation to conduct a study on how the United States got involved in Vietnam. The result was a document titled "A History of the U.S. Decision Making Process on Vietnam Policy."

Daniel Ellsberg had worked on the document and determined that the information contained therein was something the American public had a right to know. He leaked information from the top-secret study to the editors of the *New York Times*. Other newspapers picked up the story. The government went to the Supreme Court to get a restraining order to stop publication of the report. An injunction was issued and later withdrawn when the Supreme Court reviewed the information and concluded that, yes, rather than being condemned for their reporting, the newspapers should be commended for their courage in reporting the information that was of such importance to the American people.

Progressive Magazine Case 1979

Howard Morland researched and wrote a story on how easy it was to get information on how to build a hydrogen bomb. The government found out about the story and sought to ban its publication. The Justice Department filed suit in a federal court and obtained a temporary restraining order against publication of the article. The case was dropped before it reached the U.S. Supreme Court.

Hazelwood v Kuhlmeier 1987 (U.S. Supreme Court)

The case arose from a suit by journalism students at Hazelwood East High School in Missouri. They went to court after their principal, Robert E. Reynolds, deleted two pages from the May 13, 1983 issue of the *Spectrum*, a student newspaper produced as part of an elective course called Journalism II. Reynolds pulled the pages because of two stories about teen pregnancy and divorce. In his view, the articles did not adequately disguise the identities of girls who had been pregnant or the anonymity of a parent who was getting divorced. Further, he said references in the first story to sexual activity and birth control were inappropriate for younger students to read.

In a 5-3 ruling, the Supreme Court gave school administrators broad latitude to suppress controversial stories. **"A school need not tolerate student speech that is inconsistent with its 'basic educational mission',"** Justice Byron White wrote for the majority. School officials may impose reasonable restrictions on the speech of students, teachers, and other members of the school community.

Tinker v Des Moines Independent Community School Dist. 1969 (U.S. Supreme Court)

John Tinker, 15 years old, his sister Mary Beth Tinker, 13 years old, and Christopher Echardt, 16 years old, decided along with their parents to protest the Vietnam War by wearing black armbands to their Des Moines schools during the Christmas holiday season. Upon learning of their intentions, and fearing that the armbands would provoke disturbances, the principals of the Des Moines school district resolved that all students wearing armbands be asked to remove them or face suspension. When the Tinker siblings and Christopher wore their armbands to school, they were asked to remove them. When they refused, they were suspended until after New Year's Day.
    The Supreme Court said:
        The wearing of armbands was "closely akin to 'pure speech'" and protected by the First Amendment. School environments imply limitations on free expression, but here the principals lacked justification for imposing any such limits. The principals had failed to show that the forbidden conduct would substantially interfere with appropriate school discipline.
7-2 ruling

Do online research on the following:

California Assembly Bill 2581 which took effect Jan 1, 2007. Explain the reason for the bill and give your opinion. This bill relates to state law affecting high school student's First Amendment rights.

United States v Reynolds 1953 (**U.S. Supreme Court**) How do you feel about the ability of the executive branch to withhold information the public may have the "right to know?"

***War Powers Act* 1975**: Under what circumstances may the President go to war without the approval of Congress and how long can he keep troops in harm's way without Congressional approval?

Morse *et al.* *v Fredrick* 2007 (U.S. Supreme Court)
"Bong Hits 4 Jesus": Go to the course blog for more info on this case. Select one court opinion which was NOT a majority opinion and discuss. Student rights to freedom of expression.

The "I Love Boobies" bracelet case: ***Easton Area School District v Brianna Hawk and Kayla Martinez*, 2013.** Student rights to freedom of expression.

WikiLeaks:

Julian Assange 2010–11
Research this topic and write a one-page summary including your opinion based on the court cases you have studied so far. (Attach the typed opinion to this study guide page with a staple)

Edward Snowden 2013–
Former CIA information technical assistant who leaked classified material about NSA's secret programs to collect phone records and Internet data on American citizens as well as foreign leaders.

Ongoing conflict between Apple Co. and the U.S. Government regarding encryption codes protecting IPhone user's privacy.
Should the government be able to force Apple to create a way to access the phone records of private individuals, with a warrant, when national security is threatened? This is an ongoing issue at the time this edition of the study guide is published.

Study Guide Issues for Discussion

What about the government's reluctance to release information related to?
    The Vietnam War
    The Gulf War
    The Iraq War
    Afghanistan War
    War on Terror

Study Guide Questions

Under what circumstances do you feel the government of the United States has the right or obligation to censor information in which the public may have an interest?

Do you agree with the principles established by the *Hazelwood v Kuhlmeier* case? Explain why yes or no.

Do you see parallels between the rights of the media during the current international conflict and the principles involved in the *Schenck v U.S.* case?

Please attach typed double-spaced responses to the required research topics on this page, as you cannot respond in the original space provided.

Chapter 5
Freedom of Expression and Press Responsibility

Terms

Libel: False published defamation
Slander: False spoken defamation

Four elements of libel:

1. **Defamation**–hurt ones' reputation, damage their earning power, hold them up to ridicule, make them seem ridiculous, cause them to be shunned.
2. **Identification**–not necessarily just a name needed.
3. **Publication**–must be in print or broadcast.
4. **Negligence**–plaintiff must show that the media did not do their job right. They did not act reasonably or as one might expect them to act.

Four best defenses against a libel suit:

1. **Truth**—This is the number one defense in the United States. Is the information TRUE and can you prove it is true? Should it be required by a judge?
2. **Privilege**—Is the information "a matter of public record"? Is the information taken from sources the "public has the right to know"? The Congressional Record, Board of Trustee minutes, Associated Student Government meeting records, budget of public institutions and more are examples. Court records are also public record unless a judge seals them.
3. **Fair comment and critics**—If a person is "in the public light," a movie star, athlete, elected official etc., they are open to critique by the media.
   Note: *Milkovich v Lorain Journal Co.* 1990

　　　　The Supreme Court noted in this case that in some circumstances opinions may often imply an assertion of objective fact. William Rehnquist speaking for the majority reversed a lower court ruling that had supported columnist Ted Diadium's assertion, in a sports column, that a high school wrestling coach lied to a judge about a brawl that took place after a match between two teams, was protected under the fair comment and criticism defense against libel.

　　　　As a result of the fight, the state (Ohio) athletic board placed the teams on probation which would have precluded participation in the playoffs. Parents went to court to get the ban lifted which they did after testimony from the coach and principal of the school was given to absolve the leadership of responsibility in the conflict. Diadium subsequently wrote the column critical of the testimony and behavior of the coach. **The Supreme Court ruled in the case that assertions of criminal wrongdoing may not be protected opinion.**

4. **Absence of Malice**— Since the 1964 *New York Times Co. v Sullivan* Supreme Court case, public figures and public officials must prove that the media acted with actual malice before they can win damages in a libel suit. In other words, the plaintiffs must prove in court that the media knew ahead of time that the information they published was false and defamatory and printed it anyway. Justice William Brennan, writing for the majority, said that the media may need some "breathing space" in performing the functions the founding fathers sought when they drafted the First Amendment to the Constitution.

   The original case (*Sullivan v New York Times Co.*) revolved around an advertisement placed in the Times by the Committee to Support Dr. Martin Luther King and the Struggle for Freedom in the South.

   The $4,800 full-page ad was critical of the tactics used by the Montgomery, Alabama police in addressing a protest by students held at Alabama State University. The ad accused the police of intimidating the students. There were 650,000 issues published. There were 394 subscribers in Alabama and 35 subscribers in Montgomery County.

   Attorneys for Police Commissioner L.B. Sullivan were able to point out several falsehoods in the ad that were defamatory.

   1.   The ad said the students were on the steps of the administration building singing "My County Tis of Thee" when they were singing "The Star Spangled Banner."
   2.   The ad said that the police surrounded the campus. They did not. The ad stated that the police padlocked the dinning hall to starve the students into submission.
   3.   The ad said Dr. Martin Luther King had been arrested seven times (the *Times'* own recorders supported that he had only been arrested four times) Other details were not exactly correct and the attorneys were able to bring witnesses to the stand that felt that Sullivan was the person being criticized.

   The Montgomery Court awarded Sullivan the $500,000 in damages he had sued for. The Alabama Supreme Court upheld the ruling. The U.S. Supreme Court reversed the lower courts' findings in this case.

Go to the course blog for video on this issue.

Do an online search for:

Twibel Case: Defamatory information posted on Twitter

***Gordon and Holmes vs. Love* case**
In 2010, Courtney Love accused her former attorney Ronda Holms of bribery. "I was f
____devastated when Ronda J. Holmes esq. of San Diego was bought off."

In Love's case, the Twitter user , not the social media site is liable for the defamation. As a third-party publisher, social media sites such as Twitter are protected by Section 230 of the Communication Decency Act

Sarah Jones, former Cincinnati Bengals cheerleader *v The Dirty.com*

Study Guide Activities

Do a computer search for court cases dealing with who is a public figure or official for the purposes of a libel lawsuit. What were the results?

Do a search to locate any recent libel cases related to media personalities. What were the results?

Do you feel the *New York Times Co. v Sullivan* case gives the media too much freedom? Why yes/why no?

Do an informal survey (25 people) to see if they feel the media has too much freedom in America or not enough.

List names of publications you feel most often push the boundaries of libelous speech.

Student Notes

Chapter 6
Privacy Law

Fourth Amendment U.S. Constitution

The right of the people to be secure in their persons, houses, papers, and effects, against unreasonable searches and seizures, shall not be violated, and no warrants shall issue, but upon probable cause, supported by oath or affirmation, and particularly describing the place to be searched, and the persons or things to be seized.

Harvard Law Review Essay by Samuel D. Warren and Louis D. Brandeis 1890 (later a Supreme Court Justice)

They put forth the concept that there should be a right of privacy either under the common law or state statutory law regarding an individual's "right to privacy."

This right should protect prominent persons from gossipy reporting of their private affairs.

> *"The press is overstepping in every direction the obvious bounds of propriety and decency. Gossip is no longer the resource of the idle and of the vicious, but has become a trade, which is pursued with industry as well as effrontery."*

Appropriation: Protects individuals from unauthorized commercial use of their names, photographs, and other aspects of their public persona. (face, body, voice, etc.)

Intrusion: Unduly intruding into ones' physical solitude or seclusion or private affairs. Snooping, eavesdropping or intruding into someone's reasonable right to peace and quiet.

    Example: Jackie Onassis: Photographer Ron Gallela took a photo 24 feet from Jackie and 30 feet from her children.

False Light: Do not put people in a false light. Do not take something in one context and put it into another context especially if the new context may be defamatory.

Private Facts: Private information that may be offensive to a reasonable person. Not of legitimate public interest.

Do an online search for:

1974 Privacy Act

Ron Galella

Jackie Onassis

Vanessa Williams

Sean Penn

Other privacy suits by major public figures

Erin Andrews v Michael Barrett and Marriott 2016

Hulk Hogan v Gawker 2016

Video Voyeurism Act 2004: Case regarding disseminating images of a "person's private parts" when the person has a reasonable expectation of privacy regardless of private or public location. Note the actual provisions of the act and list them here.

Can a person take a picture of you anywhere, any time?

Please refer to your textbook and/or do an online search for the latest laws regarding Copyright. What would constitute "fair use" of copyrighted material?

Who owns a tattoo? Professional athletes now having to ask for copyright waivers from tattoo artists.

Do an online search for the SCOTUS case: **Utah vs Strieff** 2016 (regards police right to stop and search) At the time this case was scheduled for hearing, Justice Antonin Scalia had just died leaving the course with 8 justices. If there is a 4/4 deadlock, the case could be reverted back to the Utah Supreme Court. How did that court rule in this case.

Kentucky V. King SCOTUS
What did the court say regarding warrantless searches?

Chapter 7
Media Ethics

A sense of what is right and what is wrong is essential to a society dedicated to justice and equality for all. Aristotle, the esteemed Greek philosopher, initiated the "golden mean" a philosophy espousing the concept of avoiding extremes and seeking more moderate means. The media concept of being fair and balanced comes from this basic principle.

German philosopher Immanuel Kant (1724–1804) developed the concept of the "categorical imperative." He sought a more philosophical approach to issues related to ethical behavior and decision making. He thought people need not dictate what is right or wrong in every circumstance. Hard thinking, debate, and discussion can lead to a common good based on input from as many sources as we can gather. This theory exhorts people to identify and apply universal principles, i.e., to find principles that most people would be comfortable living with in most situations. The ethical codes that journalism associations develop could be put in this classification.

British-born John Stuart Mill, in the mid-1800s, came up with what became the basis for the libertarian concept related to social and political philosophy. Basic to this concept was the idea that people should be able to think and do pretty much what they want as long as they do not hurt someone else. The concept correlates with our democratic principle of majority rule. The emphasis is on the greatest good for the greatest number of people.

This utilitarian philosophy supports the journalistic concept of "the people's right to know." This concept puts the public interest ahead of government interests. This concept is alive and well today with the Libertarian Party. *The Orange County Register* newspaper has been called the flagship publication of the Libertarian Party. Adherents to this philosophy want a limited role of government in business and social issues. They also are strong adherents of the strict interpretation of the U.S. Constitution. The term "laissez-faire" applies here in that, economically, libertarians want the market place to dictate business climates, not government regulation.

Through online or other resources, define the following terms:

Plagiarism: The practice of taking someone else's work and using it without permission.

Junkets:

Freebies:

Payola:

Plugola:

On/Off the Record:

Shield laws: Laws that protect reporter's sources or confidential information.

Again, **do online research on:**

Janet Cooke:
"Jimmy is 8 years old and a third-generation heroin addict, a precocious little boy with sandy hair, velvety brown eyes and needle marks freckling the baby-smooth skin of his thin brown arms."[1]

Cooke, who was 25 at the time, won the Pulitzer Prize for this article, "Jimmy's World." Her resume listed a BA from Vassar, magna cum laude (she attended one year). The University of Toledo had no record of her earning a master's degree there.

"Jimmy's World" was published in September 1980. The AP (Associated Press) started the investigation into her background after she was named a Pulitzer Prize winner.

[1] Lead to *Washington Post* article by Janet Cooke, "Jimmy's World."

Check the course blog for more info

Study Guide Activities

Rent and view the movie ***Shattered Glass.*** What are the ethical issues involved? What were the results and consequences of these issues?

Do a computer search on Jason Blair, *New York Times* reporter. What were the ethical issues involved? What were the results and consequences of these issues?

Do an online search for 2013 Fox News reporter Jana Winter. She had written a exclusive story regarding the contents of a notebook belonging to the Aurora, Colorado shooting suspect James Holes. Where was the case heard and why?

Do a computer search for journalism "Codes of Ethics."

What protection do Bloggers have when ordered to give up sources?
Search online for blogger Robert "KC" Johnson
He had posted information regarding a Duke University lacrosse team rape case.

Do research to find out the policies of two of your local newspapers with regard to accepting freebies or free trips.

Movies dealing with these issues you may want to rent or view through online sources:
All the President's Men
Spotlight
Absence of Malice

Student Notes

Chapter 8
Talk Is Cheap—Free Speech Is Not

The Supreme Court, while outlining some limits to free speech, ruled on cases that limited government's latitude in limiting citizens' freedom of expression.

Chaplinsky v New Hampshire 1942 (U.S. Supreme Court)

New Hampshire had an ordinance that said you shall not address words that are offensive, derisive, or annoying to anyone lawfully in a public place, nor call him by any offensive or derisive name.

Walter Chaplinsky, a Jehovah's Witness, was arrested for "evangelizing" on the "harlot" Catholic Church and on saluting the flag. Local citizens called the police because Chaplinsky was causing a disturbance. When arrested, he called the marshal a "God damned racketeer" and a "damned Fascist" and the whole government of Rochester Fascists or agents of Fascists. Chaplinsky was arrested for violating the above ordinance.

Justice Murphy, writing for the majority, said: the "right of free speech is not absolute at all times and under all circumstances. There are certain well-defined and narrowly limited classes of speech, the prevention and punishment of which have never been thought to raise any Constitutional problem. These would include…the insulting or 'fighting words,' those which by their very utterance inflict injury or tend to incite an immediate breach of the peace."

Chaplinsky was further defined by *Gooding v Wilson* 1972 (Supreme Court). The "fighting words" must be in a face-to-face confrontation and lead to an immediate breach of the peace.

Village of Skokie v National Socialist Party 1978 (Illinois Supreme Court)

In 1976, the National Socialist Party planned to peacefully demonstrate in Skokie, Illinois, a community with a large Jewish population, to protest the racial integration of nearby Chicago schools. The protest was prohibited by village officials who said the Nazis failed to obtain $350,000 worth of liability and property damage insurance as required by a Skokie Park District ordinance quickly passed when the officials found out about the planned march. In addition, the village ruled that a member of a political party cannot march in a military-style uniform and ruled that it is not permissible to disseminate material intended to incite racial hatred.

State and federal courts in Illinois invalidated all the ordinances, ruling that they were discriminatory or abridged constitutionally protected rights of free speech. The

Illinois Supreme Court rejected the contention that the display of such symbols as a swastika did not constitute "fighting words," sufficient to "overcome the heavy presumption against the constitutional validity of a prior restraint."

Peaceful demonstrations cannot be totally stopped or prohibited solely because they display (Nazi symbols) that may provoke a violent reaction by those who view them. A speaker who gives prior notice of his message has not compelled a confrontation with those who voluntarily listen.

R.A.V. v St. Paul 1992 (U.S. Supreme Court)

In 1982, St. Paul, Minnesota enacted a local hate-crime ordinance and created a new criminal offence: the bias motivated disorderly conduct crime. Under this ordinance, anyone who "places on public or private property, a symbol, object, appellation, characterization or graffiti" that "arouses anger, alarm or resentment in others on the basis of race, color, creed, or religion" was guilty of the misdemeanor offence of disorderly conduct. The city amended the law in 1989 to specifically include a burning cross or a Nazi swastika in the prohibitions, and in 1990 to prohibit actions based on sexual prejudice.

In 1990, Robert A. Viktora, a 17-year-old, reportedly a high school dropout and "skinhead," was joined by some other minors in placing a crude cross in the fenced yard of Russ and Laura Jones, the only Black family in a working-class neighborhood of St. Paul.

Court appointed attorney Edward J. Cleary, though not endorsing the youth's behavior, agreed to take the case because he, like many in Minnesota, felt that even though the actions were "despicable and deserved punishment" the law needed to be challenged on the basis that many felt it was overly restrictive of citizens' First Amendment rights.

On June 10, 1992, the case made its way to the Supreme Court.

On June 22, the Court overturned R.A.V.'s conviction in essence saying the St. Paul law was overly broad and overly restrictive.

Justice Antonin Scalia writing for the majority said: "Let there be no mistake about our belief that burning a cross in someone's yard is reprehensible. But St. Paul has sufficient means at its disposal to prevent such behavior without adding the First Amendment to the fire."

Scalia said that governments may not punish those who "communicate messages of racial, gender, or religious intolerance" merely because those ideas are offensive and emotionally painful to those in the targeted group.

The Court was unanimous in overturning the St. Paul hate speech ordinance, but they disagreed about the legal rationale for doing so. White, Blackman, Day-O'Connor, and Stevens argued that the ordinance was unconstitutional only because it was overly broad and not limited to expressions that could lead to violence under the "fighting words" test.

The other five justices joined the majority opinion in taking a much broader view of the First Amendment right of those who engage in "hate speech." They said that any law is unconstitutional if it singles out expression of "bias-motivated hatred" for special punishment. While the majority did not specifically overturn *Chaplinsky v New Hampshire*, they made it clear that the "fighting words" doctrine cannot ordinarily be used to suppress the expression of racial, religious, or gender-based hostilities.

The Court said that government must not single out expression on certain favored topics such as race and creed but not on others, such as homosexuality, union membership, or political affiliation.

Brandenburg v Ohio 1969 (U.S. Supreme Court)

The Supreme Court upheld the Klansman's right to make an offensive and bigoted speech at a Klan rally, as long as the speech did not create an imminent danger of violent acts.

Cohen v California 1971 (U.S. Supreme Court)

Paul R. Cohen, a 19-year-old department store worker, was criminally prosecuted for appearing in a Los Angeles County courthouse wearing a leather jacket bearing the motto "Fuck the Draft."

He was convicted of violating that part of California Penal Code 415 which prohibits "maliciously and willfully disturbing the peace or quiet of any neighborhood or person...by offensive conduct."

Justice John Marshall Harlan, writing for the majority, reversed the conviction:

> *"While the particular four-letter word being litigated here is perhaps more distasteful than most others of its genre, it is nevertheless often true that one man's vulgarity is another's lyric. Indeed, we think it is largely because governmental officials cannot make principled distinctions in this area that the Constitution leaves matters of taste and style so largely to the individual."*

Texas v Johnson 491 1989 (U.S. Supreme Court)

Gregory Johnson and friends were arrested for violating a Texas law (Texas Penal Code, 42.09) that prohibited citizens from burning a state or national flag in a manner that offends...prohibited the desecration of a venerated object. Johnson and friends burned an American flag at the 1984 Republican National Convention in Dallas to protest the policies of President Ronald Reagan. He took the flag and lit it on fire on the steps of the convention center and he and others walked around the flag chanting "red, white, and blue, we spit on you." He was convicted and sentenced to one year in jail and fined $2,000. The Fifth District of Appeals in Dallas upheld the conviction. His attorney appealed Johnson's conviction to the U.S. Supreme Court on the basis that the Texas law was overly restrictive on his client's First Amendment rights.

In a 5-4 decision, the Court ruled that flag burning, especially in a political context, is a protected form of symbolic speech. The court noted that a "disturbing the peace" assertion was invalid. They also ruled that burning the flag would not fall under the "fighting words" exemption in the *Chaplinsky* case. Justice J. Kennedy said that no matter how distasteful the result, the First Amendment compelled it (the ruling) because the defendant's acts were speech in both the fundamental and technical sense. Justice Brennan, writing for the majority, said:

> *"We are aware that desecration of the flag is deeply offensive to many. But the same might be said, for example, of virulent ethnic and religious epithets, vulgar repudiations of the draft, and scurrilous caricatures. There is a bedrock principle underlying the First Amendment, it is that the government may not prohibit the expression of an idea simply because society finds the idea itself offensive or disagreeable. Punishing desecration of the flag dilutes the very freedom that makes this emblem so revered and worth revering."*

This Supreme Court decision proved very unpopular around the country. Many citizens expressed their anger over the fact that the Court had ruled that there were actually circumstances that might allow a person to desecrate that flag. These citizens wrote their respective Congressional representatives, which led to the passage of the **Flag Protection Act**, which made it a federal crime, punishable by one year in jail and a $1,000 fine, for desecrating the American flag.

After the Act became law, there were demonstrations across the nation. One of the new wave of flag burnings occurred on the steps of the national capitol building, resulting in four arrests and initiating the following test case.

United States v Eichman et al. 1990 (U.S. Supreme Court)

Shawn Eichman, a Revolutionary Communist Party member, along with other revolutionaries (including Mark John Haggerty and three others), staged a demonstration before a crowd of reporters and photographers. Witnesses reported hearing the defendants shout "burn, baby, burn" and "stop the Fascist flag law." The Supreme Court came back in the same 5-4 majority ruling the Flag Protection Act unconstitutional. Justice Brennan, writing for the majority, said:

U.S. District courts and U.S. Supreme Court reaffirmed the ruling in the *Texas v Johnson* case and added: *"Even assuming such a consensus (a national consensus supporting a ban on flag desecration as asserted by the government representatives in court) any suggestion that the governments' interest in suppressing speech becomes more weighty as popular opposition to that speech grows **is foreign to the First Amendment.***

John Doe v University of Michigan 1989 (721 F. Supp. 852,853)

In February of 1987, in response to incidents of racism and racial harassment on campus, the University of Michigan adopted a policy that prohibited "stigmatizing or victimizing individuals or groups on the basis of race, ethnicity, religion, sex, sexual orientation, creed, national origin, ancestry, age, marital status, handicap, or Vietnam-era status." In addition, the policy prohibited "such behavior if it involves an express or implied threat to or has the purpose or reasonably foreseeable effect of interfering with or creates an intimidating, hostile or demeaning environment for individual pursuits in academic, employment, or extracurricular activities."

John Doe was a Michigan psychology student who feared that discussion of certain theories about biological race and gender differences might be perceived as racist and sexist and therefore punishable under the campus policy.

The Federal District Court ruled the policy unconstitutional. The court said: "It is an unfortunate fact of our constitutional system that the ideals of freedom and equality are often in conflict."

Virginia v Black 2003 (U.S. Supreme Court)

In August of 1998, a 25-foot-high cross was burned at a rally of the Ku Klux Klan in Cana, Virginia. The burning was witnessed by a county sheriff and resulted in the arrest and prosecution of Barry Black for violation of Virginia Statute Section 18.2-423. The statute makes it a felony for any person to burn a cross with the intent to intimidate any person or group of persons; it also provides that cross burning constitutes a *prima facie* evidence of an intent to intimidate.

The Supreme Court of Virginia invalidated the conviction. The court relied on *R.A.V. v St. Paul*. In *R.A.V.*, the High Court ruled that a municipal cross-burning ordinance violated the First Amendment because the law improperly punished expression on the basis of the expression's content.

The Court reiterated that speech can be regulated only if it falls into well-defined categories: incitement constituting a clear and present danger to the government, commercial speech, fighting words that create an immediate danger of physical violence and obscenity and child pornography.

The Supreme Court held in *Black* that the operative language of the Virginia law, by specifically requiring an intent to intimidate and not including specified targets—on its surface—limited the law to true threats, which may be proscribed. A "true threat" is defined as one whereby the speaker "means to communicate a serious intention of an intent to commit an act of unlawful violence to an individual or group of individuals." This is not protected speech.

However, in *Black*, the court said that the addition of the provision for *prima facie* evidence, amounting as it did to a presumption of the intent to intimidate, rendered the statute unconstitutional on its face.

The jury that convicted Black had been told by the judge about the *prima facie* provision of the statute. On that basis, the court held Black's conviction to be improper because the *prima facie* provision removed any possibility that the act could be considered protected speech. Justice Sandra Day O'Connor wrote that the cross burning at the Klansmen meeting was not intended to threaten anyone present, it is communicative in nature; the *prima facie* provision ignores this distinction.

Study Guide Activities

Do an online search for:
Nichols v Chacon **1998**
110 F.Supp.2d 1099 (W. D. Ark, 2000).

Federal: An arrestee's display of his middle finger in an upward gesture, commonly referred to as "flipping someone off," "the bird," or "giving someone the finger," did not constitute "fighting words" and, thus, was protected as free speech under the First Amendment in a civil rights action brought under 42 U.S.C. sec. 1983. The court ruled that the arresting police officer was not entitled to qualified immunity in the lawsuit. It said the arrestee-plaintiff's gesture was clearly established as protected, free speech at the time when the officer issued a ticket to the arrestee for disorderly conduct.

"While we agree the gesture utilized by Nichols was crude, insensitive, offensive, and disturbing to Chacon's sensibilities, it was not obscene under the relevant Supreme Court precedent, did not constitute 'fighting words,' and was protected as 'free speech' under the First Amendment to the United States Constitution. We also believe that this right was clearly established on August 6th of 1998 when Chacon arrested Nichols.

Accordingly, we hold as a matter of law that Chacon is not entitled to qualified immunity and that his arrest of Nichols violated Nichols' First and Fourth Amendment rights."

Snyder V Phelps 2011 (U.S. Supreme Court)

Westboro Baptist Church—Note the courts majority ruling in this case.
The church is infamous for their protests expressing hatred for gay persons in the military, often picketing military funerals because they feel America's growing acceptance of homosexuals stems firstly from the military.
What did the lower courts award? What did the Fourth Circuit Court rule? What ultimately did SCOTUS rule? Also, who were the defendant's attorneys?

Do an online search on "freedom of expression." List the top five sites you found.

Read and find out if the sites you listed mention any of the court cases in this lesson.

Do an online search on the *Virginia v Black* case. Summarize the dissenting opinion in the case.

Student Notes

Chapter 9
Absence of Malice

This video can be shown in special class sessions or rented by students individually to point out the importance of the *New York Times Co. v Sullivan* Supreme Court case. This film supports lectures on media law, ethics, and methodology.

An ambitious young reporter (Sally Field as Megan) exhibits the traits of an overzealous reporter out to "get the scoop" and get it first. We find that any means justify that end. The storyline also explores the ethics of the federal government in achieving its "ends" in an investigation into the death of a local union member.

The movie shows how a private businessman, Michael Gallagher (Paul Newman), can be unknowingly drawn into a tangled web of questionable ethical behavior and learn how powerless we are when confronted with the powers of the press and government.

Issues related to the movie to be discussed and/or covered on exams:

- Powers of the FBI (executive branch of the federal government)
- Fourth Amendment—Invasion of privacy (by both the newspaper and the federal government)
- First Amendment's guarantee of the "public's right to know"
- Shield laws
- Right to print defamatory information if "to the best of your knowledge, the information is true," after convincing yourself that you have been "reasonable and prudent" in your investigation to make sure you are not negligent
- Power of the Fourth Estate to print what they want
- Illegal searches and seizures, trespass, search warrants
- What constitutes a credible source for a story in the paper?
- Do newspapers print only the TRUTH?
- What is the process gatekeepers use to decide what does or does not go in the newspaper?
- Does the fact that you print private information about a person make them more credible as a source for a story?
- What rights do public figures and public officials have?
- Listen carefully to what James J. Wells from the U.S. Department of Justice has to say at the end of the movie. How does he sum up the roles of government and newspapers?
- What ultimately happens to the characters of Quinn and Rosen in the movie? Why do they end up the way they do?

Absence of Malice is a Sydney Pollack film released in 1981. Runs 117 minutes.

Student Notes

Chapter 10
Newspapers

In 1776, the Continental Congress adopted the Declaration of Independence; the text of the document was published in the *Pennsylvania Evening Post* of July 6. The next year, the Continental Congress authorized Mary Katherine Goddard, publisher of the *Maryland Journal*, to print the first official copies of the Declaration with the names of the signers attached.

Four Elements of News

1. Impact
2. Proximity
3. Timeliness
4. Credibility

Gatekeepers for the print and broadcast media use these guidelines to determine, in priority order, what goes into their respective news reports.

The most important story on the front page usually appears in the upper right side of the front page in more traditionally designed newspapers. The reason for this is that the reader looks at the paper nameplate and their eye drops to that spot. Editors use print font size, style, and number of decks in headlines to lead readers through the front page of their newspaper. Serif typeface is the easiest to read. Sans serif may look cleaner and more modern and is usually used in headlines and news graphics.

In Orange County, we have two competing newspapers with very different philosophies on design. The *Los Angeles Times* (*L.A. Times*) is more traditional in its news layout, while the *Orange County Register* (*O.C. Register*) is more likely to experiment with more modern design features. *O.C. Register* was noted for its early use of color in its newspaper, winning a Pulitzer Prize for its color photography of the 1984 Los Angeles Olympic Games.

Visit the website given below to see newspaper front pages across the United States.

http://www.newseum.org/todaysfrontpages/flash/

Study Guide Questions

Contact an editor of a local paper and ask them their policy on:

Use of anonymous sources

Policy on freebies

Policy on junkets

Impact

Some gatekeepers say, "Seems that life threatening situations have the most impact in our society." What are some of these situations and why do they make front-page news?

Many professional writers say, "Those who can write will be worth their weight in gold." Why so? What do you think?

Discuss editorial pages' design and philosophy. What elements are in the paper's nameplate and what does that tell the reader, right away, about the paper?

Consult your text and/or do an online search for the following and be prepared to identify them on an exam:

Johann Gutenberg

Publick Occurrences both Forreign and Domestick, 1690 Benjamin Harris

New England Courant, James Franklin

Pennsylvania Gazette, Ben Franklin

John Peter Zenger

What was the impact of the early colonial press?

Penny Press

Horace Greeley

Yellow Journalism—where did we get the term?

Newspaper Wars in New York Between Joseph Pulitzer (*St Louis Post-Dispatch*) (*New York World*) and William Randolph Hearst (*San Francisco Examiner*) (*New York Journal*)

Muckrakers

Henry Luce

USA Today

Minority Newspapers

Declining Competition in the Newspaper Industry

Impact of Blogs on Newspaper Circulation (web log)

Impact of online sites like Craigslist on newspapers.

What do you feel is the future of newspapers in the United States and the world?

List some tabloid newspapers in your region.

List some of the special sections newspapers are adding to reach a wider audience.

Student Notes

Chapter 11
The Power of Owning the Press

Background on the *L.A. Times*

The history of the *L.A. Times* can really be directly linked to the past and present development of Southern California.

Harrison Gray Otis

Harris Gray Otis was born on February 10, 1837 in Marietta, Ohio. His parents were named Stephen and Sarah Otis. He was the youngest of 16 siblings. His uncle was a senator from Massachusetts. He worked on the family farm and went to school during the three months of winter.

- At age 14, he became a printer's apprentice for the *Noble County Courier* in Ohio.

- In 1859, he married Eliza A. Wetherby and established a home in Louisville, Kentucky.

- At age 23, Otis was elected a member of the 1860 Republican National Convention that nominated Abraham Lincoln.

- Otis and Eliza left Kentucky for Ohio where he enlisted as a private in the Twelfth Regiment of the Ohio Volunteer Infantry at Camp Dennison, Ohio, June 25, 1861 to fight on the side of the North in the Civil War. He fought in 15 battles and was wounded twice. He received four promotions and two brevets to major and lieutenant colonel. He was cited for gallant service.

- He worked as a Washington correspondent for the *Ohio State Journal*. He was once the managing editor of the *Grand Army Journal*, the first Union soldiers' paper established in Washington after the war.

- He came to California in 1876. On March 11, 1876, Otis took control of the *Santa Barbara Press* newspaper, which he published for four years. He came to Los Angeles when he learned that the newest newspaper, the *L.A. Daily Times*, was for sale. In 1882, he bought a quarter interest in the *Times*. He became the editor for the *Times* as well the *Los Angeles Mirror*. He made $15 a week. Wife Eliza also contributed articles about women, religion, and morals to the paper.

- In 1882, Los Angeles was a dirty dusty town with a population of 5,000. In 1883, the Southern Pacific Railroad came to California with a spur to Los Angeles.

- In 1883, Otis and H.H. Boyce became co-owners of the *Times*, which had grown to eight pages. They established the Times Mirror Company. The paper printed articles about how great the climate was in Southern California.

- Otis later bought Boyce out. Boyce started the *Morning Tribune*. After which there were two morning papers: the *Times* and the *Tribune*. There was one afternoon paper: William Randolph Hearst's the *Herald and Express*.

- In 1884, one year after the Southern Pacific Railroad came to Los Angeles; the city's population was 12,000.

- In 1886, Los Angeles's population was 100,000. The Southern Pacific and the Atchison, Topeka, and Santa Fe railroads engaged in a fare war. The fare from Kansas City to Los Angeles was $1. During 1886, the volume of newspaper real estate advertising reached a figure of $100,000,000.

Harry Chandler

Harry Chandler was 27 years younger than Otis. He moved to Hollywood at age 17 (worth $500 million when he died in 1944). He suffered from pneumonia as a result of a fraternity initiation at Dartmouth College at age 17. The family doctor recommended he go to Southern California. Chandler made $19 a day hauling fruit to the central valley. He saved $3000 in two years.

- Chandler was able to gain control of the circulation (1,400 persons) list of the *Times*; he also gained control of the lists for the afternoon *Herald* and the morning *Tribune* newspapers as well. Through his control of the lists, he was able to help put the *Tribune* out of business. Within two years, he was able to put Otis's main competitor (Boyce) out of business. When the *Tribune* folded in 1890, Harry Chandler reportedly sent a third party to buy the *Tribune*'s production equipment for about five cents to the dollar. After Boyce went out of business, *Times* circulation and advertising quadrupled.

- In 1888, Chandler and Otis started the Los Angeles Chamber of Commerce. In 1894, Chandler married Otis's daughter Marian. Harry and Marian had eight children, the oldest son was Norman. In 1897, The Los Angeles Merchant and Manufacturers Association formed, led by the *L.A. Times*.

- In 1890s, Los Angeles needed a natural port. The *Times* lobbied to have the harbor built in San Pedro over the push by the principals of the Southern Pacific Railroad to have it built in Santa Monica. The organization's main objective was to keep organized labor out of Los Angeles.

- Labor strife from 1907 to 1910. The *Times* building was bombed October 1, 1910. Twenty were killed, 21 were injured. Clarence Darrow defended the culprits, the McNamara brothers.

- In 1902, the federal government with the support of Teddy Roosevelt passed the Land Reclamation Act. The executive branch set up the Bureau of Land Management.

- J.B. Lippincott and engineer J.C. Clausen, hired by the government, traveled to the Owens Valley to get the land owners to give up their water rights. At about the same time, Fred Eaton and William Mulholland went to the Owens Valley and started to purchase controlling land holdings along the river.

- At about the same time in Los Angeles, Otis, Chandler, and others formed the San Fernando Mission Land Company and started buying up cheap land in the San Fernando Valley. M.H. Sherman and Henry Huntington (prominent names in Los Angeles today) were also involved.

- The media had learned that the city was working to lock up water rights 259 miles to the north in the Owens Valley. Mulholland was working to develop a monumental plan to build an aqueduct to bring that water all the way to Los Angeles. The Los Angeles Metropolitan Water District got control of key parcels in the valley without those living there knowing the ultimate fate of their land and water in the valley. Then, with the help of the federal government and a bond issue drive led by the *Times*, the aqueduct was begun.

- On July 28, 1905, the *Times* broke the news that Owens River water would be coming 235 miles to Los Angeles. The *L.A. Times* editorialized to pass the $20 million-plus bond to build the aqueduct.

- Options and land purchases the Chandlers and others on the inside made jumped in value. Options on land purchased or optioned by the Mission Valley Land Co. reportedly increased 100-fold.

- Harrison Gray Otis died on July 30, 1917; he was 80 years old.

- Norman and Harry Chandler were instrumental in persuading Donald Douglas to relocate his aircraft building business to Los Angeles. They also played a role in the relocation of the film making industry to Los Angeles.

- Los Angeles lacked a natural harbor like San Francisco and San Diego. So, the Chandlers led a drive to bring a harbor to Los Angeles and they were instrumental in the harbor being built in Long Beach instead of Santa Monica. Collis P. Huntington of the Southern Pacific Railroad always thought the natural spot for a harbor would be Santa Monica. The Atchison, Topeka, and Santa Fe wanted it built at Redondo Beach. Norman was on the board of the Santa Fe Railroad and the Chandlers had bought some of the best properties in the San Pedro port area.

- Dorothy Buffum raised $19 million to save the Hollywood Bowl. Norman and Buff had two children, Otis and Camilla. Norman died in 1973 of throat cancer. The children paddled past the surf in Dana Point to spread his ashes.

Otis Chandler

Otis Chandler fell from horse at age seven. His mother took him to more than one hospital to find one that would ultimately save the boy's life. He was a Stanford athlete, a shot putter of Olympic caliber.

- In 1953, he was discharged from the Air Force. He and his wife Missy had two children at the time.

- Upon joining the staff of the *Times*, he was presented with a seven-page memo outlining steps for working his way through the *Times* from press room to publisher.

- He was credited with bringing the *Times* to a position of national and international prominence. He died in 2006 of Lewy body disease, a brain disorder combining some of the most debilitating characteristics of Parkinson's and Alzheimer's diseases.

Study Guide Questions

Did the owners of the *L.A. Times* make their fortunes solely on the publishing of a newspaper? Explain.

What advantage did the owners of the *Times*, the largest circulating newspaper in the region, have through the ability to "select" the news and set agendas through their editorial pages?

In what ways do you feel the ownership of a major news outlet allowed the owners to shape the development of a geographic region?
This could be true in New York, Florida, the Midwest, the South and of course, the West Coast.

Through an online search give the ownership and editorial status of the *L.A. Times* today.

How has the addition of many more media outlets, including television, radio and many more newspapers and magazines, impacted the power of the *L.A. Times*?

What is the impact of the Internet on newspapers today? Think Craigslist

What do you feel is the future of the printed newspaper?

How do you access news?

Chapter 12
Radio/Radio and Politics

In the early days of radio development, individuals built their own crystal radio sets in their own homes. A few of the fledgling stations began experimenting with entertainment programs.

One of the early station owners who used radio to acquire wealth and influence was William S. Paley, founder of the modern-day Columbia Broadcast System (CBS). Paley's grandfather was a Russian who owned a lumber mill outside of Kiev. He found that many of his Jewish friends and neighbors were the subject of discrimination and persecution. Issac Paley sensed the danger and took a trip to the United States. He liked what he saw there and came back to get his family, sell the lumber mill, and leave in 1884 for the United States. The family settled in Chicago.

Soon his sons, Sam and Jake, developed a talent for blending tobacco and sold cigars from a pushcart on the streets. The cigars were so popular that they formed the Congress Cigar Company.

Young Bill Paley (born in 1901), Sam's son, soon was attending college and working summers in the cigar factory. It was Bill, who first ran a radio advertisement for the company on WCAU Philadelphia. For $50 a week, the company got a ten-piece orchestra and a singer. They called the entertainment the "Miss La Palina" show. When Jake noticed the expenditure, he ordered young Bill to discontinue the program. Jake saw the advertising on radio as frivolous at best. However, after taking the program off the radio waves, Sam was confronted around town about why the program left the air. The company had been running print advertising for years and people did not stop him on the street to discuss the issue. Plus, after another check of the books, Sam noticed that sales had gone up with the radio advertising. Here he was confronted daily about what happened to the radio show. Soon young Bill was exonerated and the show was resumed.

To shorten the story, Sam and Jake sold the Congress Cigar Company for around $30 million right before the Great Depression to Dillon, Read & Co.

It was around this time that young Bill noticed that a fledgling radio station with a first floor office in New York City was for sale. In 1928, he bought CBS for $400,000 (with Sam and Jake's help).

The first year, CBS posted gross earnings of $1.4 million. By the third year, the company posted earnings of $4.7 million. By 1937, CBS reported earnings of 27.7 million and it owned 114 stations.

Key concept that led to CBS's profitability: Paley came up with the idea of giving his programming away for free to any stations that wanted it. In return he asked only a guarantee that if he wanted to preempt a certain time slot, the station would have to make it available to him, either for free or for a reasonable fee. This allowed his company to go to advertisers and guarantee them a huge audience at specified prime times across the nation. In other words, instead of selling the programs to the stations and having them raise the money in their own communities to pay for it, Paley gave the programs away in exchange for large audiences in prime time. Thus, he was able to offer national exposure for a company's product.

IT WORKED! That, along with his natural sense of what the general American public thought was entertaining led to CBS's success. Some of the more popular radio personalities and shows: Bing Crosby, Will Rogers, Frank Sinatra, Jack Benny, Amos n Andy, George Burns, Red Skelton, Edward Murrow.

Radio and Politics

Franklin Delano Roosevelt (FDR) is a prime example of personal/political public relations.

Across the nation, from the time of the nation's founding, very few American citizens had actually seen the president in person. For more than 150 years, they had seen pictures in print publications and read news stories about the president as related in the nation's print publications but very few had ever seen or heard the president's voice.

When FDR went live on radio with his fireside chats, the impact on the country was tremendous. Now people across the country could sit in their living rooms and listen to the president speak to them about the state of the nation and during time of war he was able to reassure them and keep them abreast of his efforts to lead the country.

In 1933, President Herbert Hoover had one person handling about 40 letters a day to the president. After the fireside chats began, FDR was receiving more than 4,000 letters a day. Stores could not keep up with the consumer demand for radios. FDR already had a special relationship with most of the print media and he was not self assured about going live on radio but he was a natural. He possessed a deep, resonant voice and his slower speech lent a sense of calm and confidence. People across the nation from that generation still remember the name of FDR's dog Fala as the dog often sat beside him during his fireside chats. As many as 50 million Americans were regularly listening to the broadcasts.

FDR died in his fourth term in office. The popularity he enjoyed with the American public was much attributed to his use of and understanding of the media both print and electronic. This led our elected representatives in Congress to initiate and later ratify the Twenty-Second Amendment to the U.S. Constitution.

Twenty-Second Amendment to the U.S. Constitution
(Ratified February 27, 1951)

Section 1. No person shall be elected to the office of the President more than twice, and no person who has held the office of President, or acted as President, for more than two years of a term to which some other person was elected President shall be elected to the office of the President more than once. But this Article shall not apply to any person holding the office of President when this Article was proposed by the Congress, and shall not prevent any person who may be holding the office of President, or acting as President, during the term within which this Article becomes operative from holding the office of President acting as President during the remainder of such term.

Section 2. This article shall be inoperative unless it shall have been ratified as an amendment to the Constitution by the legislatures of three-fourths of the several States within seven years from the date of its submission to the States by the Congress.

Names and terms needed for transfer to four-year colleges/universities.

Possible exam questions requiring text, online, library, and other research for exam questions:

Lee de Forest

Reginald Fessenden

David Sarnoff

Guglielmo Marconi

Heinrich Hertz

Radio Act of 1927

Fedcral Communications Commission

Telecommunications Act of 1996

National Public Radio

Arbitron

Amplitude Modulation (AM)

Equal Time/ Equal Opportunities Doctrine

Fairness Doctrine

Study Guide Questions

List at least four radio talk shows available in your area.

What seems to be their agenda other than to make lots of money?
According to Newsweek, Nov. 2010
Rush Limbaugh ($58.7 million annually)
Glenn Beck ($33 million annually)
Sean Hannity ($22 million annually)
Search for updated data and see if you can add other TV personalities to the list.

Do you feel that the strategy of some talk show hosts is to create an atmosphere of Fear, Anger, and Hate just to generate rating?

Listen to one or more daytime talk shows.
Do they offer air time to qualified persons with opposing points of view? If yes, why? If no, why?

After listening to a couple of the most popular talk shows, relate their agenda to what you found out about the Equal times/Equal opportunities provision and the Fairness Doctrine in the 1934 Federal Communications Act.

Student Notes

Chapter 13
Television Programming

James T. Aubrey

CBS, under Bill Paley's leadership, moved from radio broadcast prominence to television success. One of the early popular shows was *The $64,000 Question*. When it was learned that the program directors had "fixed" the show, CBS lost credibility. Paley had to do something and he fired his, then, president of the television network, Lou Cowan.

Paley replaced Cowan with an up and coming television program director, James T. Aubrey.

When Aubrey took over in December of 1959, CBS profits were about $25.2 million. When Aubrey was fired by Paley in 1964, profits were $48.6 million. Aubrey was said to have a "killer instinct" for the lowest common denominator. He was a master at providing the least objectionable programming. A *Life* magazine article about him after his fall from CBS said, "No man in history ever had such a lock on such enormous audiences."

His formula: Rural comedies, detective stories, the 3 Bs (broads, boobs, and busts), no old people acting old, no physical infirmities, NO SOCIAL ISSUES, no maids.

Aubrey wanted programs that required as little thinking as possible. He demanded happy endings. His programs: *The Beverly Hillbillies, Mr. Ed, Green Acres, Petticoat Junction, The Munsters, 77 Sunset Strip* (while at ABC), *Gunsmoke, Have Gun—Will Travel, The Red Skelton Show, Father Knows Best, Wanted: Dead or Alive, Perry Mason, Route 66, Barbra Streisand specials, The Wild, Wild West, The Danny Kaye Show* (a variety show).

Other interesting notes regarding Aubrey:

- Nicknamed "the Smiling Cobra" by John Houseman.
- He was the most press-shy (if not the most written about) of modern show business executives.
- Treated his boss, Bill Paley, with disdain.
- Aubrey was the man, the monarch, on the 20th floor of CBS at a time in the early 1960s when CBS could be compared to JFK's Camelot. (It was Paley's company but Aubrey's network, the saying went.)
- The bottom line: In 1963, CBS under Aubrey had 12 of the top 15 night-time series and all 12 of the top 12 daytime series.
- Aubrey interview quote: "Jack Kennedy was a friend of mine," Aubrey mused late on a recent Saturday. "We used to talk about this whole thing of being 'ladies' men.' People thought we got away with a lot more than we really did... I'm certainly no example of clean living. But as I always said, 'If a man can be indicted for liking pretty girls, I'm guilty.'"

- Aubrey once expressed what he felt was the thing that separates the men from the boys. "In my opinion, the one thing in terms of leadership that stands out, is not intelligence or ability. Those who operate most effectively, those I respect most, simply are not afraid. And most people are afraid, they're scared of decisions."
- Aubrey played end on the Princeton football team in 1938.

Students must do an online search to get more information on James T. Aubrey.

Study Guide Activities and Issues

Possible exam essay: Compare and contrast James T. Aubrey's formula for television programming success with television programs today.

Please see the study guide chapter on "New Media" for latest developments in TV viewing options which have impacted TV viewer's habits and TV programming.

Through online, text, and other research methods, identify:

Vladimir Zworykin

David Sarnoff (as relates specifically to television)

When and where was television first introduced to the American people?

Milton Berle

Philo Farnsworth

Nielsen: What is a television program's rating? Share?

People Meters

Sweeps (four times a year)

Zippers, Zappers, Flippers, TiVo, VCR and now DVR viewer's habits.

Do you feel that some television "news" programs set an agenda rather that just report the news and let you analyze the information?

What news sources do you trust the most?

Student Notes

Chapter 14
Television and Politics

The electronic media has transformed politics in the United States. As pointed out in a previous unit of study, the impact of radio was immense. Most of the nation had participated in the democratic process having never heard or seen the president other than in the print media.

In the minds of many media scholars, television changed politics forever in the 1952 presidential campaign between Dwight David (Ike) Eisenhower and Adlai Stevenson. It is interesting to note that the candidates were approached by CBS's Bill Paley about the possibility of a nation-wide television debate between the candidates. Eisenhower's television consultant, David Schoenbrun, turned down the invitation.

Efforts were made to make Ike more TV friendly. He was asked to change his military-like bearing. Instead of chin in, chest out, he was advised to lift his head and relax his shoulders and chest thus showing more cheekbone than bald head. He was also approached about the use of makeup to dull the facial glair presented by the lighting necessary in early television technology. Ike was the first presidential candidate to use one-minute television commercials. He was also, with the help of Paley, the first presidential candidate to announce his candidacy live on television. Later, after he was elected, Ike became the first president to be broadcast live from the White House on TV.

The 1952, Republican convention was also notable because Richard Nixon, the vice presidential nominee, was accused of some improper use of campaign funds and he went live on television to refute the charges. The famous "Checkers speech," (Checkers being Nixon's dog which he said was the only gift he and his wife Pat had accepted as related to the campaign) was viewed by thousands and Nixon's words and demeanor swayed the American people and the Republican party to stay with his vice presidential nomination.

In a 1982 book by George Ball, titled *The Past Has Another Pattern*, the author writes:

> *"Stevenson would, I knew be repelled by the idea of using thirty second, or even one minute spots with only a scattered handful of nationally televised half-hour speeches. He still sincerely believed that a campaign should be used to educate people, not narcotize them by an endless succession of asinine political commercials. Spots could not convey ideas, only create fleeting artificial impressions, thus putting a premium on manner and personality. 'Sooner or later' I predicted in an informal speech in New York: 'Presidential campaigns would have professional actors as candidates who could speak the lines.' I did not know how presciently I spoke."*

At the 1952 Republican convention, Walter Cronkite and Edward R. Morrow were anchoring the television broadcast. They were setting new standards for political coverage in America. They found it difficult to ask their questions from up in the control booth and their man on the floor had to compete with legions of print media reporters. While Nixon was being questioned about campaign contributions on the floor of the convention by print-media reporters, the television anchors in the control booth reportedly told their representative on the floor holding a microphone to put his earphones on Nixon. He did as he was told and Nixon was now listening only to the questions posed by Cronkite and Murrow and the print reporters were just standing around staring.

Most political science courses, when dealing with the impact of television on politics, focus on the famous 1960 debates between Richard Nixon and John F. Kennedy.

There were four debates. Kennedy is credited with legitimizing television and polling systems for presidential politics. Kennedy's father used family money to hire Lou Harris who developed a system for finding out the values and needs of the electorate and helping Kennedy's speech writers address those issues.

Books and other print media relate that the Kennedy camp arrived in Chicago a week early for the debates realizing how important they could be. Nixon on the other hand shunned the advice of his media guru Ted Rogers and stayed on the campaign trail until hours before that first debate. There were issues regarding use of makeup that can be researched.

Those who listened to the debate on radio felt Nixon came out on top. However, those viewing the debate overwhelmingly chose Kennedy as the winner. The importance of "reaction shots" in the first televised debate was an important part of the later evaluation of the impact of the TV debate.

It is interesting to note that surveys and forums have found that three quarters of the American people believe that the press has a negative impact on the presidential campaigns with many adding that television campaign coverage leads candidates to perform for the cameras rather than focus on issues.

Study Guide Questions

Does a relentless negativism, enhanced by the criticism in ad campaigns, lead to a public perception that the race is much more negative than political observers think?

Do you feel the media may be able to shape public discourse? Does the media set the agenda for public discussion, whether intentionally or unintentionally? Important issues presented by the media include but are not limited to: color of ties; personalities of the wives and the wives' haircuts, clothes, makeup; balloons falling to the floor at the convention. CNN recently hired a comedian to find "entertaining" sidebars at the convention. America is not ready for some serious political discourse according to their news producers. The gatekeepers pick the issues and sound bites to feed to the large, anonymous, heterogeneous mass of receivers.

Does the candidate who can shape the mediated political discourse, who can control the issues of the campaign through careful media manipulation, win the race?

Do the media fixate on who is winning and losing instead of what the candidates are proposing?

Do political ads define the nature of the presidency by stipulating the attributes a president should have?

Is it difficult for the average American to rely on news to correct or balance political advertisements when Americans are more exposed to and conditioned to advertising formats?

Media corporations are high-powered businesses in a highly competitive capitalistic economic system. They have always sought the unusual, the titillating, and the sensational.

Are today's media outlets becoming less balanced? If less balanced, is this polarization of news coverage reflective of a more politically polarized society?

Should the media, even though in competition for corporate profits, hold themselves to a higher standard of credibility?

In 2013 Newsweek listed the annual income of top television personalities:
Glenn Beck, $33 million, Sean Hannity, $22 million, Bill O'Reilly, $20 million
Jon Stewart, $15 million, Laura Ingraham, $7 million,

Student Notes

Chapter 15
Obscenity and Pornography

Lecture and Notes

The impact of sexually explicit material in our society is debated daily. During the 1960s, a presidential commission was formed to explore the dangers of pornography and later in the 1980s another panel was convened to determine the nature and extent of the effects of obscenity and pornography in the United States. Here is a brief outline of court cases that will help you to explore the issue from an academic point of view:

Of special note will be our discussion of the findings of both the 1960 study done under President Lyndon Johnson and the 1986 Meese Commission report under President Ronald Reagan.

Tariff Act of 1842

This Act prohibited the importation of all indecent and obscene prints, paintings, lithographs, and engravings. It was later expanded in 1857 to include written material.

Regina v Hicklin 1868

QB (Queens Bench) 360 bans all material that tends to deprave and corrupt those whose minds are open to immoral influence. This case traces attempts to censor sexually explicit material back to England. The Hicklin test: "whether the tendency of the matter charged as obscene is to deprave and corrupt those whose minds are open to such immoral influences and into whose hands a publication of this sort might fall."

Of note is the fact that many felt that an entire publication could be considered obscene if any portion could deprave and/or corrupt.

Federal Anti-Obscenity Act 1873

Ban from the mail all obscene, lewd, lascivious or filthy books, pamphlets, pictures, papers, letter writing…Known as the Comstock Law for Anthony Comstock, the federal agent charged with ferreting out immoral materials.

Prurient (Latin root): To itch, to yearn for, to be lascivious, arouses an obsessive or morbid interest in sex.

Roth v United States 1957

Samuel Roth convicted for violating federal obscenity statutes barring the mailing of obscene materials.

The Supreme Court ruled that a work is obscene if:

- the dominant theme of the material taken as a whole appeals to a prurient interest in sex,
- the material is patently offensive because it affronts contemporary community standards relating to the description or representation of sexual matters,
- the material is utterly without redeeming social value.

Memoirs v Massachusetts 1966

Memoirs of a Woman of Pleasure (Fannie Hill)

The eighteenth-century novel by John Cleland included many sexually explicit passages. Supreme Court reaffirmed the Roth ruling and went on to say that if the work had any redeeming social value, no matter how minimal, it is protected by First Amendment. Lower courts convicted. Supreme Court reversed.

Stanley v Georgia 1969

Robert Eli Stanley was convicted of violating Georgia state laws regarding the possession of obscene materials in one's own home. Stanley was suspected of running a betting operation in his home; the police, while searching his residence, found three reels of pornographic films.

Justice Thurgood Marshal, writing for the majority, said:

> *"If the First Amendment means anything, it means that a state has no business telling a man sitting alone in his own house what book he may read or films he may watch. Our whole constitutional heritage rebels at the thought of giving government the power to control men's minds."*

Miller v California 1973

California courts found Marvin Miller guilty of sending unsolicited obscene advertising through the mail in violation of state law.

In this case the Supreme Court reaffirmed that obscenity is not protected by the First Amendment but went on to give state legislatures better guidelines regarding what may be legally obscene.

A work is obscene if:

- "the average person, applying contemporary community standards" would find that the work, taken as a whole, appeals to the prurient interest...
- the work depicts or describes, in a patently offensive way, sexual conduct specifically defined by the applicable state law.
- the work, taken as a whole, lacks serious literary, artistic, political, or scientific value.

Chief Justice Warren Burger also included some definitions of what may be "patently offensive."

1960s Commission on Obscenity and Pornography

Democratic President Lyndon Johnson

- Three years and $2 million to study the "puzzle of pornography"
- Basically the commission found no link between viewing sexually explicit material and subsequent anti-social behavior.

Findings will be discussed in class. Do a computer search on the results of this study.

1980s The Meese Commission

President Ronald Reagan's attorney general Edwin Meese convened a panel of 11 people, most of them prominent conservatives:

"to determine the nature, extent, and impact on society of pornography in the United States and to make specific recommendations to the Attorney General concerning more effective ways to which the spread of pornography could be contained consistent with constitutional guarantees."

- The study found a direct relationship between viewing sexually explicit material depicting violence and aggressive behavior toward women and incidents of the same behavior toward women.
- The commission found a link between viewing sexually explicit materials depicting women in situations of degradation, subordination, domination, or humiliation and the incidence of different nonviolent forms of discrimination against or subordination of women in our society.

Ashcroft v the American Civil Liberties Union 2004

The Supreme Court 5–4 upheld a judge's order that kept the government from enforcing the Child Online Protection Act of 1998. That Act would impose a $50,000 fine and six months in prison for the operator of a commercial website that posted "patently offensive" photos or descriptions that were available to minors. Website operators could defend themselves by requiring a credit card number or an adult access number to enter the site.

The justices stopped short of declaring the law unconstitutional. Instead they sent the case to a court in Philadelphia for a trial to decide whether software filters would work as well as a criminal law in shielding children from online pornography.

Consult your text and/or do an online search for:

U.S. v Extreme Assoc. **2005**

What did the material at issue deal with?

What did the Supreme Court rule in this case?

What was the key element of the "Miller Test" that was a determining factor in the Court's ruling?

Study Guide Questions

Do a computer search to find the *Ashcroft v ACLU* case and summarize one of the minority opinions in the case.

Do searches on the following and be able to explain or identify on an exam:

Anthony Comstock

Butler v Michigan 1957 (Laws cannot ban sexually explicit material from adults just because the material may be considered harmful to children.) Consider Section 343 of the Michigan Penal Code which makes it a misdemeanor to sell or make available to the general reading public any book containing obscene language "tending to the moral corruption of youth. What did Justice Frankfurter say in this case? (Mr. Butler sold the offending book to a police officer.)

***Reno v ACLU* 1997** (Internet is entitled to the highest First Amendment protection.)In 1997, a group of organizations, including the American Civil Liberties Union (ACLU), challenged the "indecent transmission" and "patently offensive display" provisions of the 1996 Communications Decency Act. These provisions made it a crime to send offensive Internet material to persons under age eighteen. The district court found for the ACLU. On behalf of the Federal Government, Attorney General Janet Reno appealed to the Supreme Court.

The Supreme Court invalidated both provisions of the Communications Decency Act (CDA) of 1996, because they violated the First Amendment's guarantee of freedom of speech. Justice John Paul Stevens wrote an opinion in which six other justices joined fully.

Justice Stevens reviewed the operation of the Internet and the difficulty of verifying the age of an Internet user. Justice Stevens pointed out several problems with the act: It did not define "indecent," it did not allow parents to authorize their children to access restricted materials, it applied "to the entire universe of cyberspace" rather than to well-defined areas. Moreover, the Internet is not a "scarce" commodity like the airwaves, so there is less justification for governmental regulation. Finally, the regulated materials do not just appear on the computer screen, but must be actively sought out.

***Hannegan v. Esquire, Inc.*, 327 U.S. 146 (1946),** was a <u>U.S. Supreme Court</u> case argued between the <u>United States Postal Service</u> and *Esquire* magazine. In a unanimous decision, the Supreme Court ruled that the USPS was without statutory authority to revoke a periodical's second-class permit on the basis of objectionable material that was not obscene.

Jacobellis v Ohio 378 U.S. 184

Appellant, manager of a motion picture theater, was convicted under a state obscenity law of possessing and exhibiting an allegedly obscene film, and the State Supreme Court upheld the conviction.

***New York v. Ferber*, 458 <u>U.S.</u> <u>747</u> (1982),** is a precedential decision given by the <u>United States Supreme Court</u>, which ruled unanimously that the <u>First Amendment</u> right to free speech did not forbid states from banning the sale of material depicting children engaged in sexual activity. SCOTUS on first examination of a statute specifically targeted against child pornography, it found that the state's interest in preventing sexual exploitation of minors was a compelling "government objective of surpassing importance." The law was carefully drawn to protect children from the mental, physical, and sexual abuse associated with pornography while not violating the First Amendment.

What are current efforts by the federal government to stop the spread of obscenity and pornography?

Go to 60Mins.com website and do a search for segments they have produced relating to the effects of pornography in our society. Summarize one in the space below.

Chapter 16
Magazines

The development of the magazine industry has played an important role in American history. Early magazines gave writers more time to do in-depth reporting and became a vital instrument of early muckrakers. Today magazines are a great example of segmentation of the media. Magazines are able to reach so many "niches" appealing to diverse reader values, needs, interests, beliefs, and attitudes.

List three magazines you view on a regular basis?
1.

2.

3.

What do these magazines offer that you cannot get through other media outlets?

Next time you are at an airport, note how much time you spend in the stores that display magazine titles.

Do you find yourself looking at magazines you have never noticed before? What are some of the new titles you are drawn to?

Do you find that if you buy a magazine at the airport, you are likely to read it more carefully than you do the ones you subscribe to at home? (You have to admit, being strapped in at 35,000 ft makes for a pretty "captive" audience.)

Study Guide Activities

Do text and online search for:

Henry Luce

Time/Life Magazine

Modern trends in magazine production. Note the impact of the Internet on the magazine industry. Also note the move of magazine to online formats.

List three magazines you purchased off the stand in the last month.

Do you feel that "women's" magazines "cultivate" values like how women look and what they feel about their role in society? Explain.

Go to a local Barnes and Noble or Borders bookstore and go to the magazine section. List the magazines that appeal to young girls 10–13, then 14–18. List the advertisements most prominent in these publications.

1.

2.

3.

4.

5.

6.

7.

8.

9.

List four magazines that you feel would most appeal to men. Say why you think they may appeal to this demographic and list the advertisements most prominent in these publications.

What are "zines" and what is their role in society?

Go to the AdWeek website and search for the current list of their ranking of the year's "Hottest Magazine." What are their criteria for their ranking?

Student Notes

Chapter 17
The Muckrakers

The role of muckrakers in American media history has been a major factor in giving citizens here a quality of life that has been arguably the envy of the modern civilized world. Their efforts to investigate social ills or injustices in society were instrumental in initiating reforms. Throughout U.S. history, the media, empowered by the First Amendment to the U.S. Constitution, have used their guaranteed freedoms to give the public information they have both the need and the right to know.

During the academic term of this course, students are required to watch the *CBS News Magazine, 60 Minutes*. This requirement is not meant as an endorsement of the program as the "be all, end all" of television investigative programming. However, over the years, it has established a high level of credibility in the area of investigative news production. It is considered by many to be an example of modern-day muckraking. The program does generate important and many times controversial topics that make for excellent classroom discussion and debate. It is a good example of the "Power of the Fourth Estate."

It rarely beats popular programs like American Idol or Dancing with the Stars in the ratings but it many times does make the top 10 rated programs and thus shows "hope for our democracy."

Class Activity:

Form groups of two or three students. Together, research a selected or assigned "muckraker." (many are listed at the end of this study guide lesson)
Prepare a 3–5 min. PowerPoint to present to the class.
Be sure to include:
1. Name and pictures
2. What they investigated and what they found
3. What was the impact of their published investigation

Study Guide Activities

Names and terms you will be required to know for exams. Use online searches, text, or library sources to elaborate on the contributions of the following:

Teddy Roosevelt: Where did the term "muckrakers" originate?

Horace Greely: *New York Tribune*. First to separate fact from opinion in the newspaper.

Jacob Riis: An investigative journalist. Wrote *How the Other Half Lives*

Lincoln Steffens: *The Shame of the Cities*, a series of articles on how city government institutions work together to effect their own agendas.

Ray Stannard Baker: *McClure's* Magazine.

Charles Russell: Wrote about Georgia chain gangs' abuse, leading to prison reform.

Ida Tarbell: Investigated and wrote a 19-part series on the monopolistic excesses of Standard Oil and J.D. Rockefeller.

Upton Sinclair: Wrote *The Jungle*. Led to the Pure Food and Drug Act.

David Graham Phillips: Exposed corruption in the election of senators by state legislatures, leading to the Seventeenth Amendment to the U.S. Constitution.

Teapot Dome Scandal: President Harding and Secretary of the Interior Albert Fall.

Edward R. Morrow: McCarthyism.

Drew Pearson: The muckraker with a Quaker conscious.

Tad Schultz (also spelled Szulc): Bay of Pigs.

Daniel Ellsberg: *The Pentagon Papers*.

Carl Bernstein/Bob Woodward: *All the President's Men*—the Watergate Scandal.
We again mention here, the movie *Spotlight*. *This was a movie dealing with the Boston Globe's investigation into abuse by the Catholic Church.*

List some modern-day examples of journalistic "muckraking." (Think information related to government spending, war conduct, business scams, insider trading, political corruption including bribes, etc.) Note the number of bloggers engaging in investigative research regarding issues of public concern.

Student Notes

Chapter 18
Persuasive Media: Advertising

Use text, library, and online sources to familiarize yourself with the historical background regarding advertising.

Advertisers use words and images to persuade us to take some action. Most often the purpose of commercial advertising is to get us to part with some of our hard-earned money. Political ads use words and images to persuade us to vote for a certain issue or candidate.

Through your educational journey, instructors have put a premium on thinking logically. Logical thinking is the kind of thinking we do when we consider the results of certain actions. Logical thinking is based on evidence. Logical thinking requires putting words together in statements and putting statements together to arrive at conclusions. It is important to realize that we all occasionally engage in other forms of mental activity, including daydreaming, reminiscing, and making random associations. Students, however, must make important distinctions between the benefits of these forms of thinking and logical thinking.

Some common blocks to our logical thinking process take into account our respective beliefs, values, needs, and attitudes. Some of these become a preconceived prejudice or ready-made judgments. Many times strong emotions, influenced by values and beliefs, can block our logical thinking process.

Again, one of the great things about this course is that we can find current media examples for this exercise to discuss in class. Here are some common fallacies of logical thinking that people in the persuasive media business use to influence us.

1. **Hasty Conclusions** (Secundum Quid): This fallacy occurs when a generalization is made before enough specific items have been examined. Keys to this fallacy come when we hear the word "all" or the words and images used infer that all the items should be included.
   Examples:

2. **Appealing to Authority** (Ad Verecundiam): It is natural that we develop a certain level of respect for parents, teachers, clergy, doctors, and other professionals. We also associate a level of authority with items presented as statistics, charts, and more.

   However, when these symbols are used out of context or are presented in a way where the authority is not named or verified, we should be careful. Another aspect of this fallacy is the appeal to potential incompetent authorities. This fallacy is

sometimes referred to as the "big name" fallacy. We need to make sure that the person being used as an authority on a product or issue really does know a lot about the subject.
Examples:

3. **Appeal to the Crowd** (Ad Populum): This is one of the most popular of the advertising/propaganda techniques. There are three parts to this fallacy:

> a. Flag waving: This fallacy appeals to our love of America and American institutions and symbols to get us to take an action or buy a product we might not otherwise consider.
> Examples:

> b. Bandwagon: Most of us want to feel we belong. This fallacy either says or shows "everybody" getting behind the issue or product and "you do not want to be left behind."
> Examples:

> c. Reverse bandwagon: Here we pick up the people who "are not like everyone else." They are the independent operators who do not like being like everyone else. So they become part of a group of millions to whom advertisers appeal with certain ads.
> Examples:

> d. Tear jerking: It is important to be caring and even sympathetic to causes or issues. But let's be logical in evaluating how much of our contributions really go to the cause being promoted and how much goes to "administration." Commercial-product advertisers use this fallacy as well.
> Examples:

4. **False Analogies:** Analogies are comparisons. We use comparisons often to help make a point. Advertisers, politicians (and, yes, your college instructors) know this, so we need to check to make sure that the things being compared have enough points in common.
Examples:

5. **Faulty Dilemmas:** This fallacy occurs when only two choices are given when more actually exist. Key words in this fallacy are "either/or."
Examples:

6. **The Hidden Major Premise:** This fallacy relies on our acquired knowledge about inductive and deductive logic. The classic form of deductive logic is a syllogism. A syllogism has three main parts. First is the major premise, which usually begins with the word "all." It is followed by the minor premise which is

linked to the major premise but is more detailed. Finally is the conclusion. A=B, B=C. Therefore: A=C.

All mammals are warm blooded. Whales are warm blooded. Therefore: Whales are mammals.

In first grade, the teacher holds up a picture and asks us what we can learn from looking at this picture or what can we deduce from the picture? The fallacy occurs when advertisers, with words and images, lead you to a conclusion that has not been supported by a major premise. They purposely fail to STATE the premise upon which the conclusion is based.
Lots of examples:

7. **Meaningless Words:** Words have both denotative and connotative meanings. Advertisers can use words is such a way and with special emphasis so that the words seem to have special meaning when they do not.
Examples: Smoother, mellower, better tasting. It "conditions" your skin, "Come up to the Kool taste", etc.
Other examples:

8. **You Too** (Tu Quoque): This fallacy occurs when we rotate a charge upon one's accuser. Two negatives only add up to a positive in math, not in our social or political life. Two wrongs do not make a right. This fallacy is often found in political advertising.
Examples:

9. **After This Because of This** (Post Hoc, Ergo Propter Hoc): We will not be using this fallacy to evaluate advertising. However, this argument is often tried in political debate. It is an error in the understanding of the cause and effect relationship. It is assumed that just because an event follows another in time, the first is the cause of the second.
Examples:

10. **Begging or Ignoring the Question** (Argumentum Ignorare): A question is posed in an ad but never directly answered. A public figure or official is asked an important question but spends time talking about everything but the answer to the question.
Examples:

11. **Getting Personal** (Ad Hominem): Many times in political debate, candidates will stop addressing the issues and start attacking the personal life of their opponent. This fallacy is also many times referred to as "name calling" or "mudslinging."
Examples:

Student Notes

Tear three ads out of a magazine that you think are really well done. Then, after analyzing them in light of the "common fallacies", list the fallacies you think the advertiser may be using in each respective ad.

Other Terms and Issues Covered on Exams

Advertising agencies

Consumer advertising

Creative boutiques

Marketing

Federal Trade Commission

First advertisements in colonial America

Evidence of advertising in Roman society

Ad copy

Caveat emptor

Current trends in coordinating television "advertising pods"

Current trends to make television ads more entertaining (List at least three examples from current television advertising.)

Abraham Maslow's Hierarchy of Needs (from the bottom)

1. Physiological: hunger and thirst.
2. Safety: law and order (security from danger).
3. Belongingness and Love: to be accepted.
4. Esteem: to achieve; to be competent.
5. Cognitive: to know; to explore.
6. Aesthetic: order and beauty in the universe.
7. Self-actualization: realize your own potential; be self-fulfilled.

How do advertisers play to these "needs" to add value to their respective products? Give three examples of advertisements on television that play specifically to one or more of Maslow's list of human needs.

Tear three ads out of a magazine and identify which level of Maslow's Hierarchy of Needs the ad appeals to.

The course/study guide blog has flash card elements for this lesson as well as Quizlet questions.(Go to reedsmassmedia.wordpress.com)

Chapter 19
Persuasive Media: Propaganda

The world of words includes connotations and denotations. Words can be used in different ways with different effects. Propaganda takes advantage of this fact. As you have learned in the "logical thinking" unit on advertising, words used in certain contexts illicit very emotional responses. Here we again see how words and images are used to persuade individuals and/or groups to take a course of action they might not ordinarily take.

The book/video *Faces of the Enemy* by Sam Keen, a noted author, social observer and commentator, gives some examples of how words and images are used to effect an end. The dictionary definitions for the word **propaganda** are:

1. Publicity to promote something: information or publicity put out by an organization or government to spread and promote an idea, doctrine, or cause.

2. Misleading publicity: deceptive or distorted information that is systematically spread. However, there are many feelings and emotions tied to the word as well.

Generally propaganda is associated with the use of highly charged images and words to move to action. The most important lesson learned is, Keen says, that before we are moved to war, we have to CREATE an image of the enemy. He gives us several poignant examples including an example related to a 1945 U.S. propaganda film about the Japanese and another example from a 1938 Nazi film about Jews.

Study Guide Activities

Do an online search for Sam Keen, *Faces of the Enemy* (book and film).

What insights does Keen make into "enemy making"?

What analogies were drawn in the referenced WWII Nazi propaganda films?

What did American WWII propaganda films propose Americans do?

According to Keen, before we go to war we have to create_____.

What are some of the propaganda techniques you have studied in this class that are used by America to goad citizens to actions they might not otherwise take?
Keen wants us to consider:

In the end it is easier not to talk, think, and feel. If we view our enemies as abstractions, that makes what easier?

What is the role of cartoonists?

Whose side is God on?

We are good, they are evil.
We are honest, they are liars.
We are heroes, they are villains.
Individual action versus national action

In election years, use "fact checking"
sources to hold political figures
accountable for their respective
statements in debates and in ads.

Chapter 20
Film

The impact of motion pictures on society is well documented. The digital age has marked another revolutionary era in film history. Hollywood has had a major impact on the basic values, needs, beliefs, attitudes, and more of Americans. Many felt with the advent of the video cassette and DVDs, movie theaters would go out of business. Instead they have proliferated. In fact, these new technological advances, including MP3 players, Netflix downloading of movies directly into homes, and more have enhanced the revenue of the big movie houses.

Citizen Kane Study Guide
Released 1941, RKO

Orson Welles, starred, directed, supervised casting, and coauthored the script.

He made his mark in media production with the 1938 War of the Worlds radio broadcast.

Welles was 25 years old when he made Citizen Kane.

It took Welles six months to film and less $1 million to produce the film.

- Number One on the American Film Institute's list of the 100 Greatest Movies
- Number Four on the Writers Guild of America list of the 101 greatest screenplays ever. (After *Casablanca*, *The Godfather*, and *Chinatown*.)

Plot: Life of Charles Foster Kane (parody on William Randolph Hearst)

Lecture: Research and discuss the parallels of the movie character and the real media mogul.

Sound: echo, recorded sound effects, and music to tell the story:

Specific examples from the film:

Technique: newsreel, camera angles, flashback, zoom, lighting techniques, and use of light to set the mood for the telling of the story, also use of light and shadow to show power.

> Use of the hook: Rosebud
> Specific examples from the film:

Aging of the actors—use of makeup. Find scenes where the use of short vignettes to explain a relationship and move the story. (hints: marriage, scene near the end when characters speak in a large room with fireplace)

List some of the parallels you find in your online research between the fictional Kane character and William Randolph Hearst.

Outline here information from the course blog on Citizen Kane.
Look under: Film heading

Study Guide Activities

Through online searches, text, and other information resources identify the following:

Hays Production Code

Birth of a Nation

Charlie Chaplin

"Star system"

Motion picture rating systems

Books to read when you have time:

<u>The Chief</u> by David Nasaw

<u>Citizen Hearst</u> by W. A. Swanberg

Study Guide Questions

Possible exam essay question:
Rent the CD of *Citizen Kane*: Write a short essay explaining why the American Film Institute ranks the film the best film of all time.

Based on box office ratings at the time you are taking the course, what does the American public seem to value most on the "big screen"?

Chapter 21
Public Relations

Public relations (PR) practitioners seek free time and space in the media. Advertising is purchased time and space in the media. Through class lecture and PowerPoint presentation, the following public relations factors will be presented and discussed.

Essay question on the final exam:

What are the skills needed to effect a successful public relations campaign for a non-profit organization?

1. Learn to write a press release in the Associated Press style.
2. Network: join local and regional press clubs, local chambers of commerce, and service organizations. Contact gatekeepers and ask them to lunch.
3. Be opportunistic: Look for ways to set your business apart from the rest. Learn to read the small print and take advantage of special circumstances. Learn and study the content of the many special sections and departments of electronic media.
4. Learn to take pictures: Take classes that teach you how to take photos that look good in print. Learn the different capabilities of digital cameras and the computer software associated with them.
5. Always think and plan ahead.
6. Learn how to organize and host a press day or special event.
7. Learn how to develop and deliver a PowerPoint presentation: Know that a picture is worth a thousand words. Images should be displayed not less than three seconds and not more than five.
8. High tech/high touch: Learn to be personable. Know the importance of hand-written thank you notes.
9. Study local media deadlines. Know the four elements of news: impact, timeliness, proximity, and credibility.
10. Make sure to be honest and straightforward.
11. Learn to be a good public speaker.
12. Develop and/or subscribe to media contact data banks.

Most historians agree that the first real public relations pioneer was Ivy Lee. In 1903, Lee and George Parker opened a publicity office. During the Pennsylvania coal operators strike, Lee issued a "Declaration of Principles," which included "be open and honest." After WWI, Carl Byoir and Edward L. Bernays came on the scene. Bernays wrote the first book on public relations, _Crystallizing Public Opinion_, published in 1923.

Study Guide Activities

Please do an online search to find out more about Ivy Lee and Edward L. Bernays. List important elements of what you find:

Through text, online, and other sources define or identify:

Spin doctors

PR tactical plans

Management-by-objective PR (MBO)

Integrated marketing communications (IMC)

Areas with public relations interests: (Explain the function of each.)

1. Business

2. Government and politics

3. Educational institutions (Including sports departments)

4. Hospitals

5. Nonprofits

6. Professional organizations (attorneys, doctors, dentists, etc)

7. The entertainment industry

8. Professional sports

9. Environmental organizations

Explain the "crisis management" function of public relations. Give an example

Explain the impact of social media on public relations.
Give examples.

Create a list of public relations jobs in your geographic region.

Student Notes

Chapter 22
Impact of New Media

The impact of online delivery systems is having an immense impact on how we interact with family, friends, school, work, businesses, government, and more. Cell phones make communication faster and more mobile. The Internet makes almost all aspect of life more expedient. We are able to research movies, restaurants, doctors, lawyers, teachers, health issues, and just about every aspect of our day-to-day wants and needs. The ability to access emergency help and report crime even to the point of being able to record such with cellphone cameras, has become an important factor in everyday life. This mass communication phenomenon fueled by daily technological innovations and development can have a down side. Invasion of privacy issues, car accident impacts, human predator issues, accessibility of sexually explicit material concerns, not to mention intergovernmental "hacking" and monitoring of terrorist networks, are all being addressed by academic institutions, government security officers, and elected officials nationwide. It is incumbent upon college students to be well versed in the basics of social media and to engage in vigorous debate regarding its positive and negative impacts.

Impact:

- **Wiki's** (i.e. Wikimedia, Wikipedia, WikiCommons, WikiLeaks): Wiki means quick in Hawaiian. Wikipedia is one of the most popular resources on the Web. It is an "open editing" model which allows anyone to edit and contribute to articles. This type of forum often gets criticized as a reliable source of information.

   Study Question: Why is Wikipedia not a stand-alone reliable source for obtaining information?

- **Blogs:** Internet Web logs. These are user created sites that contain posts/articles that allow interaction with readers such as comments or links to other articles posted on the Web.
   1) In 2006, more than 12 million adults created blogs.
   2) In 2006, 39% of Internet users read blogs.
   3) As of March 17, 2011, 73% of Internet users went online to get information about the 2010 mid-term election as sited from the Pew Internet & American Life Project study.

- **Mobile devices:** smart phones, iPads, tablet computers.
   1) As of March 2011, 47% of U.S. adults got some form of news on their phone or tablet computer.
   2) Of that 47%, only 1 in 10 use an app to get their information instead of a browser.

- Lists some of the present impacts of the WikiLeaks site.

Sociological Impacts:

- **Internet groups** (i.e. Facebook, Instagram)**:** 80% of all users participate in some form of online group. **Instagram** is an online <u>mobile</u> <u>photo-sharing</u>, <u>video-sharing</u>, and <u>social networking</u> service that enables its users to take pictures and videos, and share them either publicly or privately on the app, as well as through a variety of other social networking platforms, such as <u>Facebook</u>, <u>Twitter</u>, <u>Tumblr</u>, and <u>Flickr</u>.

1) These groups include Facebook groups of organizations
- By 2010, most people had shifted to social networking instead of blogging
   1) History of MySpace and its impact on the Millennial Generation:
      a) Founded in 2003 and by 2007 boasted 188 million individual profiles
      b) It served as a place for people to put updates, pictures and music, the last allowing users to buy songs from the site
      c) In 2006, the site goes international, opening servers in the UK, Japan and France, and finally China in 2007
      d) Paved the way for the social networking giant Facebook
   2) Problems/consequences:
      a) Concerns by schools, parents and law enforcement that the publicity of social networking sites is an invitation to predators
      b) Real world example: (a girl was denied her degree because of photos on her Myspace)
   3)
   4) Some interesting updated stats from 2015:
   5) 2.4 billion people around the world use the Internet (out of 7 billion).
   6) 8.7 billion machines are connected to the Internet (including smartphones, tablets, refrigerators, soda pop machines…
   7) 78% of North Americans use the Internet.
   8) Facebook has 1.4 billion users worldwide.

   Sites such as Craigslist allow users to post items they are selling, real estate listings, and any other product they wish to share in an open forum

Political Impacts:

- April 2011: President Obama announces his re-election via an online video.
- April 11, 2011, former Massachusetts Governor Mitt Romney announced his Republican presidential bid through online video.
- After breaking off budget talks with Republican, California Governor Jerry Brown took his case to voters through a video posted on YouTube.
- Other political members have used Twitter, Facebook, and other social media not only to inform voters but also to slam their opponents as opposed to simply relying on commercials during elections.
- Candidates can directly reach voters platforms where they work and play— YouTube, Facebook, and Twitter

- In 2012, Republicans Tim Pawlenty and Mitt Romney announced their respective presidential aspirations via Facebook and Twitter.

2016 Candidate Donald Trump uses Twitter to attack other candidates.

Study Questions:

What has been the impact of Craigslist on newspapers?

Do an online search for the debate on "net neutrality" the principle that individuals should be free to access all content and applications equally, regardless of the source, without Internet service providers discriminating against specific online services or websites.

Supporters say…..?

Opponents say…..?

The FCC voted on February 26, 2015 that it could make net neutrality rules based on the powers given them in the 1934 Federal Communications Act

What is the impact of Twitter and Facebook on restaurants, retail, travel, and other businesses?

Write a short page and a half essay, typed double-spaced on how you would use "new media" to enhance a business you might start or work for.

What is the impact on society of text messaging? Remind, WeChat, Facebook Messenger, SnapChat, WhatsApp, Skype and others. Note the unique features of each.

What about the impact of new steaming television?

List the unique features of:

Apple TV

Amazon Fire TV

Google Chromecast

Roku 4

More than 100 internet video streaming service are available. A few of the more popular:

Amazon Prime

CBS All Access

Crackle

Crunchyroll

Dove Channel

DramaFeaver

HBO Now

Hulu

LucasOilRacing.TV

MLB.TV
Netflix
NFL Game Pass
Noggin
SeeSo
Sling TV
Showtime
Smithsonian Earth
Tennis Channel Plus
TheBlaze TV
Univision Now
WWE Network
YouTube Red

Note the service you use. List the cost (if any) and the unique feature that led you to subscribe.

It is appropriate to note here Facebook's work on developing its "virtual-reality" device Oculus. What is the status of this development at the time you are studying New Media?

It is also instructive to note the auto industries led by Tesla and Google toward self-driving cars. At the time you are taking this course, what is the status of this development?
This Movie is recommended: View the movie and turn in a 2-page, typed double spaced review.

The Social Network is a 2010 American biographical drama film directed by David Fincher and written by Aaron Sorkin. Adapted from Ben Mezrich's 2009 book *The Accidental Billionaires: The Founding of Facebook, A Tale of Sex, Money, Genius, and Betrayal*, the film portrays the founding of social networking website Facebook and the resulting lawsuits. It stars Jesse Eisenberg as founder Mark Zuckerberg, along with Andrew Garfield as Eduardo Saverin and Justin Timberlake as Sean Parker, the other principals involved in the website's creation. Neither Zuckerberg nor any other Facebook staff were involved with the project, although Saverin was a consultant for Mezrich's book.[3] The film was released in the United States by Columbia Pictures on October 1, 2010.

Students may want to read the book **Steve Jobs by Walter Isaacson** and/or do an online search for Steve Jobs and write and two page paper on how he impacted "new media"

List of Resources

The Structure and Function of Communication in Society in the Communication of Ideas (New York, Harper, 1948)

Milestones in Mass Communication Theories and Research: Media Effects (New York, Longman, 1983)

Introduction to Mass Communication by Black, Bryant (McGraw Hill, 1998)

Miracle at Philadelphia by Catherine Drinker Bowen

Major Principles of Media Law by Overbeck (1990)

http://www.socialhistory.org/biographies by Harrison Gray Otis, Harry Chandler, Norman Chandler

Californians and the Military, Major-General Harrison Gray Otis by Mark Denger, found at www.militarymuseum.org/Otis

Los Angeles Times, October 1, 1919, Front Page

The Powers That Be by David Halberstam

Harrison Gray Otis by Albert Greenstein

Otis Chandler 1927–2006, "A Lion of Journalism." *L.A. Times*, February 28, 2006, Special Section

"Aubrey: A Lion in Winter," *L.A. Times*, April 27, 1986, Calendar Section

Newsweek, November 8, 2010

Appendices

Please note: Power Point and/or Prezi presentations are available for each lesson. Contact the Journalism Department, Saddleback College, Mission Viejo CA, 92692.

Journalism Program Goal Statement

Many journalism programs recognize the significance of the 2005 Carnegie Corporation of New York report "Improving the Education of Tomorrow's Journalists." This report was the culmination of research and interviews with the nation's most prominent publishers, presidents, chairmen, editors, anchors, senior correspondents, and producers about the state of journalism education and what journalism schools might do to elevate the profession's standards and status.

These findings and recommendations correspond with research, interviews, and evaluation conducted by various local, regional, and state program administrative and instructional staff through sabbatical leave research and study, alumni survey, and correspondence, student survey, and test results. These findings are reflected in the educational goals of many respected college/high school journalism programs.

1. The journalism program recognizes and promotes the fact that it is understood in our country that journalism is central to the strength and vitality of American democracy. The press, an institution outside government, was included among the civic organizations and activities to be protected by the Bill of Rights. A free press, the founders believed, was essential to keeping watch on the affairs of government and creating an active, politically informed public. (Carnegie Report p.1)
2. The journalism program emphasizes the basics of the journalism craft along with analytical thinking and a strong sense of ethics. This includes the basic writing skills, as well as the paramount importance of getting the facts right. Students need to develop good news judgment and analytical skills, including the ability to separate fact from opinion and use statistics correctly. (Carnegie Report p.3 and 6)
3. The journalism program helps student reporters understand the importance of developing specialized expertise to enhance their coverage of complex beats, from medicine to economics, and help students acquire first-hand knowledge of the societies, languages, religions, and cultures of other parts of the world.
4. The journalism program seeks to identify and channel the best writers, the most curious reporters, and the most analytical thinkers into the profession of journalism.

Others findings of the Carnegie Corporation Report that are recognized and discussed across the journalism curriculum include:

1. Concern about the media's quest for profits and audience. The report concludes the most critical responsibility of journalists is to serve the public interest and protect our democracy.
2. The challenge for journalism and journalists is to find ways to interest readers and viewers in news that is vital to a functioning democracy.
3. The concern that much of the news has too much "edge," particularly from "talking head" shows on cable news and radio.
4. Concern that a shorter-attention span among the public forces reporters to make the news fast and exciting. This leads to concern about training prospective reporters to know even

more about complex beats if they are to deliver stories that are both shorter and more interesting.

5. The report also expressed a concern that young students aspire to become on-air television reporters and anchors without first mastering the skills of hard news reporting.

6. The report could not overemphasize the importance of upholding the ethics of journalism. They believe that the ethical ramifications of journalism must be infused throughout the curriculum, not just taught in ethics classes.

7. The report mentions the importance of working on the college newspaper as an excellent preparation for a journalism career.

Course Research Paper

Students transferring to a four-year college or university must exhibit a proficiency in writing a research paper using proper documentation. In this course, students will be required to turn in a 3–5 page mini-research paper.

Students may select other media-related topics but only upon instructor approval. Students must cite from at least three different sources in the text of their mini-paper.

The accepted method of documentation for this paper will be the Modern Language Association (MLA) method. MLA uses parenthetical references within the text keyed to a Works Cited list at the end of the mini-paper.

A typical reference would include the author's name and a page number. If you use the author's name and the title of the work cited in the text, then the page number is all that is required at the end of the paragraph. Please check your English course text for more examples.

The college's Learning Assistance Program (LAP) also provides resources for review of this method of documentation. The college library also provides a 2–3 page handout outlining the proper MLA format. It is pretty much expected that, upon high school graduation, students have been introduced to this or some other universally accepted method for attributing information in a research paper. To quote or paraphrase information from another source without giving credit can lead to charges of plagiarism.

Many students turn to the Internet for research. Please remember that information and articles must be properly cited in the text and on the works cited page. These citations most often include authors' names and pages cited or brief article titles and page number if the article is not authored.

Works Cited pages should include only works cited. If other sources were used and you would like to include them, please label the reference page a "Works Consulted" page.

Remember, even Supreme Court opinions are authored and, of course, opinions on the opinions are authored.

Note: Examples offered by course instructor in class.

Mini Papers Topics

1. The impact of Internet gambling on society.
2. The impact of on-line pornography on society.
3. The impact of cell phones on society.
4. Career options for journalism and communications majors.
5. The polarization of American: radio and television news.
6. Polarization of America: radio talk shows.
7. The impact of the internet on newspaper circulation. The future of newspapers in America.
8. The impact of the Internet on magazines. The future of magazines in America.
9. The impact of cell phones on the motion picture industry.
10. The impact of the Internet on the music industry.
11. The impact of the Internet on the motion picture industry.
12. The level of basic knowledge of and understanding of the U.S. Constitution by students in the eighth grade locally.
13. How important is the First Amendment to the U.S. Constitution to high schools students locally? Nationally? How many know the four freedoms listed in the First Amendment? How important is "the public's right to know?"
14. How important is the First Amendment to parents locally? (Minimum of 50 surveys.)
15. What is the impact of social media on society?

Students must use primary research methods. (Surveys: at least 50) Survey questions must be presented to the professor prior to distribution. In the 3–5 page paper, relate the findings of your primary research and link it to research on the topic you do on the Internet. Use at least two Internet sources. Provide a thesis statement and a conclusion that sums up your findings.

Term Project Course Requirements
An Introduction

Former students email the journalism program chair from their status as upper-division students at four-year colleges and universities stating that the term project they completed for their Mass Media and Society class was one of the most important assignments they completed, not just in the course, but some add that it proved to be one of the most important assignments completed while an undergraduate student. Some students are able to go back to the institution or business where they conducted their interview for the project and obtain an internship to fulfill their upper-division requirement in that area. Many students conduct an interview in an area in which they are interested only to find out, after the interview project, that this is NOT an area of communications they would like to pursue.

It is suggested that you select a media job you think you might like to have one day. It is important that you begin the process of scheduling your interview within the first few weeks of class. People working in the media, as with most professions, are very busy and need plenty of lead-time to set time aside for an interview. Students are encouraged to move outside their own circle of friends and relatives for interview possibilities. All students MUST clear their term project subject with the course instructor **prior** to the interview.

Term Project Guidelines
Project grade weight to be determined by instructors

First: Call a local or regional media source and tell them you are enrolled in a Mass Media and Society course and you need to interview someone at a media-related business for a class term project worth one quarter of your semester grade.

It helps to have a tape recorder or other recording device. It also helps to have a camera because you are **required** to have a picture of you with the person you interview, at the place where they are employed, included on the cover/title page of your report.

What area of media you are most interested in; public relations, print journalism, advertising, T.V., radio, etc? Try to pick a person with a broad background in the area of your choice. Pick someone who can answer most of the provided questions. If the media personality you chose cannot answer all the questions, maybe they can direct you to someone at the business who can. It is possible to interview someone outside your local community or region with the instructor's permission.

Next: Go IN PERSON and conduct an interview at the person's place of business. The interview MUST be in person and not over the phone. Get a picture of you with the person, with you, at the person's place of work. NO HOME BUSINESSES! Person interviewed must be a full-time employee.

Make sure to take a recording device to record the interview but also take written notes in case something goes wrong with the recording. Be sure to get permission to record from the person you interview before beginning the formal interview.

1. Background and history of the publication or business.
2. Publication circulation, estimated audience, or number of clients.
3. The geographic area served by the business.
4. How many editions, programs, or services are associated with this business or publication?
5. What are the demographics and psychographics of the audience served?
6. What are the gatekeeping policies of this media source? Who makes the editorial decisions? Who are the gatekeepers?
7. What or who provide the main competition?
8. Where do the revenues come from to support this media business?
9. If they have advertising, how much does it cost and to whom do they sell? Does the business accept community feedback?
10. What jobs are available in this business? What is the best entry-level position? What are the wages one could expect for various job descriptions within this media business? (Be sure to ask for salary ranges, do not ask for the specific salary of the person you are interviewing) Is the position paid hourly, salaried, do they pay stringers or freelancers?
11. Does the business sponsor internships?
12. How does the person you are interviewing like his or her job? What are their specific duties and responsibilities? What are the positive and negative aspects of their job?
13. What educational and/or vocational training is necessary for most full-time positions at this business? What are the best places to get this education or training?
14. What are the job benefits? (Insurance, perks, freebies, payola, junkets, other) These questions serve as a guideline. You are expected to develop your own questions both before and during the interview. Not all the questions apply to all businesses so improvise and come up with some of your own questions.
15. What is the "online" presence of the business? What do they feel is the impact of online delivery systems?
16. What is the future of print journalism?
17. What is the impact of social media?
18. Try to relate some of your class lecture, terms, and issues you have discussed in class. Ask them questions about how pertinent the information you have learned is to the real world of mass communication.
Be sure to include your evaluation of the assignment at the end of your interview.
No Q and A formats. Write the report as a personal essay or feature

story. The reports should be typed double spaced, 8–10 pages long.

Cover page:

Term Project
Journalism 1, Mass Media and Society
Professor J. Mike Reed

Your Name
Date
Time your class meets

(Put the picture in this space!!)

Name of the business you visited
Address of business
Phone number of business
(Number you used to make your contact for interview)
Name and title of the person you interviewed

Please staple the cover page to your report for presentation to the professor. It is preferred you do not use cover folders.
5 extra credit points may be awarded for reports handed in the week
before due date.
Projects handed in late may have points deducted at the instructor's discretion.
No projects accepted after last regular class meeting.

Student Special Project:
Native Americans in the Media

Voices and Dreams

Native American
History, Literature, Art, and Culture

Project created as part of a 1997
National Endowment for the Humanities
Seminar

Stated objectives in the course outline for JRN/CA 1, Mass Media and Society reveal that students will engage the topic of ethnic minorities in the media. The course deals not only with treatment of women and racial minorities but it also explores the effects of under representing and misrepresenting women and minorities in the media.

The summer 1997 "Voices and Dreams" seminar at Saddleback College presented several valuable resources for exploring the treatment of Native Americans in the Media.

Students will use these resources to fulfill the mini-paper or special survey requirements for the media course.

To fulfill the "Treatment of the Native American" in the media requirement, the student will read, discuss, and answer short essay questions relating to the content of the four listed chapters in the book *Shadows of the Indian* by Raymond William Stedman.

Chapter 4, Indian Talk
- Lone Ranger radio broadcasts and telecasts
- TV Yancy Derringer series
- Last of the Mohicans
- Nick of the Woods

Chapter 8, The Enemy
In novel and film, virtually all surprise attacks on peaceful travelers from concealed position were the work of Indians.

Chapter 13, Mea Culp
- Stagecoach
- The Way West
- Cheyenne Autumn
- Soldier Blue
- A Man Called Horse
- Fort Apache
- Little Big Man
- I Will Fight No More Forever

Chapter 14, Lingering Shadows
Important media issues reviewed

Students are required to view and review at least three films from the following list. The reviews must deal with the portrayal of Native Americans in the film, as well as, what they feel the effects of these portrayals are on society in general.

List of Films:

Stagecoach
The Way West
Cheyenne Autumn
Soldier Blue
A Man Called Horse
Fort Apache
Little Big Man
I Will Fight No More Forever
Last of the Mohicans
Dances with Wolves

Lesson Objectives

Give students a view of the social impact of images created in the media of minorities especially Native Americans.
Students will become aware of the effects of media portrayals socially, politically, and economically.
Students will explore, in discussion and written essays, ways the media can effect change to more fairly represent Native Americans in the media.

Questions for Discussion and Possible Essay Exam

1. Is the vocabulary attributed to Native Americans in broadcast and film media demeaning? Why yes, why not? Examples?
2. Do the Indians belong to the feather-bonnet tribe? (all one big tribe syndrome)
3. What is the impact of comic interludes built upon the effects of firewater? (Interesting to note that alcohol was a problem in the U.S. Calvary)
4. Are the Indians portrayed as an extinct species?
5. Are the Indians either noble or savage?
6. Are portrayals patronizing? How so? Examples.
7. Is the Indian's humanness recognized? (Do they have homes, families, emotions other than mindless fury?)
8. Aside from the menacing chief or the lovely princess, do the Indian characters have personal names? Daily tasks? Amusements other than drinking or torturing?

Written Projects Should Include:

- An introduction with a thesis statement.
- Written reviews and evaluations of the content of each of the four chapters from *Shadows of the Indian*.
- Written two-page reviews and evaluations of the content of each of three movies from the required lists.
- Paragraphs dealing with aspects of the eight listed question above.
- Conclusion
- Works Cited Page
- Cover Page: (Title of project, student name, name of course, day and time course meets, date)
- All work should be typed, double spaced in a serif typeface.

Reckless 2:

Nobody's Girl

Reckless 2:

Nobody's Girl

Keisha Ervin

www.urbanbooks.net

Urban Books, LLC
97 N18th Street
Wyandanch, NY 11798

Reckless 2: Nobody's Girl Copyright © 2014
Keisha Ervin

ISBN 13: 978-1-62286-926-8
ISBN 10: 1-62286-926-5

First Mass Market Printing August 2015
First Trade Paperback Printing September 2014
Printed in the United States of America

10 9 8 7 6 5 4 3 2 1

*This is a work of fiction. Any references or similar-
ities to actual events, real people, living or dead, or
to real locales are intended to give the novel a sense
of reality. Any similarity in other names, characters, places, and incidents is entirely coincidental.*

Distributed by Kensington Publishing Corp.
Submit Orders to:
Customer Service
400 Hahn Road
Westminster, MD 21157-4627
Phone: 1-800-733-3000
Fax: 1-800-659-2436

Who wants that perfect love story anyway?

—Jay-Z featuring Beyoncé,
   "Part II (On The Run)"

Prologue

The sun barely kissed the afternoon sky as Farrah placed a cardboard box on top of her king-sized bed. For months she'd dreaded this moment. Her children had asked her repeatedly to gather her late husband's belongings, since she was downsizing and moving into a small apartment. But Farrah just couldn't bring herself to do it. Her husband's things were all she had left of him.

They were her most coveted and cherished treasures. She couldn't part with them and place them into storage. It would be like acting as if he never existed, like the love they shared wasn't the kind of love stories that were written about. Farrah couldn't box up a nearly fifty-year marriage and tuck it away in a cold, dark room. The love between her and her husband was the kind you dreamed of as a little girl. It withstood the test of time. Their love was unwavering, strong, and authentic.

She'd spent half of her life with him. They'd fallen in love quickly, fought, broke up, made up, pledged their love to God, traveled the world, and bore children together. When Farrah's husband became sick with stage-four colon cancer she was right there by his side until he looked into her eyes and took his last breath. And even though she'd wrestled with the thought of this day for months, she couldn't put off the inevitable any longer. Moving day was here. Her three children and some of her grandchildren were there, helping her pack.

"Granny," Farrah's oldest grandson Ross said, knocking softly on the door. "You okay?"

Farrah looked up at her grandson and tried her hardest to blink back the tears that begged to fall. Ross was the spitting image of his grandfather. At twenty-three years old he was tall, charismatic, and smart.

"Yeah, baby, I'm okay." Farrah sat on the edge of her bed.

"I ain't know Paw-Paw had all of this stuff." Ross looked around the room in amazement.

All of his grandfather's clothes, shoes, photos, books, awards, and memorabilia from his successful career were scattered everywhere.

"Yeah, your grandfather collected a lot of things over the years." Farrah examined the room as well.

"What's this?" Ross picked up an old photo book. "I never saw this album before." He sat beside his grandmother.

Farrah looked on somberly as Ross flipped through the album.

"You and Paw-Paw look young."

"I wasn't always an old woman." Farrah admired a picture of her when she was thirty.

Although she was eighty-one years old, gravity had been good to her. She wasn't the vibrant, youthful woman she'd been in the picture, but for an elderly woman, Farrah's beauty showed through the wrinkles and age spots on her skin. Beauty and fashion were still an important part of her life and she took pride in taking care of herself.

"Let me see that." Farrah reached out her shaky hand.

Ross handed her the photo album.

"Your grandfather was a good-lookin' man." Farrah traced the outline of his face and smiled.

"Was it love at first sight when y'all met?"

"Something like that," Farrah chuckled. "Your Paw-Paw and I had sort of a rough start."

"What happened?"

"Well . . ." Farrah took a deep breath and gazed out into space.

Chapter 1

You used to be sweet to me.
—Ledisi, "Turn Me Loose"

Every girl dreams of that *Sex and the City* moment where Mr. Big rushes to Paris to declare his undying love for Carrie, finds her, rescues her from the evil Russian, and kisses her tears away. Shortly thereafter they walk hand in hand into a life filled with Manolos, candlelit dinners, and bliss. Eight months ago Farrah James's Mr. Big, Corey Mills, aka Mills, made all of her dreams come true when he got down on one knee and put a ring on her finger. Now she was on top of the world.

Her company, Glam Squad, which she co-owned with her bestie London, was skyrocketing. Together they'd styled and done makeup for Lana Del Rey, Solange Knowles, and Rihanna. They'd even styled Lady Gaga for *Vanity Fair*'s September issue and dressed Emma Stone for the Oscars. On top of her career successes, she and Mills were planning their star-studded multimillion-dollar wedding, house hunting, and she was considering getting pregnant again.

After a bitter breakup, Farrah aborted their first baby, but now she was more than ready to bear Mills's child. On the outside looking in, Farrah and Mills's relationship was destined to fail. For three years she'd dated Mills's best friend, Khalil, but after years of dealing with his alcoholic and mindless behavior, Farrah broke things off. Distraught over their breakup, she found solace in Mills's friendship. Over time it turned romantic, despite the fact that Mills was in a six-year relationship with his then girlfriend, Jade.

After tiring of trying to make his failing relationship work, Mills left Jade and instantly made Farrah his new woman, disregarding his doubts that they could really make it work. Soon Mills's fears came into fruition when, drunkenly one night, he slept with Jade. Mills was so torn up over his infidelity that when he assumed Farrah was cheating on him with Khalil, he kicked her out of his crib. He then went on to not speak to her for weeks, although she'd told him she was pregnant.

With nowhere to turn, Farrah did what she felt was best at the time and aborted their child. However, weeks later, after Mills learned that Jade had been cheating on him for the last year of their relationship, he begged for Farrah's forgiveness and won her back. Now eight months later, she was sitting on cloud nine. Little did Farrah know, at any moment the floor was sure to fall from beneath her feet.

It was half past one and she'd been stalling celebrity wedding planner, Adore Phillips, for over thirty minutes. They had a ton of things to discuss, but none more important than the all-time-consuming seating chart. With the wedding only a month and a half away, she and Mills had to finalize who would sit where. Farrah tapped her black five-inch Louboutin Pigalle heels against the floor and eyed her watch again nervously.

She was supposed to be concentrating on the words coming out of Adore's mouth, but they fell on deaf ears. All she could think about was Mills. He knew how important this particular meeting with their wedding planner was. *I'm gonna kill him*, she thought to herself as Adore showed her pictures of the finalized menu cards.

"Excuse me, Adore. Do you mind if I give Mills a call? He should've been here by now."

"Sure thing, hon." Adore eased back out of her chair. "Just tell him to get his butt over here quick. I have a two o'clock appointment with Brad and Angelina."

"Okay," Farrah said, nodding.

"I'ma grab me a cappuccino. Would you like one?" Adore asked.

"No. Thank you. They give me headaches," Farrah politely declined.

"Okay." Adore closed the door behind her.

As soon as the coast was clear, Farrah picked up her phone and called Mills. To her surprise he answered on the first ring.

"What up?"

"Where are you?" she hissed.

"Stuck in traffic," Mills groaned.

"Which highway did you take?"

"I'm on Forty."

"Oh, my god." Farrah massaged her forehead. "Are you kidding me? How far away are you? Adore has another appointment at two o'clock."

"I'm going as fast as I can, Farrah," Mills sighed. "Just give me a minute."

"Okay, but hurry up." Farrah ended the call.

"Did you reach him?" Adore reentered the room with her cappuccino in hand.

"Yeah, he's on his way. He's just stuck in traffic. He'll be here any minute," Farrah assured.

Unbeknown to Farrah, Mills was not stuck in traffic. He was actually at Forest Park. Forest Park is one of St. Louis's largest and oldest parks. It was massive, so he didn't have to worry about anybody spotting him. Sitting anxiously on a park bench, he awaited his ex Jade's arrival. For the past eight months he'd been telling lie after lie. With the way things were going it didn't look like the lies were going to stop anytime soon. He couldn't fathom how not telling Farrah about his infidelity would lead to him living a double life. Since the night Jade called and dropped the bomb that she was pregnant, Mills had been secretly keeping in contact with her.

Since there was a huge possibility that Jade's baby was his, and he didn't want Farrah to find out that he'd cheated, Mills made sure that Jade's housing and medical bills were paid. He'd even gone to visit her after she'd given birth to a baby girl she'd proudly named Jaysin Cori Mills. Mills couldn't see any resemblance between him and Jaysin, but he'd continued to support Jade financially until his paternity test was done. His schedule was all booked up until after the wedding, so he'd already decided to take the paternity test after his and Farrah's honeymoon.

Mills had mixed feeling about taking the paternity test. A part of him just wanted to get the results so he could move on with his life and figure out what he needed to do next. But another part of him was afraid to find out the truth. If Jaysin was his, he had no idea if or how to tell Farrah. There was no way Farrah would stay with him and Mills couldn't have that. He'd worked too hard to win her trust back. For Mills, ending up alone seemed inevitable if he was the father. Mills was, overall, anxious about getting the paternity test done, so he could find the much-needed air to breathe or a shovel to dig his own grave.

As a slight October breeze swept over his skin, he spotted Jade in the distance. She walked with all of her weight shifted to the right because of the pumpkin seat in her right hand. Although Mills no longer looked at Jade in a loving or sexual way, he couldn't deny her beauty. Even after having a baby, sex appeal still dripped from her pores. Jade was made for the camera. She was aesthetically perfect. She stood five feet nine and her measurements were a dick- hardening 34-24-38.

Her butter-colored skin, blond buzz cut, full mouth, curvaceous hips, and ample behind made men and women turn their heads. But Mills wasn't fooled by her good looks. He knew what lay behind the surface was a self-centered, cold-hearted bitch.

"Hey," she said, sitting the pumpkin seat down on the bench next to him.

"What's up?" Mills replied, drily.

"It's a little chilly out today, isn't it?" Jade rubbed her hands against her arms to create body heat.

"Yeah." Mills reached into his jacket pocket and pulled out a check. "Here." He held it out.

Jade eyed him and shook her head. Since Jaysin had been born, it was the same routine every month. They'd meet in the park, he'd hand her a check, then bounce. Mills didn't try to hold the baby or ask how she was doing or anything of the sort. It was like neither of them existed. It was bad enough that she had to go through her entire pregnancy alone. Jade figured that once the baby was born, Mills would come around, but she was sadly mistaken.

Mills didn't have anything for her but a check to keep her quiet and an attitude. Yes, she'd done him dirty and broken his heart and for the rest of her life Jade would regret her actions, but their daughter didn't have to pay for her transgressions. Jaysin deserved better. She was Jade's greatest accomplishment. From the moment she was born, Jade made a vow to be a better person.

Her needs no longer mattered. Everything she did was for Jaysin. She just wished that

Mills felt the same. Jade slipped the check from Mills's fingertips and read it. Her heart instantly dropped to the pit of her stomach. The check was only for a grand.

"Listen." She took a deep breath. "I'm not tryin' to be a bitch or get all off into your pockets, but this is not enough. I need more money."

"Excuse me?" Mills screwed up his face.

"Don't even start all of that." Jade tried to reason. "All I'm sayin' is this is not enough to cover the bills, Jaysin's doctor bills, formula, Pampers, and putting food in the house. It takes a lot to take care of her, Mills. I just need a little bit more money every month."

"You got a lot of nerve," Mills chuckled. "You need to be happy that I'm even giving you that. 'Cause I don't see that other nigga giving you a dime."

Mills referred to NBA star Tyrin Rhodes, aka Rock, whom Jade had cheated on him with.

"Why would he?" Jade countered, becoming pissed. "She's not his daughter."

"That's to be determined," Mills scoffed.

"Are you kidding me? She looks just like you." Jade snatched back the blanket that was covering Jaysin's face.

Mill looked at the three-month-old baby out of the corner of his eye and saw bits of himself staring back at him. She was a gorgeous baby girl who held most of her mother's exotic looks, but her smoldering brown eyes and deep dimples reminded her of him.

"Like I said—" Mills sat up straight. "I don't know if that's my baby and neither do you."

"Oh, my god, you are unbelievable," Jade said in disbelief. "You know that she's your daughter. You just don't wanna step up and take responsibility 'cause you haven't told your so- called fiancée yet."

"What you mean, *so—called fiancée*?" Mills ice grilled her. "She is my fiancée and we're getting married in a month and a half, as a matter of fact."

"And that's fine Mills," Jade stressed. "I'm happy for you, but you need to acknowledge your daughter. I need your help and the money that you're giving me is not enough."

"Well, I don't know what to tell you, 'cause I'm not giving you no more money. You can forget that."

"What am I supposed to do?" Jade shrilled.

"How about get a job?" Mills shot.

"I can't. I don't have anybody to watch her." Jade felt her face become hot.

Tears were beginning to form in her eyes. There was a time when Mills would have never talked to her like this. He used to be sweet to her, but those days were long gone and Jade had no one to blame but herself.

"That's your problem. And just to let you know, when I get back from my honeymoon we gon' get all of this straight once and for all."

"Get what straight?" Jade furrowed her brows, confused.

"I'ma get a paternity test done."

"Wow," Jade said, stunned.

"I don't know what you sayin' *wow* for. Let's not pretend that you weren't fuckin' another nigga behind my back, let alone in my bed," Mills barked.

"Whateva, Mills," Jade said, waving him off. "Do what you gotta do, 'cause I'ma do what I gotta do."

"You do that, then." Mills stood up and placed on his shades.

As Mills walked down the trail leading to his car, Jade sat staring out into the open space. When she'd awakened that morning she hadn't suspected that things would end up this way. Mills was angry and bitter and he had every right to be. But Jade had to do what was best for her daughter, even if that meant taking things into her own hands and calling Mills's bluff.

Chapter 2

You give me reason for another day.
— Tweet featuring Bilal, "Best Friend"

Twenty minutes later Mills pulled into the parking lot of Adore's office building, only to see Farrah angrily stomping toward her car. Her long hair blew in the wind as the heel of her Louboutins clicked loudly against the pavement.

"Bay!" He placed his car into park and hopped out.

Farrah stopped mid-stride and spun around.

"What?" she huffed.

"Where you going?"

"Where does it look like I'm going? I'm going back to work." She resumed walking toward her car.

"Come here, man," Mills yelled from across the lot.

Farrah rolled her eyes to the sky and strutted over to him. Mills's dick instantly got hard as he watched her small hips sway underneath the glow of the afternoon sun. She was the quint-essential new-age Marilyn Monroe. Everything about her was timeless and unique. Farrah was a pint-sized beauty.

She reached only five feet three in and weighed only 105 pounds. Her sun-kissed skin reminded him of gold. Her light brown, slanted eyes, button nose, pink, pouty lips, and *Sports Illustrated* physique turned Mills on to the fullest. Being in the fashion industry, Farrah had an edgy swag to her that most women could never possess. She rocked both sides of her long, silky black hair shaved like Cassie and an array of small tattoos that only Mills had the pleasure of being able to find.

That day she rocked a black, sleeveless, studded T-shirt, which highlighted her black lace bra and the tightest pair of paisley-print skinny-leg jeans Mills had ever seen. His chick was the baddest and every time she stepped foot onto the scene, she murdered bitches. Mills loved her tremendously and couldn't wait until the day he made her his wife.

"What?" Farrah folded her arms across her chest and stepped into his personal space.

Mills had no place to go. She had him trapped. His back was pressed up against the driver-side door of his car and the death glare she was giving him had him sweating bullets.

"You mad at me?" He looked lovingly into her eyes and tried to pull her close.

"Is that what you called me all the way over here for?" Farrah snapped, slapping his hands away.

"I'ma take that as a *yes*," Mills chuckled.

"I don't see nothin' funny. Where were you?" Farrah rolled her neck.

"I told you. I was stuck in traffic."

"You're lyin'," Farrah squinted her eyes. "You weren't stuck in no damn traffic."

"How you figure that?" Mills tuned up his face.

"'Cause I checked and there was no traffic on highway Forty. Now tell the truth. Where were you?" Farrah asked sternly.

"Damn," Mills cocked his head back. "What are you, the police?"

"I might as well be since you hiding shit from me," Farrah shot.

"Trust me, I had every intention on coming. I just got caught up." Mills took her by the hand and tried pulling her close again.

"Caught up doing what?" Farrah allowed him to hold her this time. "'Cause I know whatever you were doing wasn't more important than this."

"If you must know, I was tryin' to plan a surprise for you li'l nosy-ass girl." Mills lied to cover his tracks.

"A surprise?" Farrah looked at him sideways.

"Yeah." Mills tried to sound convincing.

"Mmm-hmm." Farrah pursed her lips, not fully believing him. "Well, you missed everything. I had to finalize the seating chart without you, so I don't wanna hear no shit about why I got yo' mama sitting right next to yo' daddy."

"I promise I ain't gon' say shit," Mills said, laughing.

"Do you see me laughing? You know, it's bad enough that I've been practically planning this wedding by myself. You could've shown up today, Corey. That's the one thing I asked you to do and you couldn't even do that," Farrah said, visibly upset.

"You need to go head wit' all that. Who you think payin' for all this shit?" Mills snapped. "If I don't bust my ass doing all of these tournaments and fuckin' commercials and shit, there won't be no wedding."

Mills was a pro-BMX rider. He was so good at his job that he had endorsement deals with Mountain Dew, Gatorade, and Nike. His dashing good looks only added to his success. He'd done print ads for the Gap and H&M. Women went crazy over him, especially Farrah. She loved that he towered over her. Mills stood at six feet two and possessed butter-colored skin. He donned a low cut, thick eyebrows, mesmerizing brown eyes, chiseled cheekbones, kissable pink lips, and a goatee. His entire upper body was filled with tattoos and every time he flashed his megawatt smile that exposed his dimples, Farrah melted.

"Are you sure you even want to marry me?" she asked suddenly.

"Don't talk stupid." Mills looked at her like she was crazy.

"No, I'm serious, 'cause lately you've been actin' hella strange and I don't know what to think." Farrah spoke a mile a minute. "I'm tryin' my best to make this wedding perfect, make sure all of my clients are happy, find a new house, and make sure that me and you are good, but I can't do everything—"

"Shhhh," Mills stopped her mid-sentence and placed his index finger up to her lips.

"Nobody asked you to do everything. You gon' fuck around and make yourself sick stressing over this shit. The wedding and none of that other stuff matters. All that matters is that me and you are together."

"But—"

"But nothing, li'l hardheaded girl. Look, can we just take a minute and breathe?" Mills gazed into her eyes.

Farrah knew he was right. She had to calm down. With the deafening sound of the city streets behind them, she let all of her anxieties fade away and rested her head on Mills's chest. In his arms, she always felt safe. He was her best friend. She trusted him with her life. Being with Mills gave her a reason to live another day.

The love Farrah felt for him went deeper than mere words. When they took these moments just to relish each other's presence, she was reminded of why she was marrying him. He was her everything and without him she didn't know if she could go on, so she said a silent prayer to God, asking that he never take him away.

Mills and Farrah's wedding was only a few weeks away and it was the night of their joint bachelor-bachelorette party. They were having the event at the Jumping Jupiter, which was a live-entertainment performance venue. The Jumping Jupiter offered burlesque, fire-juggler, and acrobatic performances. As soon as their guest walked in they felt as if they'd been transported back in time to a place where liquor was illegal and being naughty was a sin.

Farrah couldn't have been more pleased with the space. Crystal chandeliers and velvet curtains hung from the ceilings. That night she and Mills, along with a fifty of their closest and dearest friends, had the entire place all to themselves. Everyone was mesmerized by the vaudeville decor and tantalizing men and women who hit the stage. While their guests enjoyed the mouthwatering food and breathtaking performances, Farrah sat off to the side by herself.

She slowly sipped on a glass of ginger ale while their guest sipped on chilled glasses of Perrier-Jouët that had been specially flown in for the event. With all of the laughter and music surrounding her, Farrah found it hard to fully enjoy herself. She couldn't take her eyes off of Mills. He was killin' every dude in the spot. His swag was impeccable. Mills was rockin' the hell out of a black custom Tom Ford fitted blazer, black T-shirt, black jeans, and a pair of Air Jordan 3's. To cap off the look, he got his 2 Chainz on and rocked two gold rope chains.

But his well-put-together ensemble wasn't what had Farrah trippin'; it was the look of fear that hid behind his eyes that had her shook. She could feel his energy from fifty feet away. She could tell just by looking at him that he had a lot on his mind and that it had nothing to do with work or their wedding day. Farrah wished that she could pinpoint exactly what was stressing him. But no matter how hard she searched, she couldn't find the location of his agony. It didn't help that every time she asked what the problem was, he got upset and emotionally pushed her away.

All Farrah wanted was to fix him, because they couldn't go into their marriage with things the way they were. She'd already begun to make things up in her mind, like he was cheating or wanted to back out of the wedding, but didn't know how to tell her. Farrah took a deep breath and exhaled all of her worries. *Mills loves me*, she reminded herself.

No relationship was easy and she and Mills were just going through a rough patch. Things would get better. Besides, leaving him wasn't an option. Farrah was in it for the long haul. She just prayed that whatever the problem was wouldn't break him—or better yet, them.

"What's wrong wit' you?" London plopped down beside her.

"Nothing." Farrah shot her a small smile.

"Who you think you foolin'?" London arched her eyebrow. "This is me. I know you better than you know yourself."

"Ugh. I hate that you know me so well." Farrah hung her head and laughed.

"Then stop frontin' and tell Mama what's wrong." London nudged her with her shoulder.

"I don't know. I might be trippin,' but I just feel like it's something going on with Mills."

"Like what?" London took a small sip of her drink.

"I don't know." Farrah shrugged her shoulders. "He won't tell me, but I know it's something."

"I personally think you're reaching. It's probably just pre-wedding jitters. All men go through it."

"Nah," Farrah said, shaking her head. "I think it's more than that."

"I don't know. The only thing I can tell is you just pray and ask God for discernment. He'll show you what you need to know."

"You're right. I will. Maybe it's just me. I have been hella stressed-out lately. Planning this wedding and dealing with finding a house is driving me nuts."

"Then quit worrying yourself. We suppose to be kickin' it. Put a smile on your face, pretty girl, and let's go dance." London moved her shoulders.

"You know, I love you more than Miguel loves a good enema, right?" Farrah joked.

"I love you too, friend," London laughed.

While the performers took a brief inter-
mission, the in-house DJ began to play A$AP
Rocky's hit "Fuckin' Problems," featuring 2
Chainz, Drake, and Kendrick Lamar. As soon as
Farrah stood up she and London started to twerk
it. Farrah loved to dance. When her feet hit the
floor it felt like the only thing that mattered was
her and the beat. Mills watched from afar as she
did her thing. Farrah had no idea that in a matter
of seconds he was about to give her a surprise of
a lifetime. Although it was a last-minute idea,
Mills came through in the clutch like always.

"Ay yo." Mills's pot'nah, R & B singer Teddy,
approached him with a perplexed look on his
face. "There's a dude outside sayin' he got a
package for you."

"Bet," Mills replied, excited.

"What's going on? You straight?" Teddy quizzed.

"Aww yeah. I just got Farrah an early wedding
gift 'cause the other day we had an appointment
with the wedding planner and I missed it 'cause
I was with Jade," Mills whispered so no one else
could hear.

"My dude, you gotta get that handled," Teddy
said worriedly.

"I know. I just need a little more time," Mills
stressed.

"A'ight, you keep on waiting. She gon' fuck around and find out on her own," Teddy warned.

"I feel you, but I'ma get everything straightened out as soon as we get back from the honeymoon."

"A'ight," Teddy replied, still unsure. "Now, what's up wit' this surprise?"

"I'm gettin' ready to show her now." Mills eased his way through the crowd over to Farrah.

"You came to dance wit' me?" She beamed.

"Nah, I got something I wanna show you, though." Mills signaled to the DJ to cut the music.

"Sorry to interrupt the festivities, but I wanted to take out the time to say thank you to all of you for coming and celebrating our pending nuptials. Farrah and I couldn't be happier or more grateful to have each and every one of you in our lives." Mills paused as their guests began to clap and whistle.

"As you all know, the reason why we're here is because in less than a month I will be marrying my best friend, my biggest fan, my everything, the love of my life, Farrah."

Never the one to be the center of the attention, Farrah buried her face in the crook of Mills's arm.

"I love you." Mills kissed the top of her head. "And if you'll follow me, I have something to show you outside." He led her and the rest of the crowd outside.

Farrah was floored when she found a brand new, fully loaded, chrome Mercedes-Benz G63 AMG SUV.

"You didn't? This is not mine, is it?" She looked up into Mills's eyes for confirmation.

"It ain't mine," he laughed.

"OMG, this is too much." Farrah walked over to the car in awe. "It's beautiful." She slowly glided her fingertips across the hood.

"You like it?" Mills asked.

"I love it." Farrah ran over to him and wrapped her arms around his neck. "You didn't have to do this."

"I told you I had a surprise for you."

"I thought you were just playing," Farrah giggled.

"What I tell you about thinkin'?" Mills leaned down and kissed her lips.

As he tenderly kissed her lips, Mills's hands roamed Farrah's back and ass.

"You tryin' to get some tonight?" She smiled.

"Why you ask me that?"

"'Cause if you keep on touching me like that you gon' fuck around and find the road map to heaven." Farrah broke away from the kiss, barely able to breathe.

"That's the point." Mills shot her devilish grin.

"You are something else. You know that? You are something else." Farrah imitated the comedian Kevin Hart.

"Shut up," Mills laughed.

"Guess what?"

"What?"

"I got a surprise for you too." Farrah stood on her tiptoes and whispered in his ear. "I think I'm pregnant."

Dizzy from worry, Mills paced back and forth across the wooden floor. In three minutes his life could potentially get worse. If the pregnancy test Farrah had just taken came back positive, Mills would have to pack his things and move to another state, maybe even another continent. How would he tell his soon-to-be-wife? "Yay we're having a baby—and, oh by the way, my ex-girlfriend Jade, whom you hate, might have a baby by me too."

Mills knew it was wrong on so many levels, but as they waited he silently prayed to God that Farrah wasn't pregnant. And yes, he knew that Farrah wanted a second try at getting pregnant, since she had hastily aborted their first child. Mills, however, didn't have the heart to tell her that for him it wasn't a good time.

"What time is it?" He anxiously wrung his hands together.

Farrah examined her watch.

"One a.m," Farrah replied.

"Damn, it's only been a minute." Mills said, annoyed.

"Calm down. You're making me nervous." Farrah unconsciously tapped her foot against the floor.

She didn't know who was more nervous: her or Mills? In two minutes her whole, entire world had the potential of getting ten times greater. Her fairy tale would be complete. If she was pregnant, she'd have it better than Carrie Bradshaw. All Carrie had was the man of her dreams and a successful career. Farrah would have the complete picture: the man, career, and the baby. Life couldn't get any better.

As another minute slowly went by, Farrah persisted in tapping her foot and praying. *Lord, please let me be pregnant. Please let me be pregnant,* she repeated over and over in her mind.

"It's time," Mills announced.

Farrah stared at him and took a deep breath. Her stomach was in knots as she gradually got up and entered the bathroom. There, on the countertop of the sink was the little white stick that held the key to her fate. Farrah took another deep breath, closed her eyes, and picked up the pregnancy test.

"What does it say?" Mills asked, nearly about to faint.

Farrah slowly cracked one eye open and gazed at the screen. There, staring back at her—sealing her fate—were two negative lines. Farrah opened her other eye and sighed.

"It's negative." She dropped her hand down to her side.

"You sure?" Mills lifted her hand to take a look for himself.

Sure enough, the results were negative. Mills was overcome with glee, but he didn't let it show on the outside.

"Damn, I'm sorry, baby." He hugged her from behind and kissed the back of her neck. "Maybe next time. You gon' be a'ight?"

"Yeah," Farrah tried to convince herself. "I'ma just get ready for bed and take a bath."

"A'ight, let me know if you need anything. I'ma go turn on this game real quick." Mills headed into the other room.

Farrah quietly closed the door and turned on the shower. Steam from the hot water immediately filled the room. Farrah rubbed the mist from the steam off the mirror and gazed deep into her own eyes. It wasn't the end of the world that she wasn't pregnant. She'd gotten pregnant once, so she knew that it wasn't impossible for her to get pregnant again. It just hurt that it wasn't happening at that very second and time.

The other real issue was that ever since the abortion she'd secretly regretted her decision. She regretted it so much it ate her up inside. If she wouldn't have acted out of emotion she would've had a beautiful baby boy or girl. But she had and now every time she came in contact with a baby a gut-wrenching sting of pain shot through her chest. Choking back the tears that drowned her throat, Farrah let the pregnancy test slip from her fingertips and into the trash.

Chapter 3

*Actions speak louder than words
and they say I don't care.*
        —Trey Songz, "Me 4 U Infidelity 2"

For days Farrah had been running herself so ragged between work and the last-minute wedding details that she didn't know her left from her right. Everyday had become a whirlwind of pure insanity, but Farrah wouldn't have it any other way. The best days of her life were ahead. Soon she would be standing at the altar before God, her family, and friends, pledging her undying devotion to the man she'd prayed her whole life for.

This was the perfect part of life that songs were written about and movies were made of. All of her dreams were in the palm of her hand. The only thing that would make it better was the little bambino she and Mills had been trying for. But they had all the time in the world for that.

As long as they had each other, she was at ease. Bogged down with client portfolios, her wedding book, mail, grocery bags, purse, cell phone, and five-inch heels, Farrah teetered into her and Mills's loft.

"Shit!" she huffed while trying to hold her phone up to her ear.

"Are you all right?" London asked from the other end of the line.

"Yeah, I was just trying not to drop anything." Farrah placed everything down on the kitchen countertop. "Whew, I'm tired." She breathed heavily.

"You sound like it, fat girl," London teased.

"Excuse you. I just weighed in this morning at the gym and I lost three pounds."

"What, from your fat-ass head?" London joked.

"Ha-ha-ha, funny, bitch. I swear, you's the biggest hater. You just better be able to fit into your dress when we go to the final fitting this weekend."

"Honey, please, I got this," London popped her lips.

"Says the person who had hot wings, salad with extra dressing on the side, mozzarella sticks, and a slice of cheesecake for lunch today." Farrah laughed while going through the mail, which mainly consisted of grocery and furniture-store ads.

"Damn, today Shop 'n Save was taking ten dollars off every fifty-dollar purchase. I should've took my ass there instead of going to high-ass Whole Foods."

"I told yo' bougie ass to stop shoppin' there. Whole Foods is a luxury, not a necessity. You better start going to ALDI, Pete's, and Save-A-Lot. Shit, I know a chick right now that'll sell you a book of stamps for a cigarette."

"You're an idiot." Farrah continued to rummage through the mail and came across an envelope from the Missouri Department of Family Services addressed to Mills.

Farrah knew she had no business opening up his private mail, but a letter from DFS only spelled trouble. As she broke the seal on the envelope she could vaguely hear London on the other end of the phone talking away, but every word out of her mouth was inaudible. Farrah's heart was beating so loud she couldn't hear a thing. She hadn't even gotten the letter out of the envelope and she was already overcome with extreme anxiety and sweat. Once the letter was in her hand and the words were in front of her eyes, Farrah felt as if she was about to die.

"Farrah," London called out to her.

"Huh," Farrah answered breathlessly.

"What are you over there doing?"

"Umm." She tried to gather her thoughts. "Nothing . . . look, let me call you back." She hung up without waiting for a response.

Feeling weak, she slowly took a seat at the dining room table. The letter felt like fire on her fingertips, but she had to reread it for confirmation. Sure enough, her eyes weren't deceiving her. DFS was summoning Mills to take a paternity test to prove that he was the father of Jade's daughter, Jaysin Cori Mills. Just seeing the name *Jaysin Cori Mills* was like a pitchfork being staked into her eyes.

Farrah didn't even know that Jade was pregnant, let alone had a child. Reading further, she realized that the baby was now four months old. In pure shock and disbelief, Farrah let the paper fall onto the table and silently began to cry. She didn't know what to think or how to feel, she was so stunned. Then it all began to sink in. Mills had cheated on her. In order for Jade to think that Mills was the father of her child, they had to have slept together.

And Jade must've been confident that he was the father, because she'd named the baby after him and given it his last name. "This muthafucker cheated on me," Farrah finally uttered out loud. "He fuckin' cheated on me." To hear the words being spoken from her lips crushed

Farrah's soul. In two weeks she was set to marry a man it turns out she barely knew.

"What am I gonna do?" she asked herself.

Farrah's mind told her to pack up her shit and go, but running wouldn't solve a thing. She still had questions that needed to be answered. Plus, she had to stick around just so she could see the look on Mills's face when she confronted him with the news. His expression would confirm whether he knew about the baby or not. Then it dawned on Farrah that she didn't have to wait to see the look on his face. His behavior over the last few months said it all.

Farrah would bet money that he knew about the baby and to prove her suspicions were right, she went fishing for evidence. She ransacked his drawers, shoe boxes, clothes—anything she could, find but found nothing. With their bedroom in disarray, Farrah placed her hands on her hips and pondered where she should search for evidence next.

"Bingo!" She snapped her fingers and ran over to his laptop.

Seconds later she was logged in and going through his files, but nothing incriminating popped up. Stumped, she bit her bottom lip, then decided to check his bank account. Scrolling through his debits, she saw that just a month prior he'd written a check to Jade Thomas in the amount of 1,000 dollars. Farrah's heart sank all the way to her toes. As she continued to go through his debits, she learned that Mills had written Jade a check every month for the last year.

The first check dated back to a week after they'd gotten engaged. Numb, Farrah printed off his account history and returned to the kitchen. *I am so fuckin' stupid*, she thought, shaking her head. Before Farrah knew it, hours had gone by and she hadn't moved an inch, except to pour herself several glasses of wine. For hours she'd sat still, like a corpse, replaying the last year in her head. Everything about it had been a lie.

Every intimate moment she and Mills shared had been cursed. Every time he'd confessed his undying love for her, was only him overcompensating for his betrayal. Every time they held in-depth conversations about their future was just a dream being sold to her on his behalf. She could never trust him again. He'd made her look like the ultimate fool once more.

All she could think was from that moment on how she would proceed. She couldn't even stop crying for a second, so how could she function in the world? With each sip of wine tears scorched her cheeks. Death was the only option to cure her pain. It was the only thing that would cease it.

Maybe if he came in and found me dead, he'd see just how much he'd hurt me, she thought, but killing herself wouldn't help any. The only thing that would happen is she'd be dead and Mills would eventually move on and probably end up with Jade, no less. Blind with rage, Farrah thought back to the first time she suspected Mills of cheating. She remembered the night like it was yesterday.

She and Mills lay snuggled up in bed, wrapped in each other's arms, watching *Unsung Millie Jackson* when a text message came through on Mills's phone. He swiftly turned over and grabbed his phone. Farrah glanced at the clock. It was 12:30 in the morning. She didn't say anything, but she wondered who would be texting Mills that late at night. The insecure girl in her wanted to ask, but the woman in her told her to chill and relax. She and Mills were straight. He'd done everything in his power to make her feel secure about their relationship—and it worked.

Farrah was at peace and comfortable with him, but for some strange reason, something didn't feel right about his phone going off so late at night. For the first time in a while, Farrah felt a glimpse of uncertainty. She'd tried her damnd-

est to ignore it, but the longer she stared at the
television screen, the more she became shaken.
Her woman's intuition wouldn't let it go. Finally
giving into temptation, Farrah glanced over her
shoulder and asked, "Who is that?"

Mills finished replying to the message and
turned off his phone.

"My agent. We gotta meet up with the contrac-
tor for the skate park tomorrow."

"Oh." Farrah focused her attention back on
the television.

As Mills retook her into his arms, Farrah's
heartbeat began to accelerate. She'd been here
before. This was the moment where things in a
relationship began to go down hill. Mills had just
lied to her and although she didn't know why,
she prayed it wasn't because of another female.

But the nervous tingling in her stomach told
her it was. Wanting desperately to give him the
benefit of the doubt, Farrah kept quiet and made
the mature decision to trust her man until he
gave reason to otherwise.

Thinking back to that night, Farrah wondered
if that's when Mills's web of lies had all started.
She quickly snapped back to reality when she
heard the sound of the front door opening. Mills
was home. The moment she'd anticipated and
dreaded all afternoon was here.

"Bay!" Mills yelled from the living room.

Farrah didn't answer, though. Her lips were glued shut by the unbearable pain in her chest.

"Bay!" Mills entered the dining room to find her sitting in the dark. "You ain't hear me? And why you in here sitting in the dark?" He flicked on the light.

Farrah ignored him and quietly took a sip of wine.

"What's wrong wit' you?" Mills asked, becoming concerned.

Farrah's bloodshot eyes glared at him with a look of pure disgust.

"Babe, what's wrong?" He reached over and tried to touch her, only for Farrah to swat his hand away.

"What the fuck you hittin' me for?" Mills grimaced, rubbing his hand.

Once again, Farrah wouldn't respond.

"Look, I ain't got time for a bunch of games. I been at work all day," Mills barked, becoming upset. "My back hurt. I'm hot and sweaty. I ain't got time for a bunch of nonsense. Either you gon' tell me what's wrong or you ain't."

Instead of replying, Farrah gave him a look that said, *Nigga, please*.

"A'ight, I see you on some 'ole other shit. A'ight, Farrah. Whatever's wrong wit' you I hope you feel better." Mills turned to leave the room when Farrah threw the letter from DFS and his bank statements in his face.

Startled by her reaction, Mills flinched and blocked his face from being hit.

"What the fuck is your problem?" he yelled.

"You!" Farrah finally snapped. "You're my fuckin' problem!"

"What?" Mills screwed up his face, confused.

Figuring her anger stemmed from the info on the papers, Mills bent down and picked them up.

"What the fuck you going through my bank account for?" He screwed up his face.

Farrah swallowed hard.

"I know we gettin' married soon, but you ain't got no business going through my stuff. That shit ain't cool, man. I don't go through yo' shit, so don't go through mine." Mills parted his lips to continue his rant, but then found the letter from DFS.

Upon sight the air in his lungs instantly ceased. Mills felt like at any second he was sure to pass out. His mouth was suddenly as dry as the Sahara Desert and the palm of his hands were so clammy they felt like jelly.

"Baby, let me explain. It ain't what you think—"

"Really? It ain't what I think?" Farrah cocked her head to the side and squinted her eyes. "Then what is it, then?"

"It ain't mine. I mean—I don't know if it is."

"Wow," Farrah sneered, folding her arms across her chest.

"I wanted to tell you. I tried to tell you—"

"When?" Farrah cut him off again. "Before or after you proposed to me?"

Mills felt completely defeated. He felt as if he was in a lose-lose situation with Farrah's line of questioning. He knew he had to choose his word carefully.

"*When* doesn't matter. All that matters is that I tried, and I swear on everything I love I tried to tell you, real talk. I just didn't know how. I just can't afford to lose you. If I did, I would lose it. You're my everything, babe." He tried to take her hand, but before he could Farrah snatched it away.

"What you won't do is touch me." She held her index finger up and shot him a look that could kill.

"I understand you're upset, but you ain't gotta be rude. I mean, it's not my fault you upset. If you hadn't have been going through my shit you wouldn't be crying right now. You ain't have no right opening my mail, so don't be mad at me. Be mad at yo'self."

Dumbfounded by his choice of words, Farrah's mouth hit the floor. *Is this muthafucka actually* *trying to blame this on m*e? she thought. Actions spoke louder than words, but everything about Mills was screaming he didn't care about her or her feelings.

"Here I was thinkin' we was past all of the bullshit," Mills persisted with his tirade. "But it's obvious you still don't trust me, so my question is: Why the fuck you marrying me then?"

Mills had never raised a hand to her, but Farrah could've sworn he'd reared his fist back to uppercut her like the bus driver from Cleveland. Having heard enough, she pushed her chair back and hopped out of her seat.

"This muthafucker crazy," she said in disbelief as she headed to their bedroom.

"Hold up! Where you going?" Mills panicked. "I ain't mean it like that." He followed behind her.

"All I'm sayin' is I fucked up. I should've told you the truth, but I knew if I did you'd leave me," he pleaded as Farrah entered the master bath and slammed the door in his face.

"Farrah, open the door!" Mills turned the knob, only to find it was locked.

"Come on! Open the door!" He knocked. "I'm sorry! Farrah, please open the door!" He knocked again, to no avail.

Afraid of what she might do, Mills pressed his ear up against the door. The sound of her crying so hard she had to gasp for air caused his heart to sink. He never wanted to cause her this much pain. He'd tried everything in his power to avoid it, but he'd fumbled her heart yet again. Distraught, he slid down the wall and sat on the floor. With his knees up to his chest, he listened as Farrah's heart continued to shatter like glass.

What am I gonna do? he thought. This time he'd pushed her to the brink of no return. There was no way she'd remain his. This one mistake had the potential to ruin everything. No amount of tears or apologies would fix it, but Mills was determined to find a way back into her heart. He'd set up residence there. It was home. She was home. This one thing wouldn't be the cause of their demise. He would say and do anything to win her trust back. Farrah just had to give him the opportunity.

Hours and hours went by before Mills realized dawn had come and he'd unwillingly fallen asleep. Outside the window before him, the sun was in full view. Groggy and sore from sitting on the hard wooden floor all night, he stretched his arms and legs. But stretching didn't stop his bones from feeling like blocks of cement. No amount of bends or twists would erase the kinks in his body, but all of that was miniscule compared to his drama with Farrah.

Farrah, he thought as flashbacks from the night before flooded his mind. Swiftly spinning around, Mills shot up on his feet. He naturally assumed that the bathroom door would still be closed and locked, but to his surprise it was wide open and Farrah was nowhere to be found.

"Farrah!" He searched the bathroom and their bedroom frantically, to no avail.

Each second that passed and her angelic face wasn't in his presence, Mills lost his willpower to breathe. She couldn't be gone. He had to find her. His life depended on it. Without her he was lost. His whole existence would add up to nothing. They'd finally begun to get it right. There was no way he could lose her now.

"Farrah!" he yelled, racing into the living area.

There he found her with a duffel bag on her shoulder, about to unlock the door and leave.

"Hold up! Where you going?" Mills's voice cracked as he ran to block her path.

Thankfully, his years of athletic training paid off and he was able to slam the door shut before she could escape.

"Move, Mills." Farrah cocked her head to the side and rolled her eyes.

"Come on, Bay, you gotta at least let me explain," Mills pleaded. "After everything we been through, you at least owe me that much."

No he didn't, Farrah thought, feeling her heart slice open.

Before Mills knew it she had reared her hand back so far she and Jesus high-fived, then she slapped him so hard his bottom lip began to bleed.

"I don't owe you shit!" Farrah's bottom lip quivered. "Do you have any idea what you've done to me? You have destroyed me! For a year you have sat there and lied to my face over and over again like it ain't nothin'! What—you get some kind of sick-ass pleasure in hurting me?"

"Nah, it ain't even like that," Mills tried to clarify.

"Shut up!' Farrah slapped him again. "You don't get to talk!"

"Yo don't put yo' hands on me no more," Mills warned, stepping into her personal space. "I understand you mad, but don't put yo' fuckin' hands on me!"

"Oh, you supposed to be big and bad now! Fuck you! What you gon' do? Have a baby on me! Oh, wait!" Farrah placed her index finger onto her chin and thought.

"You already did that. So tell me?" Farrah stood back on one leg and crossed her arms. "When exactly did you fuck her? Was it while we were together or after we broke up?"

"That ain't even important." Mills hesitated to tell the truth.

"It's obvious it's not important to you, but it is to me! Come on!" She dropped the duffel bag to the floor and held her hands up, as if to say, *Bring it on.* "You wanted to talk, so let's talk! Be real for once in yo' life! Was it good? Was it everything you wanted it to be?"

"Farrah," Mills clenched his jaw. "I love you. I swear to god I ain't mean for none of this to happen. I fucked up, but if you'll give me a chance to make it right I put that on everything I will."

"Are you fuckin' kidding me?" Farrah screwed up her face. "I give you a chance to speak and that's the dumb-ass shit you say! What don't you get? I'm done fuckin' wit you! There will be no second chance! I'm done! Me and you are finished!"

"Stop—you don't mean that." Mills shook his head.

"Okay, if that's what you wanna believe." Farrah shrugged her shoulders, then bent down to grab her bag.

"What the fuck are you doing?" Mills lost it and took her into his arms and held her tight. "You ain't going nowhere. You my baby. I love you. We can work this shit out."

"There is nothin' to work out." Farrah struggled to break loose. "Now get off of me!"

"Come on, Bay, just calm down." He tightened his grip on her. "Just breathe. Can we just breathe for a minute?"

"Fuck breathing! Can't you see I'm already dead?" Farrah pushed him with so much force that his back hit the wall.

"I have never loved nobody the way I love you." She began to cry. "Not even Khalil and look what you've done to me."

"I'm sorry," Mills said sincerely.

"Well, this time *sorry* isn't good enough." Farrah swallowed the tears in her throat and picked up her bag. "I'm done. Don't call me, don't come lookin' for me. Just leave me the fuck alone." She unlocked the door and left.

Mills wanted to continue to put up a fight, but he knew that the right thing to do at that point was to give Farrah some space. Continuing to push the subject would only make her resent him more. He hated to let her walk out the door. Watching her board the elevator was the most excruciating form of torture he would ever have to bear. However, it had to be done.

He'd pushed her too far this time. At that very moment as the elevator doors closed, Mills's lungs instantly stopped producing air. Farrah was the vital organ that he needed to breathe. He didn't know how long it would take or what he'd have to do, but losing her for good wasn't an option. Mills was determined to get his baby back.

Chapter 4

*I wish I had some weed up in my system 'cause
I'm about two seconds away from flippin' out.*
—Jhené Aiko, "2 Seconds"

As Farrah reached the door to her old apartment, she couldn't figure out if the load of her duffel bag or the load in her heart was greater. She hadn't been through anything this traumatic since her breakup with Khalil, Kimye's baby announcement, and that time when she was thirteen and got caught stealing the R&B group Total's cassette tape from GrandPa Pidgeon's. Neither of those experiences or life lessons could compare to this.

She knew eventually she would get over Khalil, Kanye's lapse in judgment, and her short stint as a thief, but what Mills had done to her would forever leave a severe scar etched across her heart. Or had she done this to herself? The day he came to her job, begging for forgiveness, a part of her knew that he was hiding something, but she loved him and wanted her happily-ever-after so much that she willed herself to look past her own woman's intuition.

Now, here she was, paying the ultimate price. Sorrowfully, she unlocked the door and instantly began to cry. In two weeks she was due to be married. She never imagined she would end up back where she started, hurt and alone.

"Farrah, is that you?" London stepped out of the first-floor bathroom with a blush brush in her hand.

On the inside, Farrah responded *yes*, but all she could summon on the outside was a head nod and a loud wail that came from the depth of her soul.

"What's wrong?" London raced over to her dressed in nothing but a black-lace bra and a black, high-waisted, pencil skirt.

Farrah wanted to answer her friend, but all she could do was drop her bag, cover her face, and cry. Worried sick, London wrapped Farrah up in her arms and hugged her tight.

"Farrah, what is it? Is it the wedding?"

"No," Farrah sobbed.

"Is it Mills? Is he hurt?" London held her at arms length and examined her.

"I just—can't—believe—he—did—this—to—me." Farrah's chest heaved up and down. "I—loved—him."

"Who? Khalil?" London said, confused.

"No! Fool!" Farrah snapped, hitting her on the arm.

"My bad." London massaged her arm. "I'm just trying to figure out what the hell yo' crazy ass is talkin' about."

"No." Farrah wiped her nose with the back of her shirt. "It's Mills." She sat down on the bottom step.

"What he do now?" London stood in front of her.

"He had a baby on me, that's what he did."

"You say what now?" London said, stunned. "Wit' who?"

"Guess."

London paused for a brief second, then gasped.

"No." Her mouth fell open.

"Yep," Farrah said, nodding. "Jade."

"I feel like I'ma faint. I gotta sit down." London slid down the wall and fell to the floor in a heap.

"Now you see how I feel," Farrah chuckled, wiping the tears from her face.

"What is yo' ass doing here? Why you ain't in jail?"

"I'm too pretty for jail—besides, his punk ass ain't even worth it." Farrah waved her hand.

"You better than me, 'cause I would be in handcuffs and a straitjacket right about now." London rolled her neck. "How did you find out? Did he tell you?"

"Hell, naw. A letter came in the mail from DFS," Farrah explained.

"Get the fuck outta here."

"Mmm-hmm." Farrah pursed her lips as Mills called her phone again for the umpteenth time.

"Is that him?"

"Yep." Farrah sent his call to voice mail.

"Remember yesterday when we were talkin' and I rushed you off the phone?"

London nodded.

"That's when I found out."

"What did Mills say when you confronted him?"

"That it ain't his. Ooh," Farrah said excitedly. "The baby is a lil' girl and guess what the bitch named her?"

"What?" London cocked her head to the side and tuned up her face.

"Jaysin . . . Cori . . . Mills. Now, how you like them apples?" Farrah pointed her index finger.

"Bitch, you lyin'?"

"I put that on my new Celine bag." Farrah held up her right hand as if she was under oath.

"Oh, she tried it," London stressed. "Jade need to get somewhere and have every seat in Busch Stadium."

"Right," Farrah agreed. "The court is ordering Mills to take a paternity test because Jade wants child support. But apparently Mills has been paying her every month for the past year. So something must've happened between them that made her mad. 'Cause why else would she suddenly decide to file papers on him."

"So whose ass you wanna kick first, hers or his? 'Cause all I gotta do is change outta this skirt."

"Girl, I couldn't fight nobody right now if I tried." Farrah placed her head down and paused. "I just don't know what to do." Tears slid down her cheeks.

"I mean, it's obvious that you still love him, 'cause love don't go away in a matter of hours. The question is, Do you love him enough to stay with him, get married, and play stepmama to his demon-seed baby?" London probed.

"I honestly don't know." Farrah shook her head. "I just can't believe this nigga been lying to me for a year straight like it was nothing. Like all of those times we talked about having another baby and this nigga already got another bitch pregnant! I mean, he sat there and let me look like a complete and utter fool. That's what hurts the most."

"Do you think the baby is his?"

"Yeah," Farrah said confidently. "It's obvious that it is. Who would give a chick money for a year for a baby that ain't his and on top of that, go to such great lengths to hide it? But let him tell it ain't his. That's all he keep on sayin'—*it ain't mine,*" she mimicked Mills.

"Idk, friend. And look, I ain't never the one to tell nobody to leave they man, 'cause I ain't the one laying up wit' you at night. Now, I'll hold your hand in the morning, but that's about all I can do—"

"Will you shut up?" Farrah laughed.

"Seriously, I don't wanna be that friend that be like, Girl fuck him, leave his wack ass alone, but girl, on the real: *Fuck his lying, trifling, bicycle-riding, blockhead ass!* Leave his ass the fuck alone! You don't deserve that shit!"

"I know I don't." Farrah laughed somberly.

"So it's obvious neither one of us is going in to work today, so what do you wanna do? Lay in the bed and go to sleep, watch a movie or get white-girl wasted?" London shot Farrah a devious grin.

Farrah needed some weed or liquor in her system, because she was about two seconds away from flippin out.

"White-girl wasted!" Farrah jiggled her titties.

"Well, come on then." London eased her way up from the floor and held out her hand for Farrah.

It wasn't even 1:00 in the afternoon and Farrah and London had consumed three bottles of peach Cîroc and a bottle of Moët. Rihanna's club hit "Pour It Up" was on and turned up to the highest volume. Stacks of twenty, fifty, and hundred-dollar bills were sprawled all over the floor. Neither London nor Farrah gave a shit if their neighbors had a problem with their midday house party. Farrah needed to relieve some stress and instead of being a weak broad who did nothing but cry into her pillow for hours, she decided to drink her problems away.

It wasn't like she hadn't been here before. This form of heartache was nothing new; only the person who caused it was different. With her glass in hand, Farrah lay on the couch, grooving like she was in her own personal music video. With her hands up in the air she sang, *"Ohhhhhhhhhhhhhh all I see is signs, all I see is dollah signs. Ohhhhhhhhhhhhhh money on my mind, money-money on my mind."*

"Farrah!" London yelled from the kitchen, holding a lit blunt between her manicured fingertips.

"What?"

"Is that a purple monkey on the balcony?"

Farrah arched her head back and looked.

"No, bitch," she giggled. "That's a squirrel."

"Oh," London replied, stumped.

"Anyway." She took another toke from the joint before passing it to Farrah.

"I'm telling you. We should throw on some Vaseline, a T-shirt, jogging pants, and some Tims and go see about that nigga."

"Who, Teddy?" Farrah said, inhaling the smoke into her lungs.

"No, dummy, Mills."

"Oh." Farrah slapped her hand up against her face, feeling stupid.

"I'm telling you, girl, right about now I'd beat his ass like Joseline did Stevie J in that therapist's office." London sparred with the air.

"I ain't tell you, girl! I slapped him . . . twice," Farrah stated proudly.

"Good. At least you got two licks in on his ass. Oh, my god." London stopped dead in her tracks.

"What?" Farrah eyed her.

"Turn the music off," London ordered, frantically.

Farrah quickly put the stereo on pause.

"What is it, girl? You see the purple monkey again?" Farrah turned to her side, alarmed.

"No . . . Whitney Houston is dead. She gone!" London began to cry.

"*Whit-ney*! Why you have to take her, lord," she yelled, to the ceiling. "She ain't do nothin' to nobody! You could've took Bobby! Nobody would've cared!"

"We love you, Whitney!" Farrah shouted.

"*And I-I-I-I-I-I-I-I-I will always love you*," London sang, hugging herself.

"I got his ass." Farrah drunkenly fell off the couch and began to crawl around the floor in search of her phone.

"Phone," she whispered. "Phone? Answer me. Where are you?"

"What are we looking for?" London got down on all fours too. "Ooh, I know. We looking for Ciara's career."

"Friend, have you seen my phone?" Farrah wiped a trickle of spit from the side of her mouth.

"Yeah, it's right here." London pulled it from her left bra cup. "Here, girl, I ain't want the purple monkey to get it."

"You know what? You's a real bitch. I would die for you."

"Awww, that's so sweet." London poked out her bottom lip.

"If this muthafucka think he gon' cheat on me and get away wit' it, he got another thang coming! I'm about to give his ass a piece of my mind." Farrah laid on the floor in a fetal position and texted Mills.

12:34: I hope yo baby look like Mama Dee

12:34: How could you do this to me?

Instead of responding back via text, Mills started to call her phone.

"What?" Farrah answered.

"Can we please talk?" Mills pleaded.

"No!" Farrah hung up the phone in his ear and texted him.

12:36: No

12:36: No

12:37: No

12:38: Nooooooooooooo

12:38: I loved u

12:39: I luv u

Mills 12:40: I love you 2

Farrah 12:41: Syke! I HATE YOU

12:42: Sorry that was uncalled 4. I shouldn't have sid that.

12:43: said

12:46: I change my mind FUCK U!!!!!!!!!!!!

Mills 12:47: Are you drunk?

Farrah 12:48: A lil, y

Mills 12:49: Farrah I love you. I can't lose you.

Farrah 12:50: Fuck u

12:51: Fuck u n yo big head mama

Mills 12:51: WHAT?!!!!

Farrah 12:53: Sorry I didn't mean that

12:54: yo mama do gotta big ass head tho lol

12:55: Am I underneath the table?

12:56: I gotta taste for some chicken

12:57: London do you want some Popeye's

Mills 12:58: Huh?

Farrah 12:58: that wasn't meant 4 u

12:59: You know what? I am so done fuckin' wit you

1:00: Done

1:01: Done, Done, Done

1:02: Done

1:03: Dooooooooooooooooooooooooone!

1:04: D

1:05: O

1:06: N

1:07: E

Mills 1:08: Will you please come home so we can talk?

Farrah 1:09: Eat 25 rectums and call me in the morning

Mills 1:10: Who the fuck u talkin 2?!
Farrah 1:11: calm down. Here I come
Mills 2:45: Where r u?
Farrah 2:46: You thought I was coming
didn't you, lol

A half an hour later, Farrah was knocked out on the floor with her phone firmly clutched in her hand. Hours had gone by and the only thing that made her wake up was the sound of her cell phone ringing. Farrah groggily stared at the screen. It was Mills. She didn't have the energy to slide the bar over to answer, let alone open her mouth to speak. Pissed because her head felt like a block of cement, she dropped the phone to the floor.

She hadn't had a hangover like this since her twenty-fifth birthday party in Vegas. Judging by the darkness of the living room, Farrah could tell it was late into the night. *How long have I been asleep?* she wondered. *And where the hell are my pants?* Thoroughly confused and extremely hungover, Farrah lifted herself and sat up.

"Ughhhhh." She held her head as a surge of pain rushed through her brain. "I feel like shit."

"Now I know how Lindsay Lohan feels," Farrah heard London say from a distance.

"London?"

"Huh?" London answered, sounding out of breath.

"Where are you?"

"Whitney, is that you?" London whimpered.

"London, I ain't got time to play wit' you. My damn head hurt now!" Farrah shouted, causing her head to pound even more. "Whitney Houston is dead. May she rest in Chanel heaven."

"I rebuke you in the name of Jesus," London mumbled.

"Where the hell are you?" Farrah tried to find her in the dark. "Ouch!" she yelled, running into the couch.

London lifted her head and examined her surroundings.

"I think I'm on top of the dining room table. Ooooh . . . and judging by my breath I think I threw up on it too." London slowly sat up.

"Time for a new table," Farrah chuckled, turning on the light.

"*Noooooo*!" London waved her hand in the air emphatically. "Turn that light off!"

"I have to find my pants!" Farrah waved her off. "And you need to find your bra."

London looked down and saw that her breasts were swinging free.

"Did we?" Farrah said wearily.

"You wish." London rolled her eyes. "At some point, yo' dumb ass started talkin' bout you were freezing, although it's the middle of August, and turned on the heat."

"Whew." Farrah wiped invisible sweat from her forehead.

"Girl, bye." London hopped down from the dining room table. "You wish you could get some of this."

"Heffa, please, I am strictly dickly. Besides, if I were gay you wouldn't be my type."

"What the hell is that supposed to mean?" London snapped, insulted. "For your information, I get hit on all the time by lesbians."

"Good for you, Ellen DeGeneres," Farrah said sarcastically, while putting on her pants.

"How long are you gon' be here again?" London joked.

"Don't get stabbed." Farrah laughed as her phone started to ring.

By the ringtone she knew it was Mills.

"I wish he would get the hint and stop calling me." She rolled her eyes and huffed.

"You're gonna have to talk to him eventually."

"It'll be a cold day in hell before I *ever*," Farrah stressed, "speak to Corey Mills again."

Chapter 5

I know I was mad, said I was pissed
but it wasn't so bad, not worse than this.
—Ledisi, "I Miss You Now"

For days, Farrah held on to the notion that she was done with Mills, that what he'd done was unforgiveable. And although the pain she was experiencing was the type of pain that felt like dying a repeated death, she was lost without him. Plus, she couldn't continue to pretend like important decisions didn't have to be made. If she was going to cancel the wedding, she needed to do it soon. The only thing that was holding her back was her conflicting feelings for Mills.

Every vein in her body hated him for his blatant lies and disrespect. On the other hand, whenever she woke and he wasn't there, her heart ached. She yearned to hear the sound of his voice, to feel the soft touch of his hand. She couldn't deny it. He was her everything.

She'd invested so much of herself into him and their relationship that being without Mills was unthinkable.

Farrah had to find a middle ground. She couldn't stay stagnant in her misery a day longer. She either had to love him or leave him. That morning she made the dreaded phone call to Mills, requesting they meet up and talk. She didn't want to have such a pivotal conversation at their apartment or her office in fear that she might snap and kill him, so Mills suggested they meet at Forest Park. With her new black Celine bag resting in the crook of her arm, Farrah's spiked, Alexander McQueen heels stomped the concrete trail toward him.

She had no idea as the sun shined down on her that she was meeting Mills in the same section of the park and on the exact bench Mills met Jade every month. Spotting her petite frame in the distance, Mills sat up straight. A slight smile crept onto the corners of his lips as Farrah's hips swayed from side to side. Mills knew Farrah like he knew the back of his hand. She was out to kill and he was her prey. Farrah looked like a chic goddess.

She wore her hair up in a top knot and donned a winged-tip eye and blood-red lipstick. A white Theory button-up with black anchors all over it was tucked inside a pair of denim booty shorts. A pair of vintage Chanel earrings and a gold men's Rolex watch completed her look. Farrah's swag was sickening. She was the perfect Bonnie to his Clyde. Now, more than ever, Mills knew that he had to do anything in his power to win her back.

"What's up?" Farrah sat down and crossed her legs without giving him eye contact.

"Oh, you extra cool today, huh?" Mills eyed her. "I don't get a *hi* or nothing?"

"Come on now, let's skip all the pleasantries. What are we gonna do?" She rolled her eyes.

"You tell me. You're the one who left," Mills shot.

"You don't have to remind me. I know what I did." Farrah rolled her neck. "I needed time to think."

"Now that you're done thinkin'," Mills snapped, "What did you come up with?"

"That I can't stand you," she responded sarcastically.

"Well, if it means anything to you—I still love you and no matter how much foul shit you say to me, that ain't gon' never change."

Farrah swallowed hard. She hated when Mills played the sweet card, because it always wound up working.

"Look, I'm hurt," she confessed.

"I know," Mills replied, seriously.

"I'm mad and I'm pissed but . . . I don't know what's worse: Being with you or without you. I have to figure something out, 'cause I can't continue walkin' around feeling like shit," Farrah confessed.

"And I'm sorry that I made you feel that way. I want you to know that I'm not giving Jade any more money until the paternity test results come back."

Farrah tried to conceal her pain, but tears scorched her eyes. Just the sound of Jade's name made her sick. She wanted to blink the tears away, but she couldn't hold them back a second longer. With her head turned to the side, she let them pour out onto the surface of her face.

"I just can't believe you did this to me," she cried. "Like, how could you sit there and hold that type of secret from me? I tell you everything. I would have never done no shit like that to you."

"'Cause you're good and I'm a piece of shit."

"I'm being serious right now," Farrah shot.

"I am too," Mills agreed. "Everything about you is pure and everything about me is tainted and I sometimes find myself wondering am I good enough for you."

Caught up in his confession, Farrah sat quietly, staring out into space. She wondered if Mills knew how broken she really was, would he feel the same way about her? Sometimes she questioned whether it was him or her that needed saving more. The only thing Farrah knew for certain was that from the time she was a little girl she yearned to be loved by someone and to give that same kind of love in return.

She wanted love to be like it was in the movies, uncomplicated and magical. She was sick of questioning herself and the men in her life. She thought after Khalil she was done with the torture of nonstop drama. And no, Mills wasn't cussing her out or being emotionally abusive, but he still found a way to make her feel like she was two feet tall.

Dying from being so far away from her, but yet so close, Mills scooted closer and wrapped his arm around Farrah's shoulder. Farrah wanted to forbid him from touching her, but her mouth, nor her heart, had the willpower to object.

"I'm lost without you," Mills whispered into her ear.

Here this nigga go, quoting Robin Thicke songs, Farrah thought, rolling her eyes.

"Word?" Mills spoke, noticing her sour expression. "The last few days without you have been miserable. I need you to come home. We can work this shit out."

"How?" Farrah whipped her head to the side and gave him full eye contact.

Streaks of tears showed through her Covergirl Queen Collection foundation.

"I don't have a blueprint of how. I just know that we can."

"We can't work nothing out if that baby is yours," Farrah responded. "So I'm gon' ask you again and please, for both our sakes, don't lie."

Mills gazed so deep into Farrah's eyes he swore he could see the depths of her soul. What laid there was a yearning to learn the truth, confusion, fear, sorrow, and undeniable pain. Mills hated that he'd done this to her. He'd reduced her to nothing with one lie. She'd been nothin' but an angel to him. She'd tried her damndest to shield him away from anything that could potentially crush his heart.

And although telling her his greatest fear—that Jade's baby might indeed be his— was the right thing to do, Mills once again found himself unwilling to admit the truth. There was no way he could do it, especially when the end result would be him losing her for good.

"I told you . . . that baby ain't mine," he said with a stone look on his face.

"You sure?" Farrah asked as a tear strolled down her cheek.

"It's not mine."

Chapter 6

*Love done got me trapped again man
how did I do dis shit.*
　　　　　—Webbie, "Lovin U is Wrong"

Softly, the melodic sound of Stacy Barthe's song "Touch" filled the room while Farrah sat quietly getting the finishing touches to her makeup done. Farrah felt every word of the song as if they were her own. The line *It'd probably be easier if you just were never around. Then I could concentrate on things I can't even think about now* really resonated with her as she prepared for her and Mills's wedding ceremony. In less than an hour she was about to become Mrs. Cory Mills and she honestly didn't know how she felt about it. Nervous butterflies fluttered in her lower belly. She had so much anxiety that she wanted to vomit.

But Farrah was determined to go through with their nuptials. Mills had sworn up and down, left and right, over and under that the baby wasn't his. And no, Farrah didn't believe him 100 percent. but she did believe in his love for her. She just prayed that would be enough to get her down the aisle. Besides, the only thing that got her to the ceremony site was the fact that two days prior, Mills had gone and taken the paternity test to further prove his innocence. Now they both sat idly by, awaiting the results.

In the meantime, Farrah felt like she was walking around with a shadow over her life. If she was being honest with herself, she knew deep down she should have postponed the wedding until after the results came in. As much as she wanted to believe Mills was telling her the truth, he had already proven himself a liar, so it was hard for her to give him the benefit of the doubt. Farrah was driving herself crazy, thinking of what would happen if it turned out the baby *was* Mills's. She couldn't see herself playing stepmother to him and Jade's child. That baby would be a constant reminder of Mills cheating on her and she couldn't live like that for the rest of her life.

Just knowing that there was a possibility that Jade had had Mills's baby made her feel more guilty of getting her own abortion. She thought she had moved past it, but lately all she could think of is how different things might have been if she had continued with the pregnancy. Maybe if she hadn't rushed her decision to get the abortion, he would have never slept with Jade and this whole nightmare would have never happened. Things got so messed up when she told Mills about her pregnancy, though. Sitting in her white dress, getting the final touches on her makeup done—instead of enjoying her day, all she kept thinking of was the night she showed up at club 2720 Cherokee and told Mills about the baby.

They hadn't talked in two weeks, but Farrah was sure things would work themselves out once he found out she was carrying his child. When she showed up to the club, she walked in just in time to see Jade grinding her ass all up on Mills. When Farrah confronted him and told him she was pregnant, he lashed out at her and had the audacity to say the baby might not be his. To make matters worse, Farrah's ex, Khalil was there too and when he heard she might be pregnant by Mills, one of his pot'nahs he lost it and tried to fight Mills. Hurt and confused, Farrah felt desperate to make the whole situation disappear, so she decided the abortion was the best thing to do. That way she could just move on and have no ties to this man who had broken her heart.

But of course, like always, Mills begged and pleaded his way back into her life and once again, she found herself laying in his arms. She didn't know what it was about Corey Mills that just turned her into putty in his hands. One look at him and it was like she was under his spell. Right now, though, in this moment, Farrah was really having doubts about going through with this wedding. This was the day she had been dreaming of all her life and instead of laughing and enjoying every second of it, she felt like with every minute that passed, her world was crumbling before her eyes. It was like she was looking at her life in slow motion and until those paternity results came in, everything she did was insignificant.

"Are you all right?" London stopped applying M.A.C Mineralize Finishing Powder to Farrah's face and asked.

"Why you ask me that?" Farrah eyed her quizzically.

"'Cause you look like you saw ghost. No matter how much bronzer I apply you still look as pale as Anne Hathaway," London joked.

"I'm fine," Farrah lied.

"Farrah," London pursed her lips together. "Let's not play silly games today. What's wrong with you?"

"I'm just a lil' nervous, that's all."

"You're more than nervous, sweetie. Look at you. You're shaking," London pointed out.

Farrah gazed down at her hands and sure enough, she was shaking like a leaf.

"It's just pre-wedding jitters," she said, shrugging, trying to sound convincing.

"Look . . ." London pulled up a chair and took her best friend by the hand.

"I'ma say this and then I'ma shut up. If you're having any doubts about this wedding, we can dip. You do not have to go through with this. Everyone will understand and if they don't, fuck 'em."

"I'm good. I just need a few moments to collect myself," Farrah said as she stood to take a good look at herself.

"Okay, fine," London said, putting both hands in the air. "I'ma give you your space. I need to run and get some gum out of my car anyway. Lord knows I need to be chewing on something to keep from stopping the wedding when they ask if anybody has any objections." London smirked as she walked out of the room.

Farrah's chest heaved up and down as she eyed her wedding gown from afar. It was a gorgeous, jaw-dropping, Marchesa mermaid-style dress with a sweetheart neckline and layers of tulle at the bottom. Always the one to be fashion forward, instead of wearing a veil, Farrah wore her hair slicked back into a chignon with a satin headband. Off to the side of the headband lay a beautiful silk flower pendant attached.

Over five million dollars' worth of Harry Winston diamonds were loaned to her for the special day. London had given her a soft pink and brown smoky eye with a pale pink cheek and lip. This was the way she'd envisioned herself looking on her wedding day. She'd always hoped and dreamed she'd get here, but Farrah never really thought it would come true. Now that the moment had arrived and was in reach, how could she possibly let it go? Yes, she and Mills were going through a trial, but maybe it was just a test to see if they could withstand the hard times.

Her thoughts were interrupted as London came back into the room.

"Okay, I'm gonna ask you one last time. Are you sure you wanna go through with this? Just say the word and we out dis bitch!" London said, keys and purse in hand.

"Girl, I'm sure," Farrah replied as a she took a deep breath and got ready to walk toward the church doors.

This was her fairy-tale moment. Farrah's happily-ever-after was so tangible she could taste it. Yet . . . and still her legs were begging her to run, but instead of moving, they were firmly planted in place. London was right: She could just get up and walk away, but she'd come too far to turn back now. Farrah was determined to step out on faith. She just prayed that she could trust Mills and that she wasn't making the biggest mistake of her life.

The doors to the church sanctuary opened and Farrah took the first step toward the rest of her life. *This is it,* she thought, as Babyface's "Every Time I Close My Eyes" played through the church speakers. Farrah began her walk down the aisle and it was as if she was in a fairy-tale wonderland. Everything was exactly how she had always dreamed it would be. The entire church was adorned with gold and silver crystal chandeliers hanging from the high ceilings. There were white calla lily clusters tied with a cream silk ribbon hanging on the edge of the pews and a beautiful, handwoven diamond-embroided runner laid from the foyer of the church leading up to the pulpit. Deep red rose petals were scattered atop of the runner and Farrah looked like a queen as she swiftly made her way toward her husband-to-be. If only for

this moment, she felt like everything was perfect.
She looked at Mills, standing at the front in an
all-white custom-made Cavalli suit and their
eyes locked. She could have sworn she saw a
hint of fear or hesitation behind his eyes, but
she quickly dismissed it as she placed her hand
in his and they were instructed to turn and face
the pastor.

The salty, intoxicating smell of the Medi-
terranean Sea sent Farrah's senses into shock,
causing her eyes to pop open and her to jump up
in a rush. There she was, in a king-sized bed that
wasn't her own and in a bedroom that wasn't
her own. Farrah had no idea where she was or
how she'd gotten there. All she knew was that
mountains and crystal-clear blue water were
right outside her bedroom window and that she
was on a yacht. As she raised her left hand to get
the crust out of her eye, she was blinded by the
ice on her ring finger.

Two bands filled with diamonds sat under and
on top of her five-carat princess-cut engagement
ring. Instantly, memories of her wedding day
flooded her mind. Farrah had felt so unsure of
her decision after the church ceremony that she
immediately popped a Xanax when she got to the

reception. After the ceremony, she immediately felt like she should've waited and called the whole thing off. But she'd already said "I do" and there was no turning back, so instead of dealing with her feelings, Farrah drank.

She drank so much that half the night was a blur. She didn't remember her and Mills's first dance or cutting her six-tier cake made by Sylvia Weinstock. She did, however, remember during the plane ride to their honeymoon destination in Sardinia, Italy, popping two more pills and then dozing off to sleep. Farrah had to get a hold of herself and quick.

Drinking her problems away was not going to solve a thing, so she made a mental note to lay off alcohol for a while. Hungry as hell, Farrah got out of bed in search of food and Mills. She didn't know where she was going, but the tantalizing smell of food led her in the right direction. As she walked throughout the yacht, Farrah took in its beauty. The yacht they'd rented— appropriately called *Dream*—had seven staterooms, an elevator that traveled via all four decks, a Jacuzzi, lounge area with a full bar, gym, sky lounge, and a crew of twelve.

"Good afternoon, Mrs. Mills," a short Italian woman spoke. "Your husband has been worried about you."

"My husband," Farrah repeated.

I have a husband, she thought, letting the fact sink in. *Mills is my husband.*

"Yes, Mr. Mills. He's on the second-floor deck." The woman pointed.

"Okay, thank you." Farrah smiled and headed in that direction.

Once she reached the second floor of the yacht, she spotted Mills sipping on a mimosa and reading an article in *Details* magazine. Sensing someone watching him, Mills looked up.

"There you are, sleepyhead." He got up from the table and greeted her with a kiss on the cheek. "For a minute I thought I was gon' have to call a doctor."

"Why?" Farrah asked as he pulled out her chair.

"'Cause you've been knocked out since we boarded the plane. You were poppin' Xanax like they were Skittles."

"Yeah, I'm sorry about that. I just kept on feeling like I was having a panic attack," Farrah explained.

"You cool now?" Mills examined her face, worried.

"Yeah, being next to the sea is very comforting. I feel like a new woman already." She smiled, slightly.

The aqua blue sea was breathtaking. She'd never seen anything like it, except in pictures.

"I'm glad you're feeling better. Now we can start enjoying our honeymoon." Mills ran his fingers through her hair and kissed her neck.

Farrah wanted more than anything to share in his excitement, but for some reason a dark cloud rested over her head. She never imagined on her honeymoon she'd feel so disconnected from the man she'd just swore to love forever.

"You hungry?" Mills asked, pouring her a glass of juice.

"Umm." Farrah stared at the array of food and became queasy. "No, I think I lost my appetite."

"You trippin'." Mills stacked his plate with eggs Benedict, bacon, sausage, and fruit.

"I think I'ma go take a shower and get dressed." Farrah excused herself from the table.

"You're sure you don't want none?" he asked again.

"Yeah, I'm sure."

"A'ight, well hurry back!" Mills yelled after her.

The rest of the day Farrah floated along, doing what to her were meaningless activities, like sightseeing and snorkeling to appease Mills. If it were up to her, she would've gladly slept through their entire honeymoon. She'd tried boosting her excitement level, but the tortuous possibility that she'd married Mills, knowing fully well he'd cheated and possibly fathered a child, consumed her every thought.

Mills tried to pretend that he didn't notice her distant behavior, but by nightfall he couldn't fake it anymore. Farrah was miserable and it showed all over her face. She didn't deserve to feel like shit—he did. He'd willingly married Farrah under false pretenses in order to prevent his own suffering. All throughout the morning of the wedding he paced back and forth, thinking about whether or not to come totally clean to Farrah. Not only had he not confessed that there actually was a high chance that Jaysin might be his, but he'd also lied about taking the paternity test. Deep down, he knew what the results would be and he couldn't risk losing Farrah once she found out. He hated having to lie to her, but he knew if he told her everything before the wedding she would have called the whole thing off and probably never forgave him.

Mills figured they'd get married and he'd convince her of his undying love, so by the time the truth was revealed she'd be more inclined to stay—or so he hoped. He was fully aware of how wrong it was, but he loved her too much to risk losing her. He'd be completely destroyed if she was to walk out of his life, so he was willing to do anything to keep her. But now, seeing how unhappy Farrah was and knowing it was all his fault, he felt like the biggest asshole.

The light of the silver moon shone down onto the skyline of the yacht, cascading a soft glow onto Farrah, highlighting her misery. For over an hour she sat alone, gazing at her wedding ring, wondering if she had made a mistake. The only answer she could come up with was that she loved Mills wholeheartedly. But was loving Mills enough? Mills knew that giving Farrah her space was probably the best thing to do, but enough was enough. He had to ease his baby's worried heart.

As he stepped out onto the skyline of the yacht, he couldn't help but notice how beautiful Farrah was. She sat with her knees up to her chest, staring out onto the open sea. Her long, ravenous black hair and colorful maxi-dress rippled in the wind. Mills was only inches away from her, but felt as if he needed to take a bus, plane, train or bike just to get next to her.

"Can I sit?" He stood next to her.

"Yeah." Farrah scooted over.

Mills sat beside his wife and took in her presence.

"What's on your mind? You've been quiet all day," he probed.

"I think I'm just a li'l jet-lagged." She withheld the truth.

"You sure that's it? 'Cause I feel like it's something else."

Farrah couldn't hold it in any longer. An abundance of tears poured from her eyes.

"Farrah," Mills took her into his arms. "Talk to me."

"I'm scared," she sobbed.

"Scared of what?"

"That everything is gonna come crashing down and that we're not gonna make it."

"I told you, you don't have anything to worry about. We gon' be straight."

"But what if we get back home and find out the baby is yours?" Farrah lifted her head and stared into his eyes.

"I already told you it's not, though."

"I don't know," Farrah shook her head, not convinced. "I just feel like at any moment the ball is gonna drop and everything is gonna be fucked up."

"It's already fucked up," Mills objected. "We just got married and on our honeymoon, but we can't even enjoy it 'cause of this bullshit. You're my wife. Do you understand that?" He looked at her.

"This is what we've been waiting for. I'm not tryin' to beef wit' you, Farrah. I love you and it hurts me to see you so upset. The only thing I can tell you is you gotta ride wit' me. I ain't gon' let you down."

A swift wind blew through the air as Mills reached over and placed his lips upon Farrah's. Her lips tasted like honey and he immediately became addicted to the sweet taste. Farrah feverishly kissed her husband back, knowing fully well that an orgasm or two wouldn't stop the ache in her heart. Allowing their bodies to become one under the moonlight would only place the unanswered questions and excruciating pain on pause for a brief moment.

Mills lay Farrah down onto her back and lovingly peeled her dress down and away from her body. To his surprise, she wore nothing underneath. Farrah's golden skin shined bright in the darkness. Naked as well, he laid on top of her and kissed her lips once more. Neither could get enough of the other. In the still of the night, among nothing but nature, Mills slid his way down Farrah's chest.

Her supple breasts were begging to be probed by his tongue. As he held them in his hand, Mills licked and sucked each nipple until both sprouted like rosebuds. Farrah loved when he tortured her nipples with kisses. It was a sure way to get her wet. Knowing his baby like the back of his hand, Mills teasingly rubbed his throbbing ten-inch dick against the slit of her cream-filled lips.

"Put it in," Farrah moaned.

"Uh-uh." Mills sucked her bottom lip. "Not until you tell me you love me."

"I love you," Farrah groaned.

"Promise me you ain't gon' never leave." Mills stuck his dick inside her, causing her to gasp, then quickly pulled it back out.

Farrah knew that was a promise she couldn't make. She wanted more than anything for their marriage to work, but her and Mills's relationship was as rocky as the sea they floated upon.

"Say it." Mills thrust his hips hard.

The hard pump of his dick sent Farrah into a tailspin. Her body needed more. She had to release the pent-up frustrations inside of her.

"Say it. Say you ain't gon' leave." Mills held each of her thighs in the crook of his arm and pounded until she could hardly breathe.

"I'm not gon' leave!" Farrah whimpered, feeling her spirit rise from her chest.

Mills always knew how to take her to the highest height of ecstasy. Within seconds, an orgasm so intense caused Farrah's legs to shake. A current only to be described as bliss shot through her body. She would pay millions to bottle this feeling up, but nothing lasted forever. As soon as Farrah came down from her orgasmic high, all of the uncertainties she temporarily put on hold came flooding back. Staring up at the sky, Farrah held Mills in her arms. Silently, she wished upon each star that all of their drama would disappear and that they could stay wrapped up in each other's arms forever.

Chapter 7

Girl, you know you want this dick.
—A$AP Rocky featuring Kendrick Lamar,
"Fuckin' Problems"

A month had passed since Farrah and Mills's wedding and things had gotten somewhat back to normal. The paternity test results still hadn't come in yet, so on a daily basis nervous energy took up space in the pit of Farrah's stomach. She couldn't figure out why it was taking so long. On the Maury Povich show the results came back in no time. When she questioned Mills about it, his answer was that Jade hadn't taken her part of the test yet.

Aggravated with Mills, his potential dev-il-spawn baby, and all of the drama that surrounded them, Farrah decided to have a girls' night out. Farrah, London, and their secretary Camden each got dressed to the nines and hit up the new hot spot, the Rustic Goat. It was located in the heart of the city where all of the action was, so the ladies were sure to have a good time. Serving up 1990s b-girl realness in a black Brooklyn Nets snapback, a sleeveless T-shirt tied in a knot exposing her toned stomach, leather leggings, and sky-high Giuseppe Zanotti peep toe gold- studded heels, Farrah tossed her long hair to the back and entered the spot as if she owned the place.

Everybody took notice of her cherry red lipstick, gold lion-head necklace, gold Patek Philippe watch, and Hermès bag as she headed toward the bar. Farrah was dying for a drink and a mojito was sure to do the trick. As soon as the mint-filled alcoholic drink hit her palette, she felt a sense of ease.

"Umm, this is *soooo* good." She rolled her head around in a circle.

"Mmm-hmm," London stressed.

"This place is nice." Farrah took in the ambiance.

The Rustic Goat was a humongous space with beautiful aesthetics: Edison bulbs, plush mezzanine nooks, a back poolroom, and artwork, including some by Muhammad Ali. Patrons were able to look on into the open kitchen, where cooks hustled to get out dishes. Farrah couldn't wait to try the food. The menu consisted of dishes like lobster napoleon with silky avocado and sweet roasted corn, and the southern classic chicken and waffles.

"Let's get a table," Camden suggested.

The girls found a nice round table near the center of the room and posted up. For the first time in a long while Farrah found herself truly having a good time. It felt wonderful to lay all of her troubles to the wayside and let loose.

"Okay, so the other night . . ." London began telling a story. "Me and Teddy were about to have sex and he was giving me head, right." She started laughing and wouldn't stop.

"What?" Camden started to laugh too.

"I—" London bugged up laughing.

"Bitch," Farrah giggled, hitting her playfully on the arm.

"Okay-okay-okay," London calmed down. "I farted." She instantly started laughing again. "I farted in his face."

"Oh, my god." Farrah's eyes grew to the size of saucers.

"What did he do?" Camden asked.

"He just stopped and looked at me like, *really, bitch*." London tuned up her face. "I was so embarrassed."

"I know you were," Farrah said. "Did y'all finish having sex?"

"Hell yeah, his ass wasn't about to pass up this good pussy," London replied.

"Wow." Camden crossed her legs.

"I will never look at the Grammy-award–winning, *People*'s sexiest man alive, Teddy, the same again," Farrah said.

"Me either," Camden agreed.

"Aww, bitch let's not forget about the time you told us Mills's pissy ass pissed on his self in the car while y'all were house-hunting and still went in to view the house." London put Farrah on blast.

"Touché." Farrah winked.

"Speaking of Mills . . ." London played with her straw. "What's going on with the paternity test?"

"Don't ask me," Farrah rolled her eyes. "Last I heard Jade hadn't went in to take the test."

"Well, there you go." London waved her hand dismissively. "That obviously proves that the bitch is lying. She just did it to start shit between you two and it worked. She just mad 'cause y'all were getting married."

"I guess," Farrah said, shrugging. "I don't even know. I just want the shit to be over with so I can know either way."

"What if it is his?" Camden chimed in. "What then?"

Farrah sat and thought about it. She'd threatened Mills a thousand times that if the baby was his, she'd pack up her bags in less than two seconds. But secretly, in the deepest corner of her heart, she wasn't really sure if she would actually leave. To not have Mills be hers anymore would be worse than serving up stepmother realness to his baby. He was her husband and she honestly couldn't fathom life without him. But she couldn't tell her friends that. She had to continue to play the role of being strong and secure in her values. Showing weakness wasn't an option.

"I will leave his ass," she stated firmly. "Ain't nobody got time for that."

"But you just got married!" Camden stated.

"And? A ring don't mean a thing."

"Then what was the point of y'all getting' married?" Camden quizzed.

Faced with an impossible question to answer, Farrah sat speechless. Then a real answer slipped through her lips before she had the chance to stop herself.

"'Cause I didn't wanna be thirty years old and alone." Farrah stared out into space. "And loving him is better than losing him."

For a while the ladies sat quiet, each engrossed in their own thoughts of love and loss.

"Well, thanks for killin' my vibe," London joked.

"Real talk," Camden laughed. "You ain't have to get all Iyanla Vanzant on us."

"I don't wanna talk about it anymore," Farrah sighed. "I just wanna drink, laugh, and dance."

"Amen!" London lifted her drink in the air for a toast. "Round two is on me," she announced as they all clinked glasses.

After their fourth drink, all three girls were beyond buzzed and kicking it. Justin Timberlake's smooth hit "Suit & Tie" was bangin' and Farrah was grooving to the beat. She was having so much fun that she didn't even notice that she was being watched from across the room. West Coast Compton rapper J.R. and his entourage of fellow rappers and goons were in the building. He was there for his show's after party.

He and his crew were posted up in the corner of the room with bottles of Ace of Spades and Grey Goose. Chicks were sweatin' him left and right, but he wasn't trippin' off none of them. The women were all pretty and shaped like video vixens, but he knew that they were only checkin' for him 'cause he was signed to Dr. Dre's Aftermath and his debut album *Compton's Most Wanted* had gone double platinum and was a certified classic. Industry heavyweights like

Jay-Z, the Game, and Drake were all clamoring to work with him.

His U.S tour was sold out across the country and money was coming in by the boatload. All of J.R's dreams were coming true, but living life on the road was a lonely task and one-night stands with random females had already begun to get old. He wanted more and the mystery girl in a Brooklyn Nets snapback was possibly the woman to fill the empty space in his heart.

Not only was she drop-dead gorgeous, but homegirl didn't seem to have a care in the world. All she cared about was kickin' it wit' her girls and vibin' out to the music. He loved that she wasn't jockin' him. She hadn't even looked in his direction once, which made him want her even more.

"Ay, I'll be back," J.R. told his pot'nahs before stepping away.

Farrah swayed from side to side to Kendrick Lamar's sensual melody "Poetic Justice" as her and J.R.'s eyes met. She couldn't pinpoint at first where she knew him from, but she did know that he was beautiful. Everything about him from, his nappy box to his smoldering brown eyes and the dip in his walk screamed danger and sex. But Farrah couldn't turn away.

He looked to be about five feet eleven and possessed the creamiest chocolate-brown skin she had ever seen. He donned a black T-shirt and three gold chains that appeared to kiss his collarbone. A classic gold Rolex watch, black Y-3 fitted jeans, and black Givenchy sneakers summed up his simple, yet edgy, look.

"OMG, is that who I think it is coming toward us," Camden screeched, tugging on Farrah's arm.

"I think so," Farrah said, unsure.

"Is that the rapper J.R.?" London scrunched her forehead.

"Yes, he is so hot," Camden replied in a daze.

"Who's hot?" J.R. asked, standing in front of them.

"You, you're hot," Camden stated with a hint of attitude. "You *are* J.R., right?"

"I am." J.R. smiled, revealing a perfect set of white teeth.

"Fuck," Camden stomped her foot. "Even his teeth are sexy."

"His teeth are sexy, really?" Farrah looked at Camden as if she were dumb.

"I mean, look at them—they are." Camden pointed. "Smile for us again."

"No, but thanks for the compliment," J.R. responded, smiling anyway.

"Anytime." Camden winked.

"Sorry about my friend. I think she's drunk. Hi," Farrah extended her hand for a shake. "I'm Farrah, the crazy chick to my right is Camden, and the other one behind me is London."

"Nice to meet you all." J.R. shook her hand.

"I love your music," London spoke up. "Your mixtape *The Untold Stories* is everything."

"Thank you." J.R. gently held Farrah's hand in his.

"You are so sexy in real life." Camden damn near drooled.

"Is that right? 'Cause I think that your friend Farrah is pretty sexy herself in real life." He traced the curves of her frame with his eyes.

"You did not just say that," Farrah laughed.

"What?" J.R. said, confused.

"Nothin', can I have my hand back?" Farrah cocked her head to the side.

"Yeah, if you say *please*."

This negro crazy, Farrah thought.

"Please," she said sweetly.

Never one to go back on his word, J.R. reluctantly released her hand.

"Real talk, I haven't been able to take my eyes off of you since you walked through the door," he continued.

"Uh-huh." Farrah nodded, unimpressed.

"Word?" J.R. chuckled.

"I mean, aren't we a little too old to be throwing out corny pickup lines? You're supposed to be a rapper. I know you can come harder than that, playboy," Farrah said, smirking.

"Wow, okay." J.R. grinned, massaging his chin.

Deciding he'd call her bluff, he stepped into her personal space and said, "Damn ma, your ass is so fat I can see it from the front."

"*What?*" Farrah shrieked.

"Yeah, now that's a wack-ass pickup line. Me standing over there eye fuckin' you for the past hour is a fact . . . not a line. You're beautiful and I wanna get the chance to know you better." J.R. licked his bottom lip.

"I love you," Camden said in a trance.

"You sexy as hell." J.R. stepped back and looked Farrah up and down. "And from the look on your face, you think I'm sexy too."

"No, I don't," Farrah replied.

"Yes, she does," Camden rebutted.

"I know she does," J.R. answered, giving Farrah a wink and a smirk.

"*Nooooo* I don't," Farrah stressed, laughing. She could feel her cheeks getting hot from her blushing.

"You do," J.R. said, nodding.

He could tell by the look in her eyes that she wanted him and it'd only be a matter of time before he'd have her right where he wanted her.

"She sure in the fuck does." Camden bit her bottom lip.

"You both are insane." Farrah shook her head.

"Can I buy you a drink? What y'all drinking?" J.R. asked.

"I'm good. I don't think my husband would like a strange man buying me a drink," Farrah said, flashing her ring.

"Damn, I'm too late? I thought God would've gave me a li'l more time to find you, but I guess he's already blessed you with somebody else."

"That was a good one." Farrah wagged her index finger.

"That was the truth," J.R. replied, totally intrigued by her.

"You know what? It was nice meeting you and I love your music as well, but it's time for me to go." Farrah picked up her purse.

"Damn, it's like that? You just gon' leave?"

"Yeah, it's getting late," Farrah said, knowing damn well she secretly wanted to stay.

"Okay, well, should I tell my driver to pull around or are we gonna take your car, 'cause I can drive if you've been drinkin'," J.R. said seriously.

"I like you, but you're crazy." Farrah patted him on the shoulder before sashaying away.

"Damn, Farrah," London caught up with her. "You could've at least let him buy us a bottle."

"What about *I'm married* don't you two get?"

"Girl, bye." London waved her off. "Married, my ass. Ain't nothin wrong wit' letting a multi-millionaire trick his doe if he want to."

"You can't even front," Camden chimed in. "J.R. is some kind of cute."

Farrah looked over her shoulder at him and caught him eyeing lustfully at her ass. Suddenly a jolt of electricity shot through her stomach and down to her clit and she felt her pussy walls start to throb.

"He all right," she said, smiling.

Chapter 8

You're good for nothin' and
I ain't gon' cry over you.

—Twcet, "Enough"

Award season was right around the corner, which meant that the Glam Squad would be bombarded with meetings, fittings, trips to showrooms, and more. Before any of that happened, the girls had to pack up and head to France for Paris Fashion Week. New York Fashion Week had been amazing, so Farrah was excited to see what London had to offer.

She was determined to find the sickest gowns for her clients for award season. That year they were dressing Jennifer Lawrence, Naomi Watts, Halle Berry, J Hud, Cameron Diaz, and the red-carpet queen herself, the one and only Nicole Kidman. She was new on their client list and the girls were determined to give her the red-carpet moment she so desperately needed.

It was Farrah and London's busiest time of the year, but Farrah thrived on the hustle and bustle, jet-setting and long days.

This was the reason she got into the business, because in the end—after no sleep and numerous headaches—to see their clients look like works of living art, made it all worth it. On that particular afternoon, Farrah sat at her desk, going over past years' lookbooks. Her desk was swamped with lookbooks from designers like Tom Ford, Rocha, and Vivienne Westwood.

Farrah was in gown heaven and she didn't want to come down. Since her wedding, she'd submurged herself in her work. Doing so seemed to work, because it took her mind off the bouts of doubt and anxiety that plagued her about Mills. He'd been nothing but loving and understanding when it came to her feelings, but that still didn't shake the looming dark cloud that hovered over her. Everyday the feeling of her entire world crashing down intensified. It was just a matter of time before it happened.

She'd tried praying it away and pushing the negative thoughts out of her mind, but they never stayed gone too long. Farrah was driving herself mad. On the outside she seemed to have it all together, but on the inside she was a hot and utter mess. She couldn't even fully enjoy her time being a newlywed.

She loved her husband so much it hurt. To think that everything she thought to be true could potentially come to an immediate halt terrified the shit outta her. Farrah couldn't focus on any of that. She had work that needed to be done. As she immersed herself in the old lookbooks, Camden softly knocked on her door.

"Excuse me, Mrs. Mills, but these just came for you," Farrah's assistant said, handing her a vase filled with a dozen pink roses.

"Ooh, Farrah who got you those?" London asked, trying to grab the card that was attached.

"You better not!" Farrah smacked her hand away. "I don't know who they're from."

Sliding the card out of the tiny envelope, she anxiously read the card. It said:

> *I can't stop thinkin' about you. Let's have lunch . . . J.R.*

"Psst . . . this nigga." Farrah tossed the card in the trash.

"Who was it from?"

"That li'l nigga we met at the Rustic Goat."

"Who?" London died to know.

"J.R."

"Girl, you trippin'. J.R. is a cutie-pie. He so cute every time I look at him I have an orgasm."

"He cool, London, but he ain't all that," Farrah disagreed.

"Quit frontin'—you know you think he sexy as hell."

"No, I don't." Farrah tried to downplay her true feelings.

"Okay, well, he obviously likes you," London countered.

"He *thinks* he likes me," Farrah corrected.

"Oh, he likes you all right."

"No, I'm not his type. He just doesn't know it yet," Farrah replied sarcastically.

"Okay, then what did the card say?"

"That he was thinking about me and wants to go out to lunch."

"You not gon' go?"

"No, why should I? I'ma a married woman, remember?"

"'Cause he tryin' to see you, that's why," London tried to convince her. "You better go for it. J.R. is doing the damn thing. He's one of the hottest rappers out right now. He's on the *Forbes* one hundred richest entertainers list—"

"I know, I know," Farrah stopped her. "Damn, you ain't gotta run down the man's résumé to me. And why are you talking to me like I'm not a married woman? In case your ass forgot, I have a husband and I'm doing just fine, thank you very much." Farrah said, turning in her chair to face the window.

"Farrah, I know you're still hurting over this thing with Mills, so don't even try to feed me your bullshit story of how everything is hunky-dory," London stated with her hand on her hips. "I'm your best friend and I know you ain't happy about what's going on between you and Mills and this so-called paternity test that never seems to come in."

Here we go with this shit again, Farrah thought, shaking her head. "London, I really don't feel like hearing about your theory that Mills is lying about the paternity test. Everybody knows you didn't like him from jump," Farrah said, still facing the window.

As London started to reply back, Farrah gazed out of the window, pondering whether or not she should give J.R. a chance. She couldn't quite put her finger on it, but there was something about him that was very intriguing to her. Whatever it was, though, it definitely had Farrah wanting to see him again. *It's not gon' hurt to have lunch with him. I'll just treat it like a business lunch, get him to pay for the bill, and leave him alone,* she concluded.

"Farrah? Farrah? I know you hear me!" London called out.

"My bad. What did you say?" Farrah faced her.

"You weren't listening to me? Oh, hell naw. I ain't gon' be wasting my breath talkin' to you!" London yelled, grabbing her swatches and preparing to leave.

"Where you going?" Teddy stopped her as she opened the door.

"Back to my office. What you doing here?" London asked, surprised to see his face.

He hardly ever visited her at the office.

"I came to see you. Is that all right?"

"Of course," she replied, still shocked.

"Well, come show your man some love, then." Teddy held out his arms.

Walking into his embrace, London fell in love with him all over again. The year they'd been together had been the best year of her life. Teddy was everything she'd hoped for and more. Maybe his impromptu visit was his way of keeping their relationship interesting and he had something romantic planned for them. London ran her hand through his hair and caressed his locks. "I love you," he spoke softly into her ear.

"I love you too," London replied as she lovingly planted her lips on his.

"Will y'all get y'all old lovey-dovey ass up outta my office with that shit," Farrah teased.

"My bad. What's up, Farrah?" Teddy grinned, wiping his lips.

"Shit," she responded like a dude.

"Guess what, babe?" London said.

"What?"

"J.R. asked Farrah out to lunch and she won't even go."

"Why not? That's my man, he cool peoples."

"How do you know him?" London asked, surprised.

"You know I get around ma," he said, smirking.

"Yeah, a'ight, don't let me find out yo' ass doing something you ain't got no business doing," London warned.

"Chill out. But check it, let's go in yo' office for a minute. I need to holla at you."

"A'ight. Farrah, meet the man for lunch okay?" London pleaded.

"Bye London!" Farrah yelled, slamming the door in her face.

"Are you ready to go over your schedule for the rest of this week and the upcoming week?" Camden asked, walking in.

"I guess," Farrah said, frowning. "I'm loving you in all black, by the way. You look like Neo from *The Matrix*."

"Thank you, Farrah," Camden replied, giggling. "Now, are you ready?" She sat across from Farrah with a tablet in her hand.

"Like seriously, Camden, don't tell me anything that's going to stress me out, 'cause I'm already on ten as it is."

"So I should just leave then, huh?" Camden joked, standing halfway up.

"Yeah." Farrah nodded, laughing.

"All right, seriously." Camden sat back down and crossed her legs. "We have H&M coming up in two days. You're styling their holiday campaign and you're dressing Lana Del Rey— who, by the way, is the shit right now."

"Yeah, I'm obsessed with her," Farrah concurred. "I've been brainstorming on what look we want for her and I've narrowed it down to a few designers. Camden, I need you to contact them and have them send us their selection of outfit recommendations."

"Okay, no problem. You're styling her for H&M's ad campaign and the commercial and . . ." Camden paused and looked down at her tablet . . . "she also wants one outfit for a charity event she's attending in Paris during Fashion Week. Speaking of which, I've got your entire intinerary for your own trip to Paris. I'm going to print out all the details and have them on your desk first thing tomorrow morning."

"Oh, my god," Farrah groaned, slouching down in her seat. "I can't deal with this right now." She ran her fingers through her hair. She knew she had a busy schedule leading up to Paris Fashion week, but hearing it all out loud just put everything into perspective. With everything going on in her personal life and all the things she had to do workwise, her mind went into overdrive just thinking about it all.

"Farrah, darling, you know I die for you, but we can't have this. Ain't nobody got time for you to be having a mini-meltdown right now."

"You don't get it," Farrah said, pouting.

"What don't I get?" Camden uncrossed her legs. "Tell Mama why you're upset."

"New York kicked my ass. I got no sleep and I was away from my husband for a week. Now I have to style this woman for three different events, prepare for Fashion Week, and then get throught that week itself. My schedule is about to fuck me until I bleed. I'm letting the side of my hair that's shaved off grow out and it's making my head look lopsided." Farrah poked out her bottom lip.

"Okay boo, you gotta pull it together 'cause we have work to do. I have two of the interns organizing the shoes and two of the assistants are out pulling clothes at H&M for that shoot. I will be contacting the designers you're considering for Lana Del Rey, so that's one less thing for you to worry about, and while we're waiting for them to get back to us, you can put your own outfits together and pack for the trip. "

"Okay, sounds like a plan. That's fine," Farrah said. She took a deep breath to try and collect herself. As she breathed out, her phone buzzed and she rolled her eyes as she received a text message from London that read:

> 1:12: U ready 4 lunch bitch cuz I'm starvin'
> Farrah 1:13: Y r u so ghetto?
> London 1:13: Whateva hoe what u want to eat?
> Farrah 1:14: Y r u textin' me when ur office is right next door to mine lazy ass
> London 1:16: Duh cuz I ain't feel like gettin' up
> Farrah 1:17: Bread Co. sounds good
> London 1:18: ☹ I wanted Kim Van

Tired of texting, Farrah yelled, "Then why you ask me what I want to eat if you already knew what you wanted, li'l dumb-ass girl!"

"'Cause I thought you would want some Kim Van too," London laughed.

"I do have a taste for some duck and noodles and an order of special fried rice wit' no onions," Farrah replied.

"Good, 'cause I already placed the order." London cracked up laughing standing outside Farrah's door.

"Cow!" Farrah threw a book at her.

"Love you," London dodged the throw.

"Heffa," Farrah giggled, shaking her head.

"And don't forget to get me some extra packets of cayenne pepper," Camden reminded her.

"I got you," London said, leaving out the door.

A half hour later Camden knocked on Farrah's door and said, "Excuse me, Farrah, but there is a woman here to see you."

"Who is it?" Farrah looked up, confused.

"She said her name was Lisa."

"Lisa . . . I don't know anybody by the name of Lisa," Farrah replied, perplexed. "Do I have an appointment that we bypassed by accident?"

"No," Camden shook her head.

"Okay, send her back." Farrah smoothed down her shirt, then checked her teeth and hair in the mirror.

As she stood up to greet the unexpected visitor, her heart dropped down to the heel of her Valentino soles. She knew exactly who Lisa was, except Lisa wasn't her real name. The woman's real name was Jade. Normally, Jade exuded sex on a stick, but that day she looked a hot, tired mess. Her skin wasn't its usual golden color. It was a sickly, pale yellow. Dark circles and bags surrounded her eyes and she looked as if she hadn't slept in days.

Farrah almost felt sorry for her, but then she quickly remembered who she was dealing with and quickly checked herself. Jade may have looked a disheveled, homeless mess, but Farrah was pretty sure she was there to kill and destroy.

"I'm sorry for just poppin' up on you like this at your job and for lying about who I was, but I knew if I told the truth you wouldn't see me," Jade spoke politely.

"You got a lot of nerve coming to my place of business," Farrah scoffed.

"Is everything okay?" Camden asked nervously. "Should I call security?"

"Nah, I'm straight. I doubt she's crazy enough to start some stuff in my office. Close the door behind you," Farrah said, resuming her seat.

She was caught off guard by Jade's impromptu visit, but she would never allow her nemesis to see her sweat. Acting as if she had it all together, Farrah crossed her legs, intertwined her fingers, and said, "How may I help you?"

"I didn't come here to beef wit' you or anything like that—"

"Then why are you here?" Farrah cut her off. "'Cause please believe I ain't got time for no drama and I certainly don't have to time to entertain any games you tryin'a play."

Jade sucked her teeth and kept her composure.

"Look, honestly, I didn't know where else to go," she responded, truthfully.

"I'm not following." Farrah grimaced.

"I don't know if you know, but I recently had a baby girl and it's . . . Mills's."

"That's to be determined." Farrah cocked her head to the side.

"And that's the reason why I'm here. For whatever reason, Mills refuses to take the paternity test," Jade explained.

"Whoa-whoa-whoa-whoa." Farrah uncrossed her legs and waved her hands. "What do you mean, Mills refuses to take the test? He said you hadn't taken the test."

"No, ma'am, me and my daughter went in a month ago and got swabbed. Here . . ." Jade dug inside her purse. "I have proof." She pulled out a piece of paper and set it down onto Farrah's desk.

Farrah picked the paper up and sure enough, Jade had taken the test over a month ago.

"Look, I know that you two are married now and I'm not tryin' to fuck up what y'all got. I just want Mills to take care of his daughter. Having a child has really put things into perspective for me and my main priority is making sure my daughter is taken care of," Jade said humbly.

"If my memory serves me correctly, weren't you cheatin' on him wit' some NBA player?" Farrah screwed up her face.

Jade swallowed hard.

"Yes, I was, but—"

"So how you know the baby ain't his?" Farrah stopped her again.

Jade didn't even bother to respond. She simply placed a photo onto Farrah's desk and slid it toward her.

"That's why."

Farrah looked down at the picture and what stared back at her was the perfect mixture of Jade and Mills. A paternity test didn't even need to be done. Anyone with eyes could see that the baby was Mills's. Farrah's entire face filled with tears. Every inch of her wanted to break down and cry, but she couldn't, not while Jade was there. Mustering up as much willpower as she could, Farrah blinked her tears away.

"So what do you want me to do?" she asked Jade, swallowing hard.

"I just want you to talk some sense into him and tell him to do the right thing. I'm not doing this to hurt him or you. I just want the best for my daughter, that's it."

"Mills is a grown-ass man. I can't make him do anything," Farrah replied, coldly.

"And that's fine, but at least you know the truth now. I won't take up anymore of your time, Farrah." Jade turned and left as quickly as she came.

Once she was gone Camden rushed to Farrah's door.

"Is everything all right? I could feel the tension from out there."

"Yeah, just give me a minute." Farrah turned around in her chair and faced the window.

"Okay, let me know if you need anything." Camden closed the door reluctantly.

This was it. The moment Farrah had been anticipating since she said *I do*. Once again, Mills had managed to turn her from a woman of substance into a weak and pathetic fool. Feeling as if she were about to implode, Farrah closed her eyes and squeezed herself tight. With her head down, she rocked back and forth and willed the fire in her heart to stop burning.

Her entire brain was spinning out of control with questions. *What was all of this, a game?*

Does he get off on lying to me? Why would he put me through this? Why did he marry me, knowing the truth? Did he ever really love me? she wondered. *No, he couldn't have, because if he did, he would've never done this to me. He would've never destroyed me so easily,* she thought.

Farrah continued to hold herself and rock and back forth. She felt if she stopped rocking she would lose her will to live. What was she supposed to do now? Where was she to go? How would she continue on? The only things she knew for sure was that she wanted Mills to hurt how she was hurting right now. She wanted him to know what it felt like to burn, to not be able to breathe. He never knew what real pain looked like. When Jade threw him to the wolves, she'd been there to save him.

He never had sleepless nights that felt like they were never-ending. He never went days without food in his system because he was too heartbroken to eat and the food made him sick. He never was so lonely he wanted to throw up. She wanted his days to be cold. She wanted his nights to be met with tears of regret. She yearned for him to miss her so much it drove him insane.

Then, all of sudden, her mission was clear. A flip was switched inside of Farrah's head and all of her sadness was numbed. Spinning around, she grabbed her purse and the picture of the baby Jade had so conveniently left behind. On a mission to destroy, Farrah stomped her way out the door and out to her car. She could hear Camden call out for her, but nothing could stop her.

The drive from her office to her destination was short. With her Mercedes placed in park, Farrah hopped out with the picture in hand and walked toward Mills. He had no idea what was about to hit him. There he was, at the site of his new skate and bike park, going over blueprints with the developers. He didn't even notice Farrah approaching him.

"You no-good muthafucka!" she spat, pushing him.

"Farrah, what the fuck?" Mills said, caught off guard.

"I thought you had taken the paternity test? I thought the baby wasn't yours, you lousy, lying bastard!" She pushed him again.

"Mills, what is going on here?" one of the developers asked.

"Just give me a minute, Bob," Mills pleaded desperately.

"Yeah, give him a second, *Bob*!" Farrah shouted.

"What the fuck is your problem? You actin' like a crazy woman!" Mills looked at Farrah like she was a foreign object.

"If I'm crazy, it's because you made me this way! Why you have to lie to me, Mills? I asked you over and over again and you repeatedly said *no*!" Farrah cried so hard her chest heaved up and down.

"Look at what you've done to us!" Tears dripped from her eyes as she held up the picture of the baby. "Look! She looks just like you!"

Mills wanted to continue to deny the truth, but the look of utter despair on Farrah's face was unbearable.

"I'm sorry." He hung his head low.

"You're sorry? No, I'm sorry 'cause I believed you! I married you!" Farrah pushed him repeatedly.

"I didn't mean for it to go this far. I was gon' tell you the truth." Mills tried to explain as cars stopped to watch their altercation.

"Really?" Farrah snapped. "When were you going to tell me the truth, Mills, huh? When I got pregnant or when the baby was born? You ain't shit, nigga, and it pisses me off that I'm just now realizing it! I see why Jade cheated on you! And then you the dumb muthafucka that goes back and fucks the bitch! What the fuck is wrong wit' you? Do you get off on lookin' stupid? Why you couldn't just tell me the baby was yours instead of lying about it like a fuckin' pussy!"

"Pussy?" He looked over at the developers, whose eyes were wide with amazement.

"Mills, I think we're just gonna leave," Bob announced.

"No, just give me a second!" Mills requested. "Farrah, can we please talk about this at home? You're embarrassing the hell outta me." Mills clenched his jaw.

"I'm embarrassing *you?*" Farrah said in disbelief. "I know you didn't just say that! I *knooooow* you did not just say that! Nigga, you cheated on me, got a bitch pregnant, kept it a secret, then lied and said the baby wasn't yours when you knew damn well it was, but I'm embarrassing *you?* Nigga, fuck you!" Farrah mushed him in the forehead.

"Like, really go fuck yourself! Fuck yourself wit' a fifty-inch dick until you bleed, muthafucka, 'cause I'm done! You, your slut-bag baby mama and that *Jon and Kate Plus Eight–* lookin'-ass baby of yours can all go fuck yourself! You are— good for nothin'—and I'm not gon' waste any more of my tears on you!" Farrah threw the picture at him and stomped away.

Mills wanted to run after her and plead his case, but he knew that he had no case to plead. Plus, Farrah's temper was on twenty. There was no talking to her. Nothing could calm her down. He would try his best to salvage his meeting and give her a little time to breathe. Prayfully, by the time he got home she would be open and stable enough to talk. But before Mills went home he had a quick run to make.

Chapter 9

*Don't know what I'm gonna do, but I just
keep on going through changes.*
　　　—Eminem, "Going Through Changes"

"Yeah, baby, fuck me, papi!" screamed Lizzy as J.R. pounded in and out of her pussy. "Oh, baby, don't stop! I'm 'bout to cum!" she yelled. "*Aaaaahhh!*" She gave one last scream and her body went completely limp. J.R. usually loved it when she came while he was still inside her, because she would get extra-wet just how he liked it, but tonight, he just couldn't enjoy it as much as he usually did. He pulled out, grabbed a towel, and started to clean himself off.

"You want me to suck you off, babe?" Lizzy asked with a devilish grin on her face.

"Nah, not tonight. I'm good," J.R. replied without looking up at her. "You can order room service if you want. Just have them put it on my tab. I'm gonna take a shower and head out."

"It's two o'clock in the morning. Where are you going at this time of night?" she asked.

"Whoa, wait a second. Let me explain something to you, Lizzette. You are not my girl or anything remotely close to that, so don't ever let me catch you questioning me like that again," J.R. stated. "Just because we fuck from time to time does not mean we are anything more than just that: sex buddies. Do you understand me?" he questioned.

"Damn, J.R., I get it. My bad" she replied as she sucked her teeth. She knew she made him mad when he called her by her full name. He only did that when he was upset with her and he had never talked to her like that before, so that really took her for a loop. For almost a year and a half, they'd been sleeping together. She had known him for three months before they started messing with each other and from the first time it happened, he told her it was just gonna be a physical thing. Lizzy had never been the type to just be somebody's fuck buddy, but from messing with J.R., the good girl in her had completely gone out the window.

The two met when she was hired to be his assistant on a three-month tour. She knew who he was from hearing his music on the radio and reading articles about him. She wasn't the least bit interested in working for him because she figured he was just like the rest of the rappers out there, all about their money, jewelry, bitches, and cars. But while she worked for him, she came to realize how good of a guy he was. He was always nice to his fans and his staff and he carried himself well. When she struck up the nerve to come on to him, he was hesitant because he didn't want to mix business with pleasure. So the second her task of working with him was over, she showed up at his hotel wearing nothing else but a trench coat and red stilettos and it was on from there.

J.R. gave her the best sex she ever had. He was a beast in the bed and she was turned out. Lizzy did anything and everything he asked her to do and for the entire year and a half of their arrangement, she made herself his exclusive sex buddy. He always treated Lizzy nice whenever they would get together. They'd even watched a few movies in bed from time to time. So even though he said they'd never be anything more, deep down, Lizzy hoped one day that would change. After the way he reacted to her tonight, though, she was really thrown off. He wasn't acting like himself at all.

While in the shower, J.R. couldn't stop thinking about the article he'd read about the up- and-coming styling company Glam Squad. His heart skipped a beat when he saw Farrah's picture in the article. He had no idea she was a successful businesswoman when he met her at the club. With this new information, he found himself even more attracted to her. He always wanted a woman who was beautiful, sassy, and independent. And Farrah embodied all those qualities and then some. He felt a little bit guilty that he was daydreaming on a married woman, but the more he tried not to think about her, the more he wanted to get to know her better.

He would never admit it to anyone, but, J.R. was ready to settle down. Sure, it was fun to travel the world and he could sleep with pretty much whoever he wanted, but he was completely over the phase of sleeping around. When his rapping career took off, he had all types of girls throwing themselves at him and he had a crazy sex life. You name it, he did it. But after a few years of threesomes and sleeping with different types of girls, it just didn't do anything for him anymore. It all felt played out. That's why when him and Lizzy became sex friends, he was very satisfied with what they had between each other. She took care of his physical needs and he actually enjoyed her company. He was even considering spending more time with Lizzy and seeing if maybe she was wifey material, up until he met Farrah at the club. Now his mind was on an entirely different path.

He wondered if she had received the flowers he had sent her. He was really hoping Farrah would take him up on the offer and go out to lunch with him. She didn't know yet, but he was about to become her latest client.

BAM! BAM! BAM! Mills pounded his fist against Jade's door so hard he swore it was going to bleed. *Furious* wasn't even the word to describe how angry he was. He knew that Jade was ruthless, but he never in a million years thought she'd go this far.

"Who is it?" Jade asked.

"Mills," he replied.

"I'm tellin' you now, Mills, I hope you ain't over here on no bullshit," Jade said, through the door.

"Nah, I just want to holla at you for a minute." Mills tried to sound calm.

Jade slowly opened the door, stood back on one leg, and said, "What?"

"Nah, I ain't on no bullshit." Mills shook his head. "You on some bullshit." He pointed his finger at her like a gun.

"Oh really, and how is that?" Jade rolled her neck.

"Why you tryin' to ruin my life?"

"Let me explain something to you," Jade said in an even tone. "I don't give a fuck about your life. All I care about is my daughter—who, by the way, has been sick with colic for the past week. What the fuck did she do to you? I know what I did to you, but what did she do to you?"

"Hold up." Mills held up his hand. "Nobody told you have to have that baby! I didn't want to have a baby wit' you! You weren't my girl! I mean, Who fucks around and gets pregnant on some one-night shit and then wanna cry about it?" Mills barked, causing the baby to cry.

"Now you mad 'cause you got a baby that you can't afford. Then you think you gon' sweat me and interfere wit' my life! Nah, when I have a baby I wanna have a baby wit' my *wife*," he stressed.

"Not some dirty-ass bitch that goes around giving her pussy away just 'cuz a nigga said you looked nice. It wasn't even that fuckin' good. If I would'a known you was gone be a pain in my ass, I would've had you sucked my dick to ease the pain!"

Speechless, Jade reared her hand back to slap Mills, only for him to catch her hand in mid-swing and say, "I have had enough for today." He tossed her hand back.

In the seven years Jade knew Mills they'd argued and said some terrible things to one another. But he'd never been so cutthroat and merciless with his words. She didn't know what was worse: the sound of her daughter screaming or the venom he'd just spat at her. He'd torn her to shreds, but there was no way Jade could let him get away with speaking to her like that without crushing his soul as well.

"Fuck you, nigga! You wasn't saying none a dat when you was all up in my shit eating it! Maybe if you wasn't so strung on my pussy, you woulda kept your dick at home. You pussy-whipped motherfucka. And don't you be talkin' to me like I wasn't shit to you. I been wit' you for six years before I got tired of your wack-ass dick game and moved on to somebody that knew how to lay it down right! Now onto the real situation at hand. Yeah, I had a baby!" She stepped up and got in his face.

"Yo' fuckin' baby, but you know what? You right about one thing, I shoulda never had your baby 'cuz I shoulda known you wasn't gonna help me take care of it. Your daddy ain't never did shit for you and left your mom high and dry. I musta been crazy to think you was gonna be any different!"

Jade knew it was a low blow to bring up Mills's absentee father, but she had to hit him where it hurt.

"You're a raggedy muthafucka! My baby don't need you! You ain't even gotta worry about no paternity test! I don't even want you around her! Now, if you don't get the fuck outta here, I'ma call that dumb-ass, rebound bitch you call yo' wife over here to get you!"

"What?" Mills tuned up his face.

"You heard me! Get the fuck outta here!" She pushed him repeatedly until he was on the bottom step.

Pissed, Jade slammed the door behind her and took a deep breath. Putting her feelings aside, she snapped back into mommy mode and rushed to her baby. With her baby girl tucked securely in her arms, Jade tried her best to ease Jaysin's cries, but nothing worked. Overwhelmed by her daughter's nonstop wailing and the hole in her heart Mills had just put there, Jade began to cry.

She felt utterly helpless. All she had was a half a box of Pampers left and in a day or two she would be out of milk. Life for her couldn't have gotten any worse.

"I'm sorry, baby," she wept. "I'm gon' figure out a way for us to be okay. Nah, fuck that. We gon' be better than okay. We gon' be good. I'ma do whatever I gotta do to take care of you."

Unbeknown to Jade, while she tried everything in her power to soothe herself and her weeping baby, Mills had walked back into the apartment. After realizing she hadn't locked the door, he stormed back in to give Jade another piece of his mind, but instead found her distraught with tears. He'd never seen her in such a vulnerable state.

"*Shhhhhh*." She bounced Jaysin up and down. "Everything's gonna be all right. I know you don't feel good, but you gotta stop cryin'. Please stop cryin'," she begged. "I can't take this anymore."

"Let me try," Mills said from behind, causing Jade to jump.

Face-to-face, she looked inside Mills's eyes and could tell that he genuinely wanted to help.

"She won't stop cryin'." Jade handed Jaysin over to her father.

Instantly, within a blink of an eye Jaysin stopped crying. Only the sounds of coos filled the room. Stunned, Jade wiped the existing tears from her cheeks.

"How did you get in here?"

"The door wasn't locked," Mills answered, gazing down at his mini-me.

Even with a tear-stained face Jaysin's beauty shined through. She was simply gorgeous.

"Look, I gotta go to talk to Farrah, but I'll be back." He handed the baby back to Jade.

"Okay," she said, nodding, not knowing if he was really telling the truth.

Chapter 10

I know you been so through wit' me.
You put up with my foolery.
I guess you got so used to me.
  —Trey Songz, "Me 4 U Infidelity 2"

Never before in Mills's life had he driven so fast to get home. His heart was pounding out of his chest and breathing was like inhaling and exhaling knives. He didn't know what he was going to come home to when he walked through the door. For all he knew, Farrah would be waiting on him with a gun aimed at his head, ready to pull the trigger. As quickly as he could, Mills parked his car and ran into the building. After hopping off the elevator, he unlocked the door and raced into the house.

"Farrah!" he shouted, searching each room.

Mills stopped in their bedroom. It looked like a tornado had blown through. Farrah's things were sprawled everywhere, like she'd been in a rush to grab her things and go. Mills wearily stepped toward her walk-in closet and found half of it emptied. Clothes hung off the hangers by a thread. The majority of her entire purse and shoe collection was gone.

She'd left him and this time it seemed it was for good. Mills wanted to break down, but he couldn't. This wasn't how their story was going to end. She was his wife. They'd barely been married three months. When he'd married her he'd envisioned them growing old, sitting on the porch in rocking chairs with one another. He had to find her, sit her down, and talk some sense into her.

She had to know that beneath all of the rubble and carnage existed an undying love that would never go away. They were in too deep now. How could they possibly give up? Keys in hand, Mills ran to the elevator and back down to his car. Farrah had left him, but he knew exactly where she was at. The speed limit was of no concern to him as he raced down the highway to Farrah's old apartment. Finally there, he jumped out of the car and ran up the walkway to the door.

Mills knocked as hard as he could and prayed that she'd come down and speak to him. Ten minutes went by and Mills's hand was beyond sore, but he refused to stop. He knew Farrah was inside.

"Farrah! I know you're in there! Answer the door!" He pounded his fist.

"Mills!" London stuck her head out the second-floor window. "If yo' country ass don't stop bangin' on my door, I'ma call the police!"

"Is Farrah up there?" Mills stepped back so he could see her.

"No," London lied.

"Come on, London, I know that's your home-girl and you're tryin' to protect her, but that's my wife!"

"Negro, you can save that wife shit! Was you thinking about yo' wife when you got that bitch pregnant?! Oh . . . okay," London said, smirking.

"Now you know you wrong?" Mills massaged his jaw.

"I ain't wrong! It's the truth!"

"You need to mind yo' fuckin' business!" Mills shouted, pointing his finger at her.

"I am minding my shit! You on my mother-fucking doorstep lookin' like a homeless beggar! I ain't got no soup for you, so skip yo' li'l lyin'-cheatin'-ass on down the street 'cause ain't nobody over here got time for you!" London wagged her index finger and popped her lips.

"You's a silly bitch! You act like you Farrah! What, you want me or something?" Mills shot back.

"Don't nobody want you but Farrah! Farrah—" London looked over her shoulder. "You better check this sack of shit before I cut him! 'Cause if I cut him y'all won't ever be able to get back together!"

Farrah sat on the couch and rolled her eyes to the ceiling. London had completely blown her cover.

"I knew she was in there wit' yo' ol' lyin' ass! That's why I never liked you," Mills barked.

"Good! Now we can stop pretending!" London shot back.

"Farrah! Come get this crazy bitch!" Mills yelled.

"Bitch? Oh nigga, I got yo' bitch!" London took off her earrings. "You's the bitch, an ol' beggin'-ass bitch!"

"Fuck you!" Mills shot her the middle finger and grabbed his dick.

"You wish you could fuck me, nigga! But I wouldn't let you touch me if you came with a million dollars!" London said, ready to go fight.

Having heard enough, Farrah pushed London to the side and said, "Mills, just go home."

"Nah, I ain't going nowhere until I talk to you!"

"I ain't got nothin' to say to you. Plus, you owe London an apology."

"Apology? I don't owe her shit! She in our business! You heard the way she was talkin' to me!" Mills screwed up his face.

"I don't give a fuck about none of that—just go home!" Farrah closed the window.

"Farrah! Farrah!" Mills called out for her.

Back on the couch, Farrah placed her knees up to her chest and buried her face in her lap. The sound of Mills shouting her name was like hearing nails on a chalkboard. She physically couldn't take it. All she wanted was a moment to be with herself to process the days' events. Mills would never respect that. All he cared about was healing the brokenness in his own heart.

"He's gone," London announced.

"I can't stay here," Farrah whispered.

"Why?" London sat next to her friend.

"'Cause he's only going to keep coming back." Farrah closed her eyes tight as her cell phone started to ring.

She didn't even have to look at the screen to know it was Mills.

"See, he's not going to stop."

"What do you want to do?" London wrapped her arms around Farrah.

"I gotta get outta here."

***

Just when Jade thought she was about to break, just when she thought she'd withstood all she could withstand, a blessing from up above was bestowed upon her. After two more sleepless nights with a wailing, sick baby, Jade was near pulling the little bit of hair she had out. She was becoming delirious. Taking care of a sick child on no sleep was pure hell. She was starting to become dizzy and even caught herself on more than one occasion seeing double.

She needed sleep. She needed rest. She needed a miracle. It was obvious that Mills wasn't going to be of any help. Once again, he'd played her for a fool. Just when she thought they'd shared a moment and reconnected, he disappeared and resumed his act of deadbeat dad. Jade had come to the painful conclusion that she was going to be raising her daughter on her own. Although she was scared out of her mind to be a single mother, she had no choice but to somehow figure out how to survive for the sake of her and Jaysin. She didn't know how she would ever survive with no job and no money from Mills coming in.

Then she quickly remembered her mother and millions of other women who raised children on their own everyday. She wasn't handicapped. She was an able-bodied human being who could do anything she put her mind to. No, she didn't have any work experience or really any goals or ambitions, but she would work at McDonald's if that's what it took in order to provide for her daughter. While Jaysin screamed from her baby bed, Jade frantically fixed her a fresh bottle of formula, when her doorbell rang.

"Shit," she huffed, twisting the top on the bottle. "Who is it?" she yelled, stomping through the living room.

"Delivery!" a male voice said.

"Delivery?" Jade opened the door, perplexed.

"Jade Thomas?" The deliveryman looked down at his tablet.

"Yes."

"Can you sign here, please?" The man handed her the tablet.

"I didn't order anything, sir." Jade shook her head.

"Well, we have a delivery here for you, so can you please sign where the X is so we can start unloading the truck."

"Who is the delivery from?" Jade took the tablet and signed her name.

"Umm . . . it's from Corey Mills. Hey, isn't he the Gatorade guy?"

"Yeah," Jade answered as Jaysin continued to scream.

"My kids love him. Ay boys, start unloading the truck!" The deliveryman said over his shoulder.

Bewildered, Jade stepped aside as five different men began to whisk in box after box. There were cases of Enfamil and Pampers. Then boxes of toys and racks of clothes were brought in. Tears of joy rushed to Jade's eyes. She wanted to fall to her knees and thank God, but before she could, two ladies appeared.

One was her neighbor, Mrs. Whitmore, and the other was a nurse. Both were there to help her with Jaysin. Mills hadn't played her after all. Eternally grateful, Jade said a silent prayer to God and allowed everyone to do the job they'd come to do.

Mills was a man in despair. Several days had gone by and he hadn't seen or heard from Farrah. He'd tried calling her, but was met with the sound of the operator telling him that the number he'd tried reaching wasn't accepting any calls. He'd gone to her office, but the only people there were Camden, the interns, and assistants. Camden wouldn't give him any answers and he for damn sure wasn't going to call London.

He knew that Fashion Week in Paris was nearing, but he didn't know if she'd left early or was just hiding out somewhere in St. Louis. He was out of his head with worry. Mills didn't know what to do. He had to find his wife, but he didn't know where to turn or where to go. Like most men, he never thought this day would come. Mills had become so caught up in his lies that he figured Farrah wouldn't catch on. But foolishly, he'd underestimated her.

Now she was gone and there was nothing he could do about it but suffer the consequences. It sucked, because his heart yearned for its heartbeat back. Mills had actually started to believe that she'd continue to put up with his inconsiderate ways, because no matter what he did Farrah was always there. Without Farrah he felt like death was knocking at his door. Mills had never experienced this kind of torture before. He didn't even know it existed.

This shit was gut-wrenching. He would've rather for Farrah to cut him across the throat then to just fall off the face of the earth. If he could, he would rewind time and do things right. He would've never gone to see Jade that night. He would've stayed at home with Farrah and made love until the sun came up. Now he might not ever get to experience having her in his arms again.

Each night that passed, all he did was sit and reminisce on all the things they did with one another. Thoughts of them snuggled on the couch, watching movies, making love in the shower, the days they'd lay in bed and just talked about everything and anything, or how she'd fall asleep in his arms, all constantly tormented his mind.

He never knew losing someone you loved could hurt this bad. Now that she was gone Mills realized how bad he'd fucked up. He could've loved Farrah so much better. He thought he was a better man than what he was portraying. For years he looked down at Khalil for the way he treated Farrah, only to turn around and treat her worse. The cold shoulder she was giving him was well-deserved.

Surrounded by a pile of blunt leaves, Mills guzzled down his fifth glass of Jameson whiskey. The smooth, potent liquid slid down his throat with ease. For the past few days Anthony Hamilton's *Coming From Where I'm From* CD stayed stuck on repeat. Mills was worn out. Functioning on no sleep or food and missing the hell out of Farrah was getting the best of him. If Farrah didn't come save him quick there was no telling what he might do.

No amount of drinking or smoking weed would kill the brain cells inside his mind or take away the pain. Only she could cure him. Mills ran his hands down his face and blinked back the tears that stung the rim of his eyes. Millions of tears flooded his heart, but Mills—being the man he was—wouldn't dare release them. As he willed himself not cry, someone knocked on his door. Mills purposely hadn't spoken to anyone except his assistant in days, so whoever was at his door could step.

"Come on, Mills! Open the door!" Teddy said from the other side.

Mills poured himself another glass of Jameson and acted as if no one was there. Gulping down the fresh glass of whiskey, he turned the volume up on the stereo.

"Word?" Teddy shouted, knocking even harder. "Open the damn door!"

Mills groaned and swung the door open, letting Teddy in.

"Damn nigga, what?"

"Shut the fuck up," Teddy shot back. "You need to be happy I even came over here to check on yo' soft ass."

"Bite me." Mills walked back over to his island and resumed his pity party.

"What the fuck are you over here doing?" Teddy looked around, disgusted.

The loft was a wreck and it smelled like pure ass.

"Fuck!" Teddy covered his nose.

"I know you're on suicide watch, but god-damn!" Teddy opened a window. "Wash yo' ass, dude!"

"If you don't like it, there's the door." Mills motioned his head toward the door.

"Let me know when you're done with this woe-is-me-act." Teddy poured himself a glass of alcohol. "And quit hoggin' the blunt." He snatched it from Mills's hand and took a toke.

"You know, I never knew how annoying you are until now," Mills shot, rolling another blunt.

"And I never knew how much of a bitch you are until now," Teddy snapped back. "You act like you lost yo' dog, yo' fuckin' bike, and yo' girl. I know shit is all bad right now, but you gotta pull it together. You're wife is gone and you over here moping around like you Drake and shit."

"Don't you think if I knew where my wife was I'd be wherever she was at, tryin' to make this shit right?" Mills looked at Teddy as if he were stupid.

"If yo' punk ass would've answered the phone when I called, maybe you could've found out where she was at," Teddy responded.

"You know where Farrah at?" Mills perked up.

"Oh, now you wanna talk. Lousy muthafucka," Teddy chuckled.

"Just tell me where she at?" Mills spat, aggravated.

"Her and London are in Paris."

"I thought they wasn't leaving until Sunday?" Mills quizzed.

"Nah, Farrah decided she wanted to leave early."

"What, to get away from me?" Mills asked, deflated.

"I ain't wanna say it, but . . . yeah."

"What hotel they at so I can book a flight?" Mills grabbed his phone, ready to call his travel agent.

"London wouldn't tell me 'cause she knew I was gon' tell you."

"I'm so sick of that bitch," Mills said, clenching his jaw.

"Ay, don't talk about my girl like that. Just 'cause yours ain't fuckin' wit' you doesn't mean you can shit on mine."

"Nah, that crazy bitch cussed me out. Callin' me homeless and shit and talkin' about *I ain't got no soup for you,*" Mills mocked her. "Like I'm some random, pathetic beggar or something. I'm a man. You don't talk to me like I'm some weak-ass bum."

"You acting like one right now, though. And you smell like one too. Nigga, please go wash your ass!" Teddy shook his head.

"I just want my wife back." Mills grimaced, taking another glass of whiskey to the head. "I just want my wife back."

Chapter 11

Everything I want, you got it.
                    —Ciara, "Other Chicks"

Cancelling some appointments to jet-set around the world to Paris and take a few days to herself before Paris week had been the best decision Farrah made in months. She was supposed to style Lana Del Rey for H&M's Christmas campaign, but Farrah really needed the time to get away from everything. If she hadn't gotten out of St. Louis as fast as she had, she was sure to have lost her sanity. Mills would've continued bombarding her with calls and unwanted pop-up visits and once the media got wind of their separation, a media circus would have ensued.

Farrah didn't have the time nor the patience to deal with that. She had to put her mind on pause. She needed a change in scenery and different air to breathe. She didn't need Mills all up in her ear trying to convince her to come back to him. If she did decide to go back, it would be on her own merit. But running back into Mills's arms was the furthest thing from her mind.

Farrah didn't even want to breathe the same air as him. The mere sound of his name made her head hurt. Paris was the perfect distraction and stress reliever. Farrah, London, and one of their assistants were staying at the glamorous Four Seasons Hotel George V. The Four Seasons in Paris redefined luxury at its best and it was just steps away from the Champs-Elysées.

Farrah and London both had their own suite. Upon walking in you were greeted by an entrance foyer that led to a large sitting room with period furniture, while the bedroom was secluded by sliding doors. They even had their own terrace overlooking the city. Since they'd arrived earlier than scheduled, Farrah used the extra days to ponder over her marriage.

She often found herself on the terrace alone, absently staring out at her surroundings. She'd cry, question, wonder, wallow, and more than anything, pray. The only person who could bring her through this was God. Her heart belonged to Mills, but since she'd met him their relationship had been plagued with nothing but drama.

Thank God, Paris always brought a smile to her face. Every time she visited, she instantly fell in love with the city. The trip this year was a bittersweet one for Farrah because of everything going on in her personal life. She was enjoying herself, but the joy of it kept getting short-lived when she thought about all the drama that was waiting for her back in the States.

As a celebrity stylist, though, Farrah had to stay on point because Paris Fashion Week was essential for her business to continue its success. The clothes shown during Paris Fashion Week set the tone for what the entire industry followed that season. Although it was a never-ending cluster fuck of show after show, networking, fake air kisses, parties, late dinners, and no sleep, Farrah loved every second of it. This trip was one she looked forward to every year.

She and London attended all of the major shows like, Christian Lacroix, Ungaro, Chanel, and John Galliano. You name the designer and they were there. On a starry Parisian night Farrah sat front row at the late, great Alexander McQueen spring-summer fashion show. The new designer for McQueen, Sarah Burton, said in interviews that the collection was inspired by bees, so Farrah was beyond excited.

Hundreds of industry insiders, including Joe Zee from *Elle* magazine, Anna Wintour, Grey Rose from *Haute Couture* magazine, and actress

Amanda Seyfried were there. Everyone looked effortlessly chic and put together. Before the show began, Farrah and London stood in front of their seats, posing for photographers.

"Farrah, what are you wearing?" one of the photographers asked.

"McQueen, of course," she said, winking.

She was in head to toe McQueen, to be exact. To wear any other designer would've been incredibly rude and disrespectful. She wore a striking, silver twill, double-breasted suit adorned with Jacquard dragonflies. Her hair was pulled back into a sleek ponytail and sparkling gold shadow on her eyes and matte nude lipstick completed her look. Despite the ongoing pang to her chest, Farrah put on a strong face and pretended that everything in her life was peaches and cream.

She wouldn't dare let her peers see her in a vulnerable state. This was business and in business you put your personal shit aside. Besides, she'd had enough of hurting. She'd been hurting for the last four years. As the music cued and the lights went down, Farrah held out her camera to take pictures. McQueen's new designer, Sarah Burton, was a master at crafting exquisite pieces and always put on an amazing show, so she never knew what to expect.

All of a sudden a green orb of light shined bright and snowflakes began to fall from the ceiling, creating a winter wonderland. Models like Coco Rocha, Sessilee Lopez, Jessica Stam, and the number-one model in the world, Joan Smalls, proceeded to stomp the blood cells out of their feet in some of the most spellbinding creations Farrah had ever seen. While Farrah took in the show, she noticed out of the corner of her eye someone staring at her. Wondering who was watching her instead of the show, she gave the person a full view of her face.

Farrah nearly dropped her camera when she realized it was the rapper J.R. undressing her with his eyes. She would've never thought she'd see him again, let alone run into him in a whole other country. She couldn't help but notice that he looked even cuter than before. He could've been a model with his fine self. He donned a black-and-white square printed Staple shirt buttoned all the way to the top. Three thin, gold rope necklaces lay underneath the collar of his shirt. The rest of his look consisted of black, fitted Seven jeans and all-black Christian Louboutin rollerball spikes loafers. On his left wrist, he was sporting a gold submariner Rolex. This man was dripping with fashion swag.

Pursing her lips together, Farrah cocked her head to the side and shot him a look that said *really?* J.R. simply hung his head and grinned that charming, boyish grin of his, then looked back up at her. Unable to focus on the show because she was taken in by J.R.'s presence, Farrah pretended to concentrate on the rest of the show, even though all she could think of was how fine J.R. looked tonight.

"Sarah Burton just gave me life," London said, standing up to leave.

"Yeah, it was good." Farrah smoothed down her suit as J.R. made his way over to them.

"Is that . . . ?" London whispered out the side of her mouth.

"Mmm-hmm." Farrah placed her shoulders back and her breasts out.

"You miss me?" J.R. wrapped one arm around her waist and kissed her cheek.

"Why are you stalkin' me is the real question." Farrah kept her composure.

Not paying any mind to her statement, J.R. turned to London.

"I never thought I'd see London in Paris," he said jokingly.

"Damn, you remember my name?" London smiled.

"Yeah, anybody that's important to her is important to me. Ain't that right, girlfriend?" J.R. smirked.

"I'm not going there with you today," Farrah giggled.

"You look cute. You look like dessert." J.R. slid his index finger across Farrah's cheek.

It took every bit of willpower she had not to take his finger into her mouth.

"Aww, isn't that sweet." London nudged Farrah on the arm.

"Stop." Farrah shot London a stern look.

"Let me give you two lovebirds a minute." London stepped away grinning like a Cheshire cat.

"What are you doing in Paris? Are you just here for Fashion Week?" Farrah asked, trying to keep the conversation on the surface.

"I'm here for the shows and I'm finishing up my France tour. I have three sold-out concerts at Le Bataclan."

"That's what's up." Farrah gave him props. "Did you like the show presentation?

"Nah," J.R. shook his head. "It was too much weird shit. You, on the other hand, yeah, I like you. But I made that clear the first time we met."

"You sure did." Farrah turned beet-red.

"You still married?" J.R. gazed at her left hand.

"Yep." Farrah looked down at her ring and sighed.

"What was that?" he asked, concerned.

"What was what?" Farrah replied, confused.

"I saw you take a deep breath. What, your happily-ever-after turning out to be a nightmare already?"

"You are so nosy! You do realize I barely know you? I mean, you cute and all, but we ain't cool like that."

"So you finally admit it. You think I'm cute." J.R. got in her face.

His lips were inches away from hers. All Farrah had to do was lean forward and place hers upon his. Farrah couldn't front, if she was a single woman she'd allow herself to fall head over heels for this guy. On the surface it seemed J.R. possessed everything she ever wanted in a man. But Farrah was off limits.

"You going really hard for somebody you hardly know. For all you know I could be crazy." She gazed into his eyes and became lost.

"Stop being afraid. You ain't gotta be scared of me. I ain't gon' hurt you," J.R. said, seductively placing both his arms around her waist and pulling her into him.

"I'm a grown woman. Grown women don't get scared," Farrah challenged.

"If that's the case, then quit bullshittin' and let me take you out to eat."

"Oh my god," Farrah's voice cracked. "I can't with you today. It was good seeing you again, J.R. Enjoy Paris." She slightly brushed his arm with her hand before sauntering off.

"You gon' be mine sooner or later!" J.R. shouted after her.

Complete and utter silence surrounded Jade while she slept peacefully underneath the covers. Sleep had never felt so good. She'd tried getting up numerous times, but the fluffiness of her king-sized pillow and the security of her Egyptian cotton sheets kept her snuggled up in bed. As she slept she had no idea Mills was there. He'd been there for over two hours, getting acquainted with Jaysin.

Once Mills let his guard down and released his ego, he found himself madly in love with his daughter. The sight of her gorgeous little face instantly brightened his day. She was the instant mood-booster he desperately needed. When he looked at her adorable little face he saw a pinch of Jade and a whole glass of him.

He hated that he'd missed her birth and her first few months. It upset him to know he let so much time go without being around her. He'd never get those moments back, but Mills was there now and he would never leave his daughter's side again. He would raise her to be a better, stronger version of himself.

By noon, Mrs. Whitmore, Jade's next-door neighbor, had taught him how to change Jaysin's diaper and he'd given her a bottle. Mrs. Whitmore was a godsend. Ever since Mills asked her if she'd be willing to come help Jade with the baby, she had almost become Jasyin's unofficial grandmother. She'd been a great help to him and Jade. Deciding it was time for Jade to get up, Mills headed to her bedroom, while Mrs. Whitmore gave Jaysin a bath. Being inside Jade's bedroom brought back so many memories that Mills tried to bury. Jade was still living in their old apartment. Except for the baby items scattered throughout the house, she hadn't made many changes to the place since she and Mills broke up and he moved out. Memories of them making love until they weren't physically able to move, late-night talks, arguing over the remote, and more came flooding back.

He remembered when things started to go downhill for them; the nights she didn't come home and wouldn't answer his calls, and the way they'd ignore each other if they were home at the same time. He remembered when he started lusting after Farrah, and after being faithful to Jade for six years he finally cheated on her with Farrah. Walking throughout the house, he could still hear all the screaming and and hurtful words they said to each other. A lot had transpired in this apartment and among those four walls. but now all that was left of everything was just mere memories. There was no use in thinking about the past. Now that they had a child together, they both had to move forward and work things out for the sake of baby Jaysin. Mills had moved on and was a married man and Jade was just the mother of his child and nothing more.

But then why was Mills getting urges to hug or caress her? He found himself wondering if she had any love left for him. And as Mills watched her laying there, sleeping in their old bed, he was nostalgic, remembering why he'd fallen for her in the beginning. He longed to reach out and trace his fingers along her beautiful soft, skin.

Resting had done Jade wonders. Her skin went from sickly and pale and back to its radiant glow. Her blond buzz cut shone underneath the rays of the afternoon sun. Over the sheets, Mills could see the silhouette of her curvy hips and thick waist. He could see her plump breasts through the thin material of the sheets. It was undeniable how sexy this woman was even in her sleep. As quiet as he could, Mills slipped into bed behind Jade, wrapped his arm around her waist, and said, "Damn nigga, you sleep late." Jade flinched and swiftly turned her head to see who was behind her. She was beyond relieved that it was Mills and not some intruder whose ass she'd have to kick.

"What are you doing here?" she asking, feeling his hard dick pressed up against the crack of her ass.

"I told you I was gon' be back." Mills hopped out of the bed and adjusted his dick.

"What time is it?" Jade sat up and pretended like she hadn't felt the stiffness of his dick and that it didn't turn her on.

"Time for you to get yo' ass up and fix me something to eat." Mills opened the blinds.

"You have lost your damn mind and where is my baby?"

"She straight. I already fed her and Mrs. Whitmore is giving her a bath."

"Say that again?" Jade placed her index finger behind her ear. "You fed Jaysin?"

"Yeah, what you deaf?" Mills chuckled.

"Wow," Jade said in disbelief. "I guess pigs can fly." She pulled the covers back and got out of bed.

Jade wore the tiniest pair of cotton-striped booty shorts that exposed the cheeks of her ample ass. Just the sight of her behind made Mills's dick hard. Memories of him bending her over the bed, couch, or sink and his thick dick sliding in and out of her wet pussy, while the cheeks of her ass bounced uncontrollably, tortured his mind. Mills had to get out of the room quick.

"Hurry up and put some water on that." He pointed to her crotch. "It's getting' a li'l ripe up in here," he joked.

"Shut up!" Jade grabbed a pillow and threw it at his head as he walked out.

Almost an hour later Jade entered her kitchen, feeling clean and revived.

"For a minute there I thought you had fallin' in." Mills sat at the island, holding Jaysin.

"Hey, my baby." Jade kissed Jaysin on the cheek. "I can't thank you enough, Mills, for all of your help. All the things you got Jaysin and hiring Mrs. Whitmore and the nurse was so needed."

"You ain't gotta thank me. I should'a been did it. What you can do is hook a nigga up wit' some lunch. My stomach over here growlin' like a muthafucka."

"You serious about me feeding you, huh? Yo' wife didn't feed you before you left home?" Jade opened the fridge.

"Nah, she outta the country on business," Mills replied, with a twinge of sadness in his voice.

"Trouble on the home front?" Jade placed a bag of chicken wings, russet potatoes, flour, cooking oil, and various seasonings on the countertop.

"Oh word, you gettin' ready to fry me up some chicken and fries?" Mills ignored her question and smiled brightly.

"It's your favorite, right?" Jade arched her eyebrow.

"Fuck, yeah. I can't even front, yo' fried chicken is the bomb. Can't nobody hook it up like you."

"I don't think your wife would like to hear you say that." Jade began to season the chicken.

"Shit, that's real. Farrah can't even boil water," Mills joked.

"Wow," Jade arched her eyebrow and laughed.

"Yeah, Jaysin," Mills held her up to face him. "Yo' mama can burn in the kitchen, but she can't dance for shit."

"Boy, please, you better get yo' life and put it back in yo' chest. I murder the dance floor," Jade checked him.

"No, she don't," Mills looked at Jaysin and shook his head.

"I got more rhythm in my left thumb than yo' mama got in her whole entire body. But you gon' be straight 'cause we gon' put you in tap, hip-hop, and ballet classes. And as soon as you can walk, Daddy gon' get you a bike so you can learn how to ride just like me." Mills kissed Jaysin on the forehead.

An overwhelming amount of joy washed over Jade as she looked on while Mills played with their daughter. It was as if they were a real family, taking pleasure in each other's company and creating memories that would be cherished forever. This was the picture she'd envisioned while giving birth and even though she knew this moment wouldn't last long, she secretly wished this was her reality. She regretted ever having stepped out on Mills. She got so caught up with the lavish lifestyle, messing with Rock from the NBA that she lost a good man. Now here she was living in regret, wishing that somehow she could turn back the hands of time and never messed up her relationship.

Chapter 12

I'm taken back by your presence.
    —Stacy Barthe, "Never Did"

The trip to Paris had been nothing but business and a never-ending therapy session for Farrah. She'd gone to the Louis Vuitton show where head designer Marc Jacobs had the models descend down from escalators in bold checkerboard prints. She'd visited Giambattista Valli showroom and got a private viewing of his 2014 fall collection. Farrah's mission to find the fiercest award-season gowns was accomplished. She'd personally put dibs on gowns from Jean Paul Gaultier, Lanvin, and her go-to designer Vivienne Westwood.

In between attending fashion shows, she pondered what would be the outcome of her and Mills's marriage when she returned home. She lay in bed at night looking up at the ceiling and prayed constantly to God for discernment. But no matter how heavy her heart felt at times, she still made it a priority to do her best and enjoy her time in Paris. There was no use in dwelling about things she couldn't change or act on until she got back to the States.

And with that perseverant attitude and resilience to keep moving forward, there was no way she could visit Paris and not indulge in some of her favorite guilty pleasures. She and London had to have lunch at L'Astrance. A meal at Astrance could only be described as an investment.

The restaurant was quaint. Upon entrance, you were instantly taken in by its high ceilings, mirrored walls, widely spaced tables, and friendly service. Chef Pascal Barbot offered his decidedly twenty-first-century take on French haute cuisine and did not disappoint. After an amazing lunch she and London hit up her favorite vintage store, Didier Ludot. Each time Farrah set foot inside the nostalgic store, she became lost in a couture fantasy land. Each of Didier Ludot's three locations at the Palais-Royal specialized in a specific category of clothing: evening couture, ready-to-wear, and one shop of just little black dresses.

Farrah adored that Ludot specialized in vintage pieces from French designers, such as Chanel, Balenciaga, Givenchy, Balmain, YSL, Lanvin, and Hermès, to name a few. Farrah didn't have any qualms about dropping stacks on the designer duds. Shopping always served as a distraction and put a smile on her face. With all the drama in her life she needed to smile. Even though at night when she got in bed, she felt scared and weary of what might happen when she got home and faced Mills, she still did her best to have the best time in Paris.

Farrah only had two more days left to enjoy her trip and she was going to soak up every second of being in the city of love. It was an unusual sunny afternoon in Paris. Farrah and London walked leisurely down the street with tons of shopping bags in their hands. Farrah couldn't wait to get back to her suite and rest before attending the ultra-exclusive spring preview party for Stella McCartney.

Solange Knowles would be on the ones and twos and pop sensation and Karl Lagerfeld muse Azealia Banks was slated to perform. It would be a night of glitz, glamour, and incredible food and expensive champagne.

"I think I'ma go back to Didier." London stopped mid-stride.

"You don't listen," Farrah remarked. "I told you to get that Hermès cuff."

"I know, but I already spent ten grand. I ain't wanna drop another stack."

"Well, what you gon' do?" Farrah huffed.

"I'ma go back. Here, will you take my bags back to the hotel for me?" London poked out her bottom lip.

"Yeah heffa," Farrah groaned, taking the bags.

"Thanks, doll face," London air-kissed her cheek, then ran off down the street.

Bogged down with bags, Farrah continued on walking toward the hotel. As she crossed the street she was stopped in her tracks by a black Fisker bumpin' Wale's "Let A Nigga Know", abruptly stopping just inches away from hitting her. It was almost as if the driver did it on purpose.

"What the hell?" she shrieked, scared out of her mind. "Excuse you!" She hit the hood of the car, still with bag in hand.

"My bad, I ain't mean to scare you, beautiful." J.R. rolled down the window and laughed. He pulled the car over and parked on the side of the street.

"Well, stalkers are usually frightening." Farrah snapped back, realizing it was him and continued walking.

"Don't say that, 'cause that's how I feel, like a stalker runnin' into you like this," J.R. said, jumping out of his car and hurriedly trying to catch up to her.

"Well, stop stalkin' me *stalker*!" Farrah put an extra amount of bounce into her walk and picked up her pace.

"I can't 'cause I haven't gotten your attention yet," J.R. flirted as he caught up to her.

Farrah paused and smiled. She hated that J.R.'s sweet nothings always made her blush.

"Okay, you got my attention, now what?" She cocked her head to the side and placed her hand on her hip.

"You know what this is about, right?" J.R. asked as he reached for her shopping bags to relieve her of them.

"What? What is this about? 'Cause the last time I checked this shit was illegal."

"This is about me liking you and you really liking me, but you playin' hard to get," J.R. replied, with an intense look of desire in his eyes.

"I'm not up to be gotten. News flash," Farrah raised her left hand to show off her rings. "I'm married." She resumed walking.

"Where yo' husband at then?" J.R. quizzed, walking alongside of her.

"Home."

"See? And that's exactly my point. You keep telling me you're married and all, but everytime I see you all you have is a ring, but not a husband. Why you keep bringing him up for?"

Farrah stopped walking again and inhaled deep.

"Sounds like I hit a spot with that one. Now are you gon' ride or are you gon' make me walk with all these bags? I can't be seen walking around carrying all these pink and red shopping bags. Nigga got a rep to keep up with." J.R. smiled and cocked his head to the side.

"Neither one. That's my hotel across the street. I'll take it from here, thanks," she replied as she reached for the items.

"It's cool, I got 'chu, boo," J.R. said as he jerked his arms away from Farrah's reach. "What kind of gentleman would I be letting you carry all this by yourself across the street."

J.R. and Farrah crossed the street and made their way up to the hotel entrance.

"Pierre, eh . . ." Farrah paused, *"pouvez-vous prendre cela en compte dans ma chambre s'il vous plaît?"* Farrah asked as she pointed the doorman toward her bags. She hoped she had used the correct words. Over the years she had learned a little bit of French, but she really didn't know much of the language. She was limited to just a few phrases and words.

"Right away, ma'am," replied the doorman with a thick French accent. "Oh, thank God you speak English! Please tell me I didn't make a fool out myself and say the wrong phrase, Pierre?" Farrah questioned, feeling relieved that she didn't have to struggle to communicate with the man.

"No, ma'am," Pierre chuckled. "You say right thing to me." He took the bags from J.R. and walked them over to a cart where he had a concierge take it from there. Farrah thanked the man and gave him a tip.

"Look, what is this really about?" She spun back around to face J.R. and folded her arms across her chest.

"I need you to style me for my show tonight," J.R. confessed.

"You could've called my office for that."

"Not when I can ask you face-to-face." J.R. pinched the tip of her nose.

"You don't need my help. It doesn't seem like you have any trouble putting your outfits together. You look like you have that under control." Farrah examined his outfit.

J.R. resembled a ghetto thug in a green camouflage jacket, gold chain, YSL logo T-shirt, jeans, and Tims. Ironically, Farrah wore a very similar outfit. Farrah looked like a sexy round-the-way-girl. She was thugged out in an army fatigue jacket, Celine T-shirt, denim booty shorts, and Tims. A gold chain that read *Queen Bitch* adorned her neck and a diamond-studded Cartier watch gleamed from her wrist.

"That's why I came to you, 'cause you got good taste." He gave her a warm smile.

"I'm sorry, I can't do it," Farrah stated bluntly.

"Why not?" J.R. wrinkled his brow.

"'Cause I already have plans tonight."

"C'mon, wifey, I need you. I can't go out on stage lookin' tore up."

"First I'm your girlfriend, now I'm your wifey. Next thing you know we gon' be gettin' a divorce." She gave him a mock glare and grinned.

"I don't believe in divorce. Me and you gon' be together forever," J.R. said in a serious tone.

"Whatever," Farrah waved him off. "If I help you I'ma charge you extra for it being so last minute."

"That's cool."

"*Huhhhhhhhhhhhh* I can't stand you! Okay," Farrah groaned. "I'll help you."

"I knew I could count on you."

"Yeah-yeah-yeah-yeah." Farrah rolled her eyes. "What size do you wear?"

After spending the rest of the afternoon pulling clothes for J.R., Farrah made it to the venue with racks of clothes and shoes. Her assistant

Sydney was there by her side to organize and display all of J.R.'s options. It was 8:20 p.m and he had less than an hour to decide what he was going to wear. The only problem was that J.R. hadn't arrived yet.

Farrah and Sydney had been waiting patiently inside his dressing room for two hours, awaiting his arrival. Each second that passed and he wasn't there Farrah's anger increased. She didn't have time to be waiting around on some inconsiderate, cocky asshole who'd asked her to do him a favor. *I knew I shouldn't have wasted my time,* she thought, chewing on a piece of gum.

Outside the dressing room it was complete mayhem. Farrah never knew so much behind-the-scenes work went into producing an hour-long show. People kept running by frantically rushing to complete their tasks. Stagehands, sound guys, the band, J.R's publicist, entourage, and barber were all awaiting their chance to have a moment with the star, who still hadn't shown up.

What Farrah didn't know was that J.R.'s sound check had gone past schedule, which resulted in him being late for his meet-and-greet with his fans and there was no way he would cancel on his fans. Even with him skipping dinner and taking no breaks, he still wasn't able to catch up to the original time constraints. Once he did arrive, J.R. bypassed everyone and went straight to his dressing room. His intentions were never to have anyone waiting on him, especially Farrah.

"My bad, love," he huffed, out of breath. "I ain't mean to be late."

"Mmm-hmm," Farrah sucked her teeth and stood up. "Look, let's just get this over wit' so I can go. You've wasted enough of my time."

"You mad at me?" J.R. made her stop and look at him.

"What would I be mad at you for? This is strictly business, boo."

"Excuse me," J.R. said to Farrah's assistant. "What's your name?"

"Sydney." She extended her hand.

"Nice to meet you, Sydney." J.R. shook her hand. "Could you do me a favor and step out for a minute?" J.R. flashed his memorizing smile.

"Umm . . ." Sydney eyed Farrah, unsure.

"It's okay." Farrah nodded her head in assurance.

Once Sydney was out of the room, J.R. gently took Farrah by both of her arms and said, "You and I both know this is more than just business, but if that's what you need to tell yourself then I'll roll with it . . . for now. On everything I love, I ain't ask you here to be on some bullshit. I got caught up and ran behind schedule. For that I sincerely apologize. You forgive me?"

Farrah really wanted to stay upset with him and be able to give him her ass to kiss, but she was taken in by his presence. One look into J.R.'s pretty brown eyes and all of her defenses were melted.

"You good." Farrah turned her back and started rummaging through the racks of clothes. "Hurry up, we gotta get you dressed."

"Bet." J.R. pulled his shirt over his head.

"Here." Farrah spun around and damn near stumbled backwards into the racks.

"Whoa, you all right?" J.R. caught her before she fell.

"I'm okay." She accidently slapped his hand. "I just . . ." Farrah cleared her throat, trying her damnest to avoid starring at his bare midriff. "Lost my balance a little bit."

She had no idea that what lay underneath J.R.'s shirt were six rows of mouthwatering abs. His chocolate-brown complexion had a slight golden hue to it and looked soft as silk.

"Goddamn," she said in awe, giving in to her thoughts. "Nigga, is that real?" She unconsciously slid her fingertips down his stomach.

"You mean to tell me all I had to do was take off my shirt to get you droolin' over me?" J.R. beamed.

Farrah abruptly came to her senses and spat, "Chile bye. You betta check ya' e-mail. Ain't nobody trippin' off you."

"That's what ya' mouth say, but your eyes are telling me something completely different." J.R. grinned, putting the T-shirt on.

"I think you should wear these Rick Owens jeans with that." Farrah handed him the pants.

"Yeah, these are sick." J.R. unzipped his jeans.

"Uh-uh, bruh," Farrah shouted, covering her eyes. "I think not. You will go into the bathroom and change," she said, pointing.

"I bet you don't say that to all of your other male clients?"

"How many times do I have to remind you that I am a married woman?" Farrah rolled her neck.

"I'm not the one who needs to be reminded," J.R. said, smirking, and headed into the bathroom.

J.R. was well into his set. He had the entire audience in the palm of his hand. Over 2,000 adoring fans rapped along and swayed to the beat of his songs. The Parisian women in the crowd were losing their mind. They screamed, begged for the touch of his hand, and even threw

their bras and panties onto the stage. Farrah
and Sydney stood on the side of the stage and
watched with admiration while J.R. commanded
the crowd. She had originally planned on heading straight to Stella McCartney's ultra-exclusive
party as soon as she finished getting J.R. dressed,
but like everyone else in attendance, she couldn't
help but become entranced by J.R.'s tone and
mannerisms. His swag was impeccable. There
was no denying it. Once you saw him live, you
quickly realized that he had the X factor.

J.R. was born to be a star. The black snapback
with *L.A.* written in white, bold print, black-
and-white paisley print T-shirt, Rick Owens
jeans and sneakers heightened his star quality.
As the band slowed down the tempo, Farrah
found herself bobbing her head to the pleasant
sound of a song she'd never heard before.

"This a new joint, y'all," J.R. said into the
microphone. "I wrote this a couple of weeks ago.
Rock wit' me."

Unsure of what was about to happen, Farrah
looked on diligently. As the lights dimmed and
turned red, J.R. stood center stage in front of
the mic stand. The red hue from the strobe lights
seemed to be making erotic love to his cocoa
skin as he rapped in high regard for a woman he
adored. Farrah would be lying if she didn't feel

a pang of jealousy as she heard him go on and on about this amazing mystery woman he had his eyes on. Farrah kind of felt mad that J.R. had been flirting with her so much, yet all along he was feeling on somebody else. *Girl, get it together. You have no business feeling any type of way about what this dude is rhyming about,* she said to herself. She couldn't make sense of why it was even bothering her.

Then the chorus came in and the crowd went wild. J.R. had the legendary Philly diva Jill Scott on the track. The song was catchy, upbeat, and soulfully romantic. Before going into the third verse, J.R. waved his hand. Without missing a beat, the band ceased playing.

"Y'all mind if I bring somebody to the stage real quick?" he asked the audience.

Everyone roared and screamed *yes* while others pulled out their camera phones to capture the moment.

"Farrah!" J.R. turned and looked at her.

Farrah's eyes bulged.

"No," she responded, waving her hands frantically.

"She wanna act shy. Let me go get her," J.R. jogged over to Farrah and took her by the hand.

"What are you doing?" she asked, feeling as if her heart was going to leap out of her chest.

Thousands of eyes were on her. She had never stood in front of such a big crowd.

"Ain't she beautiful?" J.R. asked the audience, smiling from ear to ear.

The crowd shouted back *yes*. Embarrassed beyond belief, Farrah hid her face with her hands.

"Stop that." J.R. took her hand in his. "I wrote this song for you." He cued the band to resume playing.

She the type of girl you pray for, Wanna give your all to, Love is in her eyes, All I see is you"

J.R. rapped while holding her hand and gazing into her eyes.

With the warmth of his skin on hers, Farrah became lost in the heavenly words J.R. relayed. No one, not even her husband, had said words to her that held so much meaning. She knew that J.R. liked her, but she had no idea that his feelings ran so deep. Even though they were in an auditorium full of screaming fans, J.R. somehow made Farrah feel like it was only the two of them stading on stage. Something about his energy had her on the brink of losing control.

At that moment in time she'd do anything he pleased. J.R. had her in the palm of his hand. She was his for the taking. Before Farrah knew it the song was over. The roar from the crowd and the look of undeniable desire in J.R.'s eyes sent chills up Farrah's spine. She was hypnotized and no longer wanted to run from her emotions. Face-to-face they stood, staring into each other's eyes.

Here they were with his feelings out in the open for the world to see. Farrah could keep on pretending that his attraction for her was one-sided. But as J.R. pulled her even closer into him and placed her face in his hands, Farrah couldn't deny the lust for him that lay in every crevice of her skin.

She wanted him as much as he wanted her and when his soft lips brushed up against hers she didn't resist it. Farrah closed her eyes and welcomed the warmth of his lips on hers. She opened her mouth and invited his tongue to dance with hers. She could feel the passion in his kiss and she relished in the sweetness of his lips. Farrah kissed him with so much intensity she swore her feet levitated off the floor. Sure, she belonged to another, but she'd deal with the repercussions of her actions later. J.R. made Farrah feel like nothing negative existed in the world. There, up on that stage in front of all those people, they shared such an intimate moment. For Farrah, it was as if time stood still.

J.R. could not believe he was finally kissing the woman who had been invading his mind for the past few weeks. He never thought he'd have this opportunity. Knowing she was married, he had figured she would never let anything happen between them. So with that in mind, he hadn't seen any harm in how he'd been flirting with her. He had written the song a few days after reading the article about her. He had planned to perform it tonight, but he hadn't planned on bringing Farrah up on the stage. That had just been a spontaneous last-minute thing. Now that he knew he had her open, he no longer cared if she was married or not. This was the woman he wanted for himself and he was prepared to fight for her if he had to. You know what they say, "All is fair in love and war."

Chapter 13

At night I think of you.
　　　　—Ghost Town DJ's, "My Boo"

Nervous as hell, Farrah paced back and forth across her living room floor, wondering if she had made the right decision. *Am I moving too fast?* she thought. But then a visual of J.R.'s face would appear in her mind and she'd remember just how much she longed to see him. *Okay, Farrah,* she stopped and looked in the mirror. *This is nothin'. You're a grown-ass woman. You ain't gonna let J.R. see you sweat. You ain't got nothin' to be afraid of. Shiiiiiiit . . . look at you. You will have his tight little ass runnin' in circles.* Farrah was chuckling when the doorbell rang. *Oh shit, he's here!* Taking a much-needed breath, she inhaled deeply and smoothed down her hair. *Okay bitch, you the shit. Let's do this,* she thought, opening the door.

"What up?" J.R. traced her physique with his eyes.

Farrah looked good enough to eat, in a gray cowl-neck, padded shoulder, long-sleeve top with the back out, black-and-white geometric print, skintight leggings and pointed toe, Christian Louboutin heels.

"Damn, you tryin' to make my heart race on purpose?" J.R. admired her curvaceous frame.

"You said wear something sexy." She turned around to grab her clutch purse, giving him a good view of her plump ass.

"I did, but damn." J.R. walked up behind her and wrapped her up in his arms. "Forget the date. Why don't we just fall back and stay at the crib tonight." he kissed her softly on the neck.

The stirring feeling of his lips on her skin caused Farrah's nipples to sprout.

"No, you wanted to go out, so we're going out." She pushed him back with her butt.

"You better watch that thing. A booty like that can cause bodily harm. And if you keep backing it up like that you gon' mess around and get yourself in trouble," J.R. said with a sly smirk.

"Shut up and c'mon." She dragged him by his arm.

Outside the building she expected for them to hop in his car, but was surprised when J.R. took her by the hand and began walking up the street.

"Are we going to a restaurant over here?" she wondered, confused.

"I guess you could say that." He played coy.

"Okay." Farrah smiled in anticipation.

"But on the real ma, you look beautiful tonight." J.R. gazed down at her.

"Thank you."

"I mean, you always look nice, but tonight you must've put that extra *ump* down on it," he joked.

"You stupid," she laughed.

"But . . . ah . . . tell me. Did you buy that outfit especially for tonight?"

"No," Farrah lied. "This ain't even that serious."

"Oh word? It's not. Then why you still got the tag on it?" He placed his head down and grinned.

"What?" Farrah stopped dead in her tracks, mortified.

"Here, let me get that for you." J.R. stood behind her and reached into the back of her shirt and pulled out the tag.

She was beyond embarrassed and unable to come up with a good enough explanation other than the truth, so instead she decided she'd just play it all off. "I hope you don't think that I really went out and spent my afternoon finding this outfit for you, 'cause that's not the case. I ain't even trippin' off you like that." Even though that was, in fact, the truth. Farrah and London had spent three hours looking for the perfect dress that hugged her body as if it was handmade according to her measurements.

"Mmm-hmm, that's what yo' mouth say." J.R. handed her the tag and then retook her hand.

"Whateva J.R." Farrah turned her head to the side and laughed.

"A'ight we're here," he said, staring up at an abandoned building.

"You say what now?" She twisted up her face.

"C'mon."

"I'm not going into that death trap. Are you crazy?"

"Farrah, I ain't got time for your bougie uppity games. C'mon." He tugged gently on her arm.

"Okay, but if I see one thing crawl out at me I'ma kick everybody ass involved."

Once inside the building, Farrah was pleasantly surprised to find that it wasn't filled with broken glass and debris. The building was actually going through its final stages of renovation.

"What is this place?"

"I'm not sure, exactly. I sort of stumbled onto it and had my assistant get me the information so I could rent it out for tonight. I wanted to take you someplace that was just for us with no other people around. You're special, Farrah, and I want to treat you as such," J.R. said as he held her hand and they walked through the building toward a set of stairs.

"Oh, my God, J.R.. This is . . ." Farrah paused, unable to find the right words to convey how she felt. "Unexpected. I can't believe you did this for me." She hugged him around the neck tight.

"Thanks, ma. I'm glad you're enjoying your time with me so far. But this is nothing. We're just getting started."

"Oh really now?"

"Just wait and see."

"Wow, okay." Farrah continued to follow his lead.

"C'mon, that's not all I wanted to show you." J.R. led her up the steps to the rooftop.

Upon arrival Farrah's eyes watered with tears. J.R. had decorated the entire rooftop to look like the Garden of Eden. There were imported trees with Chinese lanterns hanging from the limbs. Thousands of twinkling lights and candles lit up the sky. And in the midst of all of that was a small table set for two. To the right of the table was a tan, suede sectional and directly in front of that was a mahogany glass top coffee table with three cylinder vases filled with floating candles and petals.

"This is too much." Farrah wiped the tears, which were falling from her eyes.

"I told you there was more," he stated. "Here, have a seat." J.R. pulled back her chair.

Once Farrah was seated, he poured her a glass of wine and revealed their entrée for the night, which was hidden cleverly under a silver dome.

"*Bon appétit.*" He lifted the lid revealing two boxes of Chinese takeout.

Overwhelmed, Farrah cocked her head to the side and whispered, "Come here."

J.R. gladly walked over to her. "Thank you," she whispered into his ear. Lovingly, Farrah took his face into the palm of her hands and planted a sensual kiss on his lips.

J.R. pulled her into him and planted his hands on her hips while Farrah glided her hands all over the back of his head. As their kiss became deeper, J.R. never let go of her as he walked them toward the entrance door. Once there, he pinned Farrah up against it as his hands roamed throughout her body.

"Stop, J.R.," Farrah managed to say in between breaths. "I can't do this," she pleaded.

"Yes, you can," J.R. whispered as he gently sucked on the bottom of her earlobe.

He hiked her dress up and slid his hand between her thighs. Before Farrah could grab his hand to try and stop him, his fingers grazed along her pussy lips and penetrated her walls and she instantly became wet. She moaned and groaned as his fingers probed and played with her insides. All she could do at this point was throw her head back in defeat as his lips made their way down her neck. With his free hand he pulled her dress down to expose her beautiful breasts. Farrah's dress was so tight she wasn't able to wear any underwear with it. He squeezed her right breast and took the nipple into his mouth. He sucked and played with her perfectly round nipple as his fingers came in and out of her cave.

"Take your dress off and lay down on the couch for me," he instructed as he took a step back and started to take his clothes off.

Without hesitation, Farrah did exactly as she was told. She undressed herself and made her way to the sectional. She was past the point of no return. She knew what she was doing with J.R. was wrong because she was still married, but her body was yearning for more of his touch.

J.R. walked over to her fully naked. This man had one of the sickest bodies Farrah had ever seen. Seeing him standing before her, the best she could compare his body to was Lance Gross from *Temptation: Confessions of a Marriage Counselor*. You would never guess this man was so perfectly sculpted and chiseled underneath the clothes. He got on top her and they were skin to skin. She could feel his hard penis throbbing against her pelvis.

"You want me to put myself inside of you?" he asked.

"Yes, baby," was all Farrah could muster.

He grabbed his manhood and teased her pussy lips with the tip of his dick before thrusting himself deep inside of her. Farrah groaned and thrust her hips as he pumped in and out of her. Without warning she felt an orgasm creep up on her.

"I'm about to cum!" she screamed.

"Say my name!" he ordered her.

Farrah was so enthralled in her body clenching up and about to explode she couldn't find the strength to say anything. She had never experienced a feeling like this. She had always considered Mills to have given her the best sex of her life, but that all changed tonight.

"Say my name, Farrah!" he stated as he pounded her even harder.

"J.R.!" she whispered.

"Nah, say it louder!" he said. "I wanna hear you scream my name while you take this dick!" he stated while he looked down at his penis getting swallowed up by Farrah's pink, plump pussy.

"J.R!" Farrah screamed as she came all over him. She was gasping for air as every nerve and muscle in her body tensed up and then released.

Farrah woke up completely winded. Her panties were wet and her pussy was throbbing. *Did I just have a wet dream?* she asked herself as she sat up in the hotel bed. Her heart was racing and she kicked the covers off of her, being that she was sweating also. She could not believe she had just experienced her first wet dream. Until now, she'd heard and read about them, but she never thought she'd have one herself. She went to bed thinking about J.R. and trying to make sense of whatever it was that she was feeling for him, but this dream just took everything to a whole new level.

She knew she had to get ahold of herself and figure out what she planned on doing, because regardless of how she was feeling, the fact was she was still legally married to Mills. She was set to fly back to the States in the next few days, so she decided she'd use that time to pray and ask God to help her work things out. She especially prayed that her decisions would ultimately lead her to the happiness she knew she deserved.

Chapter 14

The problem here is you.
—Ciara, "My Love"

Never in a million years did Mills think this would be the course his life would take. His wife was gone and for God knows how long. In the wake of her absence he found himself spending the majority of his time with Jade and their daughter. Just a few weeks prior Jade was his sworn enemy, the thorn in his side, and now she'd become somewhat of a crutch. There wasn't a day that went by that he didn't stop in to see his daughter.

In such a short amount of time he'd grown accustomed to seeing her angelic face. All of his worries instantly faded away in her presence. Being around Jade didn't hurt much, either. The strong friendship they once shared seemed to have returned. She made him laugh and made him a home-cooked meal every time he visited.

Mills sat on the floor playing with Jaysin's tiny toes. She was lying on a pink blanket on her back. Mills thoroughly enjoyed toying with her feet. They were the cutest thing he'd ever seen. Jade lay on the couch reading *Prima Donna* by Keisha Ervin. The television was on and TMZ was on. Mills wasn't paying the show any attention until he heard Harvey Levin say, *"The rapper J.R. was performing in Paris and during the show he brought celebrity stylist Farrah Mills on stage. Not only did he serenade her, but he kissed her . . . on the lips. No big deal, right? Well, it wouldn't be if Farrah was single, but she's married to BMX pro Corey Mills. I wonder how her husband is gonna feel about this? My sources say they may be heading straight for divorce."*

Mills's nostrils instantly flared. His chest heaved up and down. He was so furious he couldn't think straight. He hadn't seen or talked to his wife for a couple of weeks and here she was in Paris hugged up with another man. Mills would've never expected that she'd disrespect him like that. And as if that wasn't bad enough, she'd done it in such a public way and in front of so many people. If this was her way of getting back at him, she'd done it.

Farrah cheating on him was the worst form of betrayal Mills could think of. He had no idea she even knew who J.R. was. Mills hadn't even had a full five minutes to let all of this sink into his mind before his phone started blowing up. Teddy, his manager, publicist, *Us Weekly*, and more were calling him back-to-back, asking all sorts of questions. His manager was busy setting up a plan to do some damage control, his publicist was formulating a statement to release to the press, and *Us Weekly* was just calling to be nosy and all up in his and Farrah's business. Of course, that came to no surprise. Teddy was the only person who called out of concern for Mills's well-being and how he was taking this newly discovered information.

Mills was humiliated, pissed, and confused. He wanted to choke the shit out of Farrah. Seeing how she was all hugged and kissing on J.R., she was obviously over him and their marriage, so why she hadn't just come out and said what needed to be said was beyond him. This was torture to the highest extent.

"Are you all right?" Jade asked, sitting up.

"No," Mills screwed up his face.

"Yeah, that was a dumb question," Jade chuckled. "It's obvious you're not all right. What was that about, if you don't mind me asking?"

"I do," Mills snapped, getting up from the floor.

"Oh, honey, you finally tasted your prescription." Jade wagged her index finger. "Don't get mad at me 'cause you gettin' a dose of your own medicine," she said with a mix of sarcasm and genuine lament in her voice.

"My bad. I ain't mean to snap on you." Mills sat opposite her on the couch. "I just ain't see this shit coming. I mean, I knew she was mad and rightfully so—but damn, what the fuck was that shit about? I ain't even know she knew ol' boy." He placed his head back.

"You know I'm no fan of Farrah, but in this case you have to understand that the girl is probably tired and burned out from you. A person can only take so much and you have taken that girl to hell and back." Jade continued on: "I remember all the shit Khalil put her through. Remember how many times you and I drove her home because Khalil pulled some grimy shit on her at the club? And to leave that relationship just to then get trampled on with what you've done; poor girl must be exhausted."

Jade was being sincere with her words. Regardless of the drama going on between her, Farrah, and Mills, as a woman Jade could relate to Farrah in this instance. She knew what if felt like to be betrayed by the person you're in love with and have that person walk all over you. That's what Rock did to her when he dismissed her like she was just some groupie he was fucking, because he wanted to get back with his ex. Yeah, she was messed up for cheating on Mills like that, but she was just being true to her feelings and at the time, she really thought she was in love with Rock. It wasn't until she lost Mills to Farrah and was left completely alone that she realized Mills was the only man she couldn't live without and Rock was just a phase.

"That wasn't my intention, though!" Mills broke Jade out of her trance. "I knew it was fucked up to withhold the truth from her, but I was just doing it 'cause I knew it was going to hurt her," Mills replied, as his anger subsided a little bit from listening to the situation from Jade's perspective. His heart melted and turned into hot lava from realizing he had caused Farrah that much pain.

"I call bullshit on that." Jade went into the kitchen and grabbed them both a beer.

"What you mean, you call bullshit?" Mills grimaced, taking the ice-cold beer.

"Mills, I know you. You didn't tell Farrah about sleeping with me or the baby because you wanted to save your own ass. You didn't want to face responsibility for your actions, so you lied until you couldn't lie anymore. It had nothing to do with sparing Farrah's feelings. Tell that lie to someone else, just not me." Jade arched her eyebrow and took a sip of the beer.

Mills looked at her and took a long gulp from the bottle. Jade was 100 percent right. He'd never admit it, though, for his own selfish reasons.

"Listen, lying gets you nowhere. It only makes the situation worse. Trust me, I know, 'cause if I would've just been honest with you about how I felt we wouldn't be here now. We'd be a family, but I fucked up and now I'm suffering the consequences just like you. So learn from my mistakes and do things differently. Talk to her. Don't act out on your emotions 'cause that's when a whole bunch of reckless shit starts to happen." With that, Jade walked out of the kitchen and left Mills to think about everything she had just said.

After a seven-hour flight from Paris to New York and a two-hour flight from New York to St. Louis, Farrah finally made it home. On the plane ride home she had the chance to think over things and sort out her feelings for J.R. and Mills. The kiss between her and J.R. was unexpected, surreal, and delicious, but she was a married woman who had every intention on seeing her marriage through. As far as the dream she had, she concluded it was her body's way of telling her she needed to get some and get some fast! It'd been weeks since she'd had sex, but she wasn't an adulterer so the day after that crazy wet dream, Farrah met up with J.R., explained to him that she could never see or speak to him again. Although he seemed saddened by her decision, J.R. promised that he'd leave her alone. She'd always cherish that kiss they shared in Paris and that dream she had with him was always gonna be her dirty little secret.

Farrah had made up her mind that she was going to return home, sit down, and talk to Mills like a rational human being. Running away from their issues only made matters worse. She'd gotten wind from Camden that the kiss heard all around the world was the talk of every gossip magazine and blog. Farrah was sure Mills already knew about it and most likely was upset. She was kind of afraid of how he might react once he saw her face.

As Farrah placed her key into the lock she said a silent prayer to God asking him to cover her in the blood of Jesus. Once inside, she spotted Mills sitting at the dining room table, eating Chinese food. At once Mills stopped chewing. He was startled and disgusted by the sight of Farrah's face so much he lost his appetite.

"Hi," Farrah spoke softly.

Mills shot her the look of death and emptied his plate. Realizing this wouldn't be an easy feat, Farrah dragged her luggage down the hall to their bedroom. After switching on the light, she walked into her closet and quickly noticed that the things she'd left behind were no longer there.

"No, he didn't," Farrah said out loud to herself.

"Oh, yes I did," Mills said behind her.

Startled, Farrah spun around and faced him.

"Where is my stuff?" she asked, feeling her face turn red.

"Where it belongs . . . in storage."

"What you tryin' to say—you putting me out?" Farrah raised her voice.

"You're not so dumb after all," Mills replied, mockingly.

"Are you fuckin' kidding me? This is a joke, right? You actually moved my shit?" Farrah threw her purse down on the bed.

"Yeah, go stay wit' that nigga you was fuckin' in Paris." Mills stood in the doorway.

"First of all, I didn't fuck him—"

"Bullshit! You really expect me to believe that you didn't fuck that nigga?" Mills cut her off. "You was practically suckin' his dick on stage!"

Before Mills could blink Farrah rushed over and slapped him so hard his bottom lip began to bleed.

"What I tell you about puttin' yo' hands on me!" Mills took Farrah by the arms and shoved her into the wall.

"Don't put yo' fuckin' hands on me no more, 'cause if I hit you back you won't live to tell about it!" Mills yelled, shaking her profusely.

"Get the fuck off of me!" Farrah seethed with anger.

"I'm not playin' wit' you, Farrah. Straight up, you put yo' hands on me again you gon' be lookin' like Rihanna after the Clive Davis after party," Mills warned.

"I wish you would put your hands on me," Farrah spat.

"Yeah a'ight, try me. Put yo' hands on me again and see what happen." Mills let her go.

"You know what? It's all good." Farrah grabbed her purse and bags.

"Where you going?" Mills watched her nervously.

"Home!" Farrah said as she headed for the door.

"What the fuck you mean, home? This is your fuckin' home, but if you wanna leave that's fine by me. But before you go—" Mills reached out and grabbed her arm. "Just answer me this: Did you do it on purpose? Were you tryin' to hurt me?" Farrah could hear the pain in his voice as he questioned her.

"Everything is not about you, Mills! And no, I didn't do it on purpose. I styled him for his show and he pulled me out on stage and kissed me. I had no idea he was going to do that." Farrah inhaled and took a deep breath. She could feel the adrenaline running through her veins.

"I apologize for embarrassing you like that, but let's not forget that you are the same mutha-fucka that cheated on me wit' your ex and had a baby wit' her. So you don't get to play the victim, my dear." Farrah pointed her finger in his face. "You started all of this shit! And now that your feelings are hurt you wanna get mad and put me out? If that's the case, we can just end this shit right now." She slid off her ring. "Is that what you want?"

Mills paused and allowed his anger to subside. He didn't want to lose Farrah. There was no way he could let her walk out the door and not crumble into pieces. Sure, he'd had her stuff taken out of the room, but that was because he was expecting her to come home apologizing for what she did. He had no idea things would turn out the way they were.

"You know that's not what I want," he replied, unable to look at her.

"Then let's sit down and talk because we have to figure this shit out." Farrah allowed her bags to fall to the floor.

Overwhelmed with emotion, Farrah sat down on the edge of the bed. Before Mills sat, he went into the bathroom and rinsed the blood out of his mouth. He never would have thought Farrah had such a heavy hand.

"You ain't have to hit me like that." He spat with an attitude, returning to the room.

Every bit of Mills yearned to fuck Farrah up, but he couldn't. That was his wife and she was already emotionally hurting.

"I don't know what to do," Farrah said, ignoring his last statement. She buried her face in her hands. "I wanna be with you. I just don't know if that's possible," she confessed.

"It can be possible if we try," Mills responded as his cell phone started to ring.

He and Farrah both looked at the screen. It was Jade. Farrah's temperature immediately rose to a billion degrees. Her anger went through the roof when Mills, without hesitation, answered the call.

"Really?" Farrah shot.

"What's up?" Mills asked Jade, all the while ignoring Farrah's reaction.

"Oh, this nigga done lost his muthafuckin' mind." Farrah stood up and placed her hands on her hips.

"What hospital are you at?" Mills panicked. "A'ight, I'm on my way." He ended the call and shot up.

"I'll be back." He grabbed his sneakers and put them on.

"Where you going at ten o'clock at night?"

"Jaysin's in the hospital. She's been sick with a cough for a few days now and she stopped breathing for a minute."

Thoroughly confused, Farrah said, "So Jade calls you and you just up and leave like that? As if we weren't just having a life-or-death conversation about our relationship?"

"I don't know what to tell you. That's my family. My daughter is sick and in a real physical life-or-death situation. This shit between me and you can wait." Mills grabbed his keys. "I'll call you as soon as I can." He raced out of the room and out the front door.

Farrah stood, flabbergasted. So much had changed in the two weeks she'd gone to Paris for Fashion Week. She didn't understand when or how Mills and Jade had begun communication. What she did know was that she didn't like it one bit.

Farrah tried to be the understanding wife. She tried to be patient, but every second, minute, and hour that passed with no call from Mills while he was with Jade was the equivalent of counting down death. She'd called his phone numerous times, only to get his voice mail. Although she knew he had probably turned it off when he got the hospital, all Farrah could envision was Mills and Jade running off into an empty hospital room to tear each other's clothes off so he could penetrate her eager, wet slit.

Farrah tried to shake her insecurities off, but how could she when her husband just called another woman and child his family? Farrah didn't sleep a wink that night. All night she eyed the clock waiting for him to return home with an explanation, but by morning it was time for her to go to work and Mills was nowhere to be found. Once she was dressed and ready to go, Farrah decided that she didn't need answers to the questions that plagued her mind. She was done. She was over Mills making a fool out of her. As far as she was concerned, he was free to do whatever he pleased and with whomever he pleased.

It was well into the afternoon. Farrah sat at her desk having a long-distance conversation with editor of *Marie Claire* magazine when she heard a loud ruckus outside her door.

"Mr. Mills, wait!" Camden shouted, racing behind him. "You can't just go in there!"

"Watch me!' Mills remarked, storming into Farrah's office.

"What the fuck is this?" He stood in front of her desk holding up a piece of paper.

Stunned by his tyrannical behavior, Farrah held the receiver in her hand.

"Let me call you right back." Farrah quickly hung up the phone.

"Farrah, I'm so sorry. I tried to stop him," Camden explained, out of breath.

"It's okay, Camden. Close the door behind you, please." Farrah forced a smile onto her face.

Camden nodded and closed the door quietly.

"Have you lost your fuckin' mind?" Farrah hissed.

"Nah, but you've obviously lost yours. So you want an annulment?" Mills shook the paper.

"That's what the note said, didn't it?" Farrah responded, sarcastically.

"Why? Because I went to the hospital last night to see my daughter?" Mills mean-mugged her.

"If that's what you think, then you're sadder than I thought you were." Farrah smugly crossed one leg over the other.

"The baby was sick and she stopped breathing, Farrah. She's all right now, but the doctors say she has severe asthma. I stayed at the hospital all night because they had to give her a breathing treatment on a nebulizer machine to get her oxygen levels back up."

"And I'm sorry to hear that." Farrah sat, stone-faced. She did feel somewhat guilty that since Mills left, she never even thought or wondered if the baby was okay. But of course she wasn't about to sit there and apologize. If it wasn't for all of Mills's bullshit, they would have never been in this predicament in the first place.

"I was gonna call you, but my phone went out."

"Mmm-hmm, I just bet." Farrah stared at him blankly.

"So that's it? After everything we've been through?" Mills stood wearily.

"Exactly. After everything we've been through." Farrah nodded her head in agreement.

"Nah . . ." Mills paced back and forth, then stopped. "Fuck that! We not gettin' no annulment, no divorce, nothing!"

"Mills, I'm done." Farrah uncrossed her legs and reached into her drawer and took out some files. She calmly started looking over her paperwork and acted like Mills was no longer in her office.

"Well, I'm not! I'm not lettin' you go! You're my fuckin' wife!"

"Whom you've cheated on, lied to, had a baby on, and from the looks of it, you are now rekindling your relationship wit' your baby's mother." Farrah cocked her head to the side. "Ain't nobody got time for that."

"So that's what this is about? You think I'm fuckin' with Jade?" He eyed her.

"I honestly don't give a fuck if you are or aren't, but guess what, I'm not gon' stick around to find out. Now if you'll excuse me, I have work to do." Farrah turned toward her computer.

"You got a lot of nerve playin' the victim when the whole world saw you kissing another man!" Mills barked.

"And guess what . . . I liked it!" Farrah spat as she rose from her chair. "I enjoyed every fuckin' minute of it! Shit, right about now, I wish I *had* fucked him!" she shot with as much venom as she could muster.

Mills wanted to hit her back with something equally cutthroat and low-down, but the words wouldn't form. She'd gone too far this time, but he couldn't let her see the hurt she'd caused. Mills was a man built on pride. Showing emotion wasn't in his DNA. He'd rather play it cool and nonchalant.

"I don't wanna do this anymore! I'm done!" Farrah confirmed.

"Nothing between us is progressing. Since day one it's been one fucked-up incident after another. Every time I get a li'l comfortable, here you go dragging my heart through the mud again. I'm sick of it. I've come to the conclusion that maybe we were never supposed to be together. This whole thing was a mistake. Love isn't supposed to be like this. . . ." Her voice trailed off.

"I'm not gon' allow you to hurt me anymore, I'm not," she said in defeat.

Mills walked over to Farrah's desk, placed his hands down on it, leaned forward, and said, "I don't give a fuck about none of that. We're not getting' an annulment." Mills flicked the piece of paper across the room and walked out.

Mills had no idea what he was doing anymore. As he walked to his car, he felt like his life was crumbling before his very eyes. Mills was a victim of his own uncertainty. He'd let it take him over and as a result, his relationship with Farrah was in shambles. He'd cheated, broken her heart, had a kid with his ex, and lied to get her to marry him. Now his good girl was going bad. She'd kissed another man and even though she said she didn't sleep with him, for all Mills knew she could be lying about that. The trust they once held was gone. Mills sat in his car and thought about calling her to say how sorry he was and he was willing to forgive her for what she did in Paris, but he knew nothing he said would change her mind right now. Farrah always said actions speak louder than words, so he had to figure out a way to show Farrah how far he was willing to go to keep his marriage.

Chapter 15

But she's a good girl in a bad world.
        —Shwayze, "Cali Trippin'"

J.R. felt like he was going crazy. His schedule had slowed down tremendously since he had finished up his tour. J.R. always took some time off after he toured. It helped to rest his mind and body so he could prepare for his next album. But weeks had gone by and J.R. was still hurting from the way Farrah had deaded things between them before they even started. He promised he'd respect her wishes and leave her alone, but at the time he said it, he didn't think it would be this hard. J.R. didn't even understand why he was so distraught over this situation. He was used to just walking away from girls and not catching feelings. It was like Farrah had a spell over him and he just couldn't make any sense out of it.

What didn't make the transition any easier was how the paparazzi and magazine bloggers kept hounding him by asking questions about what was going on between him and Farrah Mills. Everywhere he went he would see the now-infamous picture of them kissing on stage plastered all over the front pages of magazines and newspapers. Word around the inside celebrity circuit was that her and Corey Mills were still married, but weren't on speaking terms. As messed up as it sounded, J.R. was happy to hear Farrah and her husband weren't talking. It was like music to his ears.

Not that J.R. was wishing anything bad upon Farrah or her marriage, but to know that she and her husband weren't on great terms meant that he still had that little window of opportunity to open. He just had to figure out how to slip in and take her for himself. And especially after he did some digging on this BMX rider Corey Mills, he definitely didn't feel bad if they were heading for divorce.

From what he found out, this dude Corey had been dogging Farrah out from jump. This guy had Farrah as the side chick in the beginning, then made her the main chick and married her. Didn't sound too bad, if it wasn't for the fact that somewhere between them getting back together and getting married, he got his ex pregnant! This was all hearsay to J.R., though. It's not like he had any proof that everything he'd heard was truth, but if any of it was true, he'd be doing Farrah a favor by breaking up her marriage to this asshole. There's no way he would ever do her grimy like that.

"J.R., the game is over. Are you okay? It's like you're here but your head is someplace else," Lizzy asked, tugging on his arm.

"Nah, I'm cool. I was just thinking about some stuff I have to take care of," he responded. "You ready to go? We're supposed to go meet up with some of the players and their girls for some food and drinks."

"Oh. Okay. Ready whenever you are," Lizzy said, grabbing her sweater.

Right now, Lizzy felt like she was in a dream. Since J.R. had come back from Paris, he had been spending more time with her and being really nice to her. He was hitting her up almost ever other day to hang out. They would order take-out and watch movies, play video games, or just blast music and dance. When he asked her if she'd fly with him to St. Louis to catch a basketball game, she had to contain herself from jumping up and down like an excited toddler. This would be the first time that he'd invited her to go out in public on a one-on-one. He had taken her to the BET Awards before, but that was more of a business-type date because it was work for him. This outing was personal and it meant everything to her that he'd wanted her to come. Lizzy felt like he was finally acknowledging that she could be more than just a fling to him.

The only thing that she found strange was that in all those times that they hung out, he hadn't touched her once. Every time she would try to rub up against him or if she would try to initiate sex, he would immediately pull away. At first, Lizzy was taking it personal, but now seeing that J.R. was dedicating so much time to her, she thought differently. She figured J.R. was really trying to get to know her more on a personal level to see if there was more of a connection there, other than just the sex.

They pulled up to Three Sixty restaurant. Once parked, they were led to the rooftop. It had been completely rented out and converted into a private party. Celebrities oftentimes were forced to close out restaurants so they could have a night out without people asking for autographs or pictures. Lizzy was completely mesmerized when they walked in. The entire rooftop was encased by glass and no matter what angle you turned, you had the most amazing view overlooking the city. From the eastside, you could see the iconic St. Louis Gateway Arch, and from the southside you could look straight into Busch Stadium. Lizzy grew up in Los Angeles. She had never been anywhere outside of California and the time she went to Las Vegas to celebrate her twenty-first birthday.

"I'm gonna go grab a drink, you want anything?" J.R. asked as he placed his hand on the arch of her back and leaned into Lizzy's ear. Just the touch of his hand and how his breath brushed her ear as he spoke made Lizzy want to fuck him on the spot.

"Apple martini, please," she said with a genuine smile.

J.R. made his way over to the bar and placed the order. As he was about to grab his phone to check his Instagram, he felt somebody push him over.

"Yo! Who da fu—" Before he could finish his sentence, his boy Rock started laughing and reached in to give him a pound.

"I gotchu' son! You shoulda seen your face, nigga. You looked like you were about to fuck somebody up!" Rock exclaimed.

"I was, nigga. You lucky I didn't knock you ass out in front of all your teammates." Rock laughed. "What's good, my dude? I ain't seen you in a minute."

"You know me. I'm good. Just chillin'. I ain't been doing shit but playing and focusing on keeping shit good between me and my fiancée," Rock explained.

"*Fiancée?* You ready to slow down like that, son?" J.R. asked him.

"Yeah, man. Yo, I ain't even tryin'a sound soft or nothing, but I love Mya. She had my son and she's a great mom. She deserve for me to put a ring on it," Rock said. "That, plus the shit that happened last year with the side chick I was dealing with, made me come to my senses."

"Oh word?" was all J.R. could reply. He had no idea what Rock was talking about and he didn't really care to ask. It'd been a minute since they'd seen each other and he was glad they were catching up; but listening to Rock talk about settling down made him think about Farrah again.

"Yeah, I got a story you could write about," Rock said, smiling. "Peep this. I'm at shorty's crib getting my dick sucked when her man walks in on us! I thought I was about to have to fight and shit, but the nigga just let me walk out!" Rock said as he laughed. "And even after all that, I heard she had his baby and they still fuckin wit' each other. I tell you, man. That dude Corey Mills is a pussy!" Rock yelled out, laughing even harder.

"Yeah, what a pussy," J.R. agreed. "Hey man, it was nice seeing you, but I gotta roll," he said as he ran back to Lizzy without waiting for a response from Rock or grabbing the drinks. He'd heard everything he needed to hear. It was funny, how when you were not looking for things everything just fell in your lap.

"Let's go," J.R. said to Lizzy as he led her by the hand.

"Uhm. Okay," was all Lizzy said. She wasn't expecting them to leave so soon, but he seemed like a man on a mission, so she knew better than to ask questions.

Chapter 16

She just wanna run over my feelings
like she drinking and driving.
                                    —Drake, "Connect"

Weeks had gone by and Farrah had barely spoken to or heard from Mills and she liked it that way. Being away from him gave her the opportunity to begin to see everything clearly. During her time alone she realized that being without Mills wasn't so bad after all. When he wasn't around, her life ran smoothly. There was no drama, lies, or deceit. She could breathe easier and wasn't met with a new set of tears everyday.

But the devil always likes to attack when one is comfortable. For Farrah, it was another regular day. That morning she'd gotten a lot done at work. Now it was time for lunch. Her stomach was growling louder than a tiger. She couldn't make it out of the building and to her car fast enough. To her dismay, when she got there none other than Mills was standing by her car, waiting for her.

In an instant her entire body became heavy and weighed down with sadness, anger, and nervousness. It was sad that one human being could make her feel so many different emotions and all at once. A part of her wanted to run back inside the building or run out into the middle of the street and get hit by a car. Either option sounded better than having a conversation with Mills. Whatever he wanted was sure to bring her nothing but misery.

Feeling trapped, Farrah stood still. She felt like Tina Turner in *What's Love Got to Do with It* when Ike Turner found her at the bus station. There, in the middle of the parking lot Farrah held her vintage Gucci bag in her hand and stared at Mills with despair in her eyes. She wished she could love him the way she used to, but she couldn't pretend that what lay underneath his mesmerizing good looks and designer duds was a manipulative man. With the weight of the world on her shoulders, Farrah slowly walked over to her car.

"You look pretty," Mills said, captivated by her presence.

Farrah looked effortlessly chic with her hair up in a bun. She rocked an oversized pair of black shades. M.A.C Candy Yum-Yum lipstick shined bright from her luscious lips. A pair of white chandelier earrings, gray Thayer blazer with the sleeves pushed up, white V-neck T-shirt, white skinny-leg jeans with a zipper at the ankle, and silver Gucci pointed toe pumps made up her outfit.

"What is it, Mills?" Farrah replied, not in the mood for pleasantries.

"I got a surprise for you."

"Whatever it is I don't want it," Farrah said, honestly.

"Yes, you do," Mills assured.

"Look, I'm about to go." She tried to push him out of her way so she could open her car door.

"Only place you're going is with me," Mills insisted.

"Why are you so damn hardheaded?" Farrah furrowed her brows, agitated.

"Let me show you what I got for you. I promise you won't be disappointed."

Farrah sighed and rolled her eyes.

"C'mon, please let me do this for you," Mills pleaded, not taking *no* for an answer.

"I don't know, Mills." Farrah tried to stand her ground.

"Quit actin' like you don't love me." He pulled her into him and hugged her.

"I don't," Farrah shot, while trying to squirm away from his embrace.

"You can't even lie good. Now come on." Mills took her by the hand and led her over to his car.

"You know I could get you locked up for kidnapping, right? 'Cause I'm clearly resisting." She dragged her feet.

"Do you ever hush?"Mills asked, opening the passenger-side door.

Almost an hour went by before they reached the destination. Farrah was outraged. She'd missed lunch and an appointment because of Mills. Now in a very pissed-off mood, Farrah sat staring blankly at her surprise. It was the house she'd been raving about for months. The home she wanted to start their life as man and wife in. The house she'd envisioned raising their children in and growing old in.

It was an architecturally award-winning 8-million-dollar mansion. It was a home that even James Bond would envy. The approximately 5,800 square foot, two-level home was divided into two adjoining structures connected by a glass-enclosed bridge, which overlooked an expansive lake view. Part one of the house held impressive entertaining areas: dining, kitchen, living, as well as the master suite. Part two of the home held three guest suites, an office, and garage. The setting was serene, secluded, and lush. The backyard was beautiful, flat, and landscaped for privacy on over half an acre, with ample room for entertaining.

The house was everything Farrah wanted and more, but as she sat looking at her dream home her stomach began to churn. The mere sight of it made her want to puke. Because of Mills's lies and infidelity the house was now tainted.

"Surprise!" Mills shouted, wondering why she looked so unenthused. "I bought the house. It's ours now."

"You mean it's yours now," Farrah countered. "I'm not living here."

"What you mean? I just bought this for us. You're my wife. Where else you gon' stay?" Mills shot her a look that could kill.

"Where I've been staying. My apartment."

"So you don't have any plans on coming home?" Mills shot her an angry look.

"Not unless you plan on not living in it." Farrah shook her head.

Mills inhaled deep and tried his hardest not to strangle her.

"C'mon, Farrah. We gotta get past all this." He slumped back in his seat.

"You're right, but I'm not ready. There is still a lot I have to think about."

"Well, can you at least get out and look at it?"

"I guess," Farrah responded, mentally exhausted. Once she got out of the car she looked up at the massive home. There was no denying her dream home's beauty. *Why did Mills have to go and fuck everything up*? she wondered.

"Farrah, you remember Karen the Realtor?" Mills acknowledged the two women.

"Yes, how are you?" Farrah extended her hand for a shake.

"Congratulations! You got your dream home," Karen said, smiling and shaking her hand.

"Karen, can you give me and Farrah a minute, please?" Mills asked.

"Sure." Karen stepped off to the side.

"You can't pretend like you're not happy," Mills said to Farrah.

"The gesture is nice, but it doesn't change anything between me and you," Farrah confessed.

"I get that, but I bought the house 'cause I wanted you to see how serious I am about making this work. I am dedicated to you and this marriage. We can make this work, babe. You just have to meet me halfway," Mills begged, taking her hands in his and carressing them.

"I don't know what you want from me," Farrah sighed, pulling her hands from his and massaging her temples.

"I want you to love me like you used to," Mills said, with his whole heart.

Before Farrah could even think of a response her cell phone started to ring. She was stunned to see that it was J.R. calling. She paused for a second, not sure if she should answer his call or let it go to voice mail. She let it ring a few more times before coming to a decision.

"Let me take this call real quick." Farrah walked off. "Hello?" She spoke in a low tone.

"I know I'm on the restricted list, but I just wanted to see what was up wit' you, li'l lady," J.R. said in a cool tone.

"Nothin' much, stalker," Farrah giggled. "You just won't stay away."

"How can I? I miss you."

A smile unintentionally crept onto Farrah's face. She didn't understand what it was about this man that could make her smile so easily.

"That's nice to know." She tried to play it cool.

"I wanna see you."

"That's not possible."

"It can be, if you get on the flight I booked for you to L.A.," J.R. countered.

"You bold," Farrah scoffed. "You just know I'm gonna agree to go see you, huh?" she chuckled.

"You know you wanna see me," J.R. said in a low, sexy tone.

Farrah paused and thought for a second. "Maybe," she replied.

"Maybe yes, maybe no?" J.R. flirted.

"Maybe you need to stop flirting with me. How about that?"

"Or maybe you need to stop frontin' and admit you wann see me. *'Cuz your mind's telling you noooo, but your body's telling you yeeesss.*" J.R. tried singing that classic line from R. Kelly's "Bump n' Grind".

"Oh my God, you tryin'a to kill me with your singing? Now I know why you stick to just rapping!" Farrah exclaimed, not able to stop herself from laughing.

"You know you liked it," J.R. said jokingly. "So are you coming to see your boo?"

"Boy, bye!" Farrah quickly hung up the phone before he had a chance to say anything else. She had to admit, she needed that laugh.

Farrah walked back over toward Mills, not feeling as angry as before, but the second she saw him, the previous emotions came right back.

"Who was that?" he asked with a sour look on his face.

"Damn," Farrah put her phone back inside her purse. "You're being very nosy. It was a business call, if you must know."

"Yeah, okay," Mills replied, as he eyed her suspiciously, not believing her.

"This was nice, but can you take me back to my office? I have work I have to take care of."

"So just fuck the house? You don't give a shit about that, huh?" His nostrils flared.

"What do you want me to do, Mills?" Farrah threw up her arms in distress. "You think 'cause you bought this house that was gonna make things better? That I was gonna come running back into your arms?" She placed her hands on her hips.

"This house does not take away the fact that you have a child with someone else. What's your plan? Your baby just gonna come over and play in the yard? We gonna laugh and smile and be one happy family?" she asked, sarcastically.

"In time, yes," Mills said, bewildered.

"Mills," Farrah closed her eyes and inhaled deeply. "It will take for Biggie to rise up from the dead and Jennifer Hudson to get fat again for that to shit happen."

"Wow," Mills responded, stunned. "You really ain't feeling me anymore?"

"It's not that I don't care about you. I'm just fed up with the bullshit and in all honesty I really feel that we just need to be separated for a while."

"But we're already separated! How much more of a separation can we possibly have?" Mills exclaimed.

"We're separated, but you're still not giving me my space. Stop pushing yourself on me."

"Is that really what you want?" Mills asked, devastated.

Farrah swallowed hard as she walked toward the front door. "Can you please drive us back to my office, Mills? I really need to get back to work," she said as she walked out of the house.

"I'm not taking you anywhere until you answer the question, Farrah," Mills said with conviction.

"Fine. I'll call a taxi then." With that, Farrah began walking down the driveway while she called a cab on her phone.

"Farrah, wait," Mills yelled out as he ran out after her. "I'll bring you back to your office."

"No, thanks. I'm good," she replied.

Once Farrah was dropped off in front of her office building, she ran back inside to tie up some loose ends and then she raced back outside and

hopped into her car. Minutes later she was home
and packing up her things as fast as she could.
Clothes, shoes, jewelry, and handbags were
tossed left and right. If she was going to L.A. to
see J.R. she couldn't go looking like a slouch. She
had to rock the best of the best outfits.

After finding both day and night looks, she
started to go through her massive shoe collection. She would take her Givenchy lace-up heels,
Aldo dalmatian slippers, Alaïa cut heels, and
more. As she tossed the fab heels into her luggage, she went through everything she'd thrown
in there and felt satisfied with what she planned
on taking. She rushed into the bathroom to get a
quick shower before heading out. There was no
way she would board a plane to see J.R. and not
make sure she was smelling and looking fresh.
Out of habit, Farrah started taking all her jewelry
off. As she hurriedly placed her jewelry in the
crystal bowl she kept on the sink specifically for
that purpose, she saw her wedding rings slip out
of the bowl, drop to the floor, and slide across the
bathroom. Swiftly, Farrah raced across the room
and picked it up. As she put them in her hand,
she looked down at them and was reminded of
Mills and the vows they made before God.

What am I doing? Farrah thought. Deflated
by memories of her wedding day, Farrah sat on

the side of her bed. She couldn't run off to L.A. to see J.R. like she was some single woman. She was married and although she'd told Mills she wanted a separation, it still wouldn't be right to spend time with another man. Yes, she was angry and felt betrayed by Mills, but what good would it do for her to turn around and do the same to him? And as much as she tried to act like they didn't, his feelings still mattered to her. She couldn't and wouldn't play him out. He was her husband and she owed him the decency of respecting that title until it was no longer valid. Reluctantly, Farrah picked up her cell phone and called J.R.

"What up, ladybug? Are you on your way to the airport?"

"Hey," she said, softly.

"What's wrong?" J.R. asked, hearing a twinge of sadness in her voice.

"Umm . . . I'm not going to be able to come."

"Damn, why not?" J.R. asked, sounding disappointed.

"It's just too much. I need to figure out what I got going on here before I jump into anything else. I like you and I don't wanna put you in the middle of all that," Farrah regrettably confessed.

"I feel you. Thanks for being honest wit' me. I wish I could've seen that pretty face of yours, but it's okay."

"A'ight," Farrah said, breathlessly. "I'll talk to you soon."

"A'ight." J.R. paused. "Farrah?" he asked to make sure she hadn't hung up yet.

"Yes, J.R.?" she responded.

"You're one of the few good ones left out there, ma. Just make sure whatever you decide, you're happy. Don't ever sell yourself short." With that, the phone went silent.

Stuck in the moment, Farrah sat staring out into space with her phone tucked into her hand. Had she made the right decision by not going? Whenever she was around J.R., he filled her with nothing but happiness and joy. Was she really going to give that up to continuously argue and fight with Mills? Yes, because he was her husband. The man she'd fallen in love with was still somewhere inside his soul. There was still hope that they could get back to a happy place. Deciding to put her heart back on the chopping block, Farrah called her husband.

"Hello?" Mills answered, surprised that she was calling so soon. After today's events he didn't think he'd hear from her for at least a week or two.

"You busy?"

"Nah, what's up?"

"You wanna have dinner tonight?" she asked, unsure of her words.

"Are you sure you want to do that? About an hour and a half ago you were screaming at me for not giving you your space," Mills asked, thoroughly confused.

"I know what I said, but I feel like I need to at least try to make this work. I don't know if it's possible, but I'm willing to try."

"That's all I've been asking this whole time," Mills said, elated that she'd changed her mind. "Yeah, that's cool. What time you want me to come pick you up?"

"Seven is good," Farrah responded, looking at the time.

"See you then."

Chapter 17

So what we gon' have, dessert or disaster?
—Keri Hilson featuring Kanye West and Ne-Yo,
"Knock You Down"

Farrah stood in front of the bathroom mirror putting the finishing touches on her hair and makeup. Since summer was winding down and it was slightly cool outside, she decided to rock a gold-collar necklace over a golden-yellow chiffon blouse, black, backless, leather, spaghetti strapped, crop top, gray asymmetrical, draped skirt and a pair of ankle-strapped, single sole heels. Her hair was flat ironed bone straight to the back. On her lips she wore a deep plum shade of lipstick that gave her a dark, sensual look.

On the outside she looked beautiful, but the inner part of her felt like one gigantic ball of stress. Her mind and emotions were all over the place. It was almost as if she was spinning out of control. She needed someone to grab her and make her stand still before falling apart, but no one—not even herself—was able to help her keep it together.

"Who you about to serve C.U.N.T. fabulousness to?" London came into her room and stood in the doorway of the bathroom.

"Mills." Farrah bucked her eyes and applied mascara to her lashes.

"Ugh," London curled her upper lip. "I thought we were done with him?"

"I can't be done with somebody I'm still married to," Farrah said, sarcastically.

"Why not?" London threw her head back. "That shit ain't nothing but a piece of paper."

"And that's exactly why yo' old ass is still somebody's girlfriend and not they wife," Farrah laughed.

"Bitch, you think I care? You ain't hurting my feelings." London folded her arms across her chest. "I ain't trying to be nobody's wife. Especially if I'ma end up looking like you."

"Really bitch?" Farrah shot London a death glare.

"I'm sorry friend, too soon." London hugged Farrah from behind.

"Get off of me!" Farrah slapped her hands away.

"But seriously, why are you going out with him? We don't like him." London pouted.

"'Cause I gotta figure this out, London. We are either gonna be together and work everything out or we're gonna go our separate ways. And in order to come to either conclusion we have to spend time together."

"I guess," London said, shrugging. "Just don't be no fool, chile."

"I'm not," Farrah replied, when the doorbell rang. "Ooh, that's Mills. Can you get the door for me? I'm not ready yet."

"You sure want me to open the door? His ass might come up dead," London half joked.

"Just go open the door." Farrah pushed her out of the room.

London giggled and took her sweet time walking down the two flights of steps leading to the front door. By the time she got there Mills had rung the bell five times.

"Who is it?" London asked, trying her best not to laugh.

"Mills!"

"Bitch-ass nigga? Is that what you said?" London yelled through the door.

"Where Farrah at?" Mills ignored her sarcasm.

"Where yo' baby mama at?" London responded, opening the door.

"Whcrc Teddy at, out with his main chick?" Mills hit her where he knew it would hurt.

"See now I'ma have to cut ya." London pulled a razor blade from out her cheek.

"London!" Farrah shouted, coming down the steps.

"*Giiiiiirl* you betta get him," London warned, walking around in circles.

"Oh my god, we're getting ready to go." Farrah quickly kissed her friend on the cheek and left.

"Ay yo, you gon' have to get her under control," Mills warned, as they walked down the walkway leading to his car.

"I know. I'm sorry. She's just looking out for me."

"Looking out for you gon' get her fucked up."

"Hi, how are you?" Farrah uttered, changing the subject.

"I'm good. How are you?" Mills asked.

"Have you looked at me?" Farrah stopped mid-stride and posed. "I'm doing great."

Mills smiled and admired her curvaceous frame. Farrah's body was always swimsuit ready.

"You do look good. You wearing the fuck outta that skirt." He eyed her thighs.

"Thanks." Farrah blushed.

"You gon' wrap 'em around my back later?" Mills flirted, opening her door.

"Let's get through dinner first," Farrah countered.

After a brief car ride, Mills and Farrah made it to Scape, located in the Central West End's historic yet hip Maryland Plaza. Scape was a restaurant with an eclectic blend of classic and contemporary food. The innovative American cuisine sat against a backdrop of warmth and sophistication. From the white linen–topped tables to the fine china to the whimsical bubble chandeliers, no detail was overlooked.

The weather that night was fantastic, so they sat outside at the back bar. The back bar was located right behind Scape and boasted a giant projection screen, flatscreen television, customized bar, enchanting greenery, cobblestone ground, and hanging glowing lights. The setting for a romantic night was there. All Farrah and Mills had to do was show up and be present. After placing their order for drinks and dinner, Mills and Farrah sat having small talk.

"I'm happy you called." Mills placed his napkin on his lap. "I wasn't expecting to hear from you anytime soon, though. I thought I was gonna have to keep stalking you." He chuckled, somewhat playing.

"I ain't even know you had that in you," Farrah laughed.

"You ain't know . . . bitch I'll kill ya'," Mills impersonated Laurence Fishburne in *What's Love Got to Do with It*.

"Till you do right by me, everything you even think about gonna fail." Farrah mimicked Whoopi Goldberg in *The Color Purple*.

"You stupid," Mills cracked up laughing.

When their laughter subsided a brief moment of silence swept over Farrah and Mills. Neither minded the quiet between the two. Silence was welcomed. It was far better than the ear-splitting bickering they'd been doing for the past few months. It'd been a while since Farrah had the chance to just sit back and bask in his presence.

Amid all of the anger she'd forgotten how handsome Mills was. The fresh haircut and line-up goatee highlighted his chiseled cheekbones. He looked sexy as hell in a thin, black sweater. Three small rope chains with different pendants hung from his neck and a black and gold Movado watch gleamed from his wrist. The physical attraction she had for him had not declined. He still could get it anyway he wanted.

"We haven't been here in a while." She looked around.

"Hell, I don't even remember the last time we been anywhere in a while. We've been wrapped up in all this bullshit for like a thousand years. All we do anymore is fight," Mills acknowledged.

"Well, if you hadn't have lied and cheated we wouldn't be fighting." Farrah smirked, crossing her legs.

"C'mon babe, let's not even get into all that right now." Mills shut down the conversation quick.

"I just bet we ain't." Farrah arched her eyebrow as the waiter placed their meals in front of them.

"Anyway, what you got going on?" Mills picked up his fork, ready to dive in.

"What don't I have going on?" Farrah sighed, rolled her eyes to the sky. "I have to pull clothes and jewelry for the BET Hip Hop Awards. I'm styling 2 Chainz's country ass. You don't know how long I've been waiting to get my hands on him. I also have to dress Wale and Meek Mill."

"That's what's up." Mills nodded his head slow. "So is ol' boy going to be there?"

"Who?" Farrah furrowed her brow.

"That nigga you kissed." Mills looked her square in the eyes.

"First of all, he kissed me and I don't know, I guess. Why?"

"'Cause if he is planning on being there, you don't need to be going then," Mills shot sternly.

"Excuse me," Farrah rolled her neck. "I didn't know you had a say-so in it."

"What, you wanna see him or something?" Mills questioned.

"If I wanted to see him, I would see him," Farrah said, bluntly.

Fuming, she shot Mills a look that said, *Nigga, if you only knew.*

"You know the media is going to have a field day if you go," Mills continued on. "They're gonna make up a story even if there is none. I don't need anymore bad publicity."

"The sad part is you're serious," Farrah scoffed, eating her food.

"You damn right I am. You already embarrassed the hell out of me once. You ain't gon' get the chance to do it again. I don't want you to go nowhere near that nigga."

"Wow," Farrah leaned back in her chair. "I see somebody's balls grew bigger. I am not going to miss out on a job opportunity that's going to expand my business just because your insecure ass feels some type of way. This is my job and I'm not going to fuck it up for you or anbody else."

"So fuck how I feel?" Mills's blood boiled.

"In this case, yes. I know this may come as a surprise to you, but this is not about you. It's about my career. You act like I fucked that man. I didn't step out on our relationship. You did that. So don't even try to put your shit off on me," Farrah hissed.

"You still on that shit? I fucked up—either you gon' forgive me or you ain't? I'm tired of you bringing the shit up."

"You're tired," Farrah said, in disbelief. "Tired of what, exactly? You tired of being a lying, cheating, no-good-ass fool? If that's the case, then yeah, I'm tired too," she snapped, not caring that people were starting to stare.

"Yo, who the fuck you think you talkin' to? I ain't that soft-ass nigga you fuck wit'," Mills declared.

"I know exactly who you are. That's the problem," Farrah shot back.

"I'm telling you now, Farrah, if you go to L.A. we gon' have a problem," Mills warned again.

"We—" Farrah sat up straight and pointed between the two of them, "ain't gon' have shit. You can't give me no ultimatums when you got a whole family across town, chile please. You better get yo' life."

"You got feelings for this nigga, don't you?" Mills fired back, feeling like his chest was about to cave in.

"If I had feelings for him, trust me, I would be with him right now. But no, I'm here stuck on stupid tryin' to work shit out wit' yo' lousy ass." Farrah threw her napkin down onto the table.

Both Farrah and Mills were so caught up in their argument that they failed to realize that half the restaurant was listening to their every word.

"If I'm such a lousy-ass nigga, then why are you here? You the same muthafucka that called me talkin' about *I wanna try to work it out*." He mocked her voice. "If I ain't shit then why you keep coming back?"

Unsure of why she kept coming back, Farrah sat silent.

"Exactly, 'cause you know you're full of shit," Mills barked.

"Maybe I wouldn't be so full of shit if you stopped feeding it to me all the goddamned time." Farrah shook her head. "Yo' ass need to get it together and stop doing all the grimy shit that you do. Maybe if you change yo' fuckin' ways we'd be all right."

"Here you go wit' that again," Mills waved her off. "Have you ever stopped to think that maybe this is me and that I'm happy wit' who the fuck I am? Maybe I don't wanna change. You want somebody to change so bad, then why da fuck don't you change then. Then maybe you'd quit naggin' and complaining every five seconds! Shit do that!"

"You are so fuckin' disrespectful. You don't give a fuck about me." Farrah swallowed back the tears that had begun to rise in her throat.

"If I didn't give a fuck about you then why would I be here? I always put you first."

"You didn't put me first when you fucked that bitch!" Farrah spazzed out. "Did you put me first when you kept yo' baby a secret? Did you put me first when you lied about taking the paternity test?"

Feeling as if it were Groundhog Day, Mills shook his head and sneered. He was so sick of her bringing up the same shit over and over again.

"How many times you gon' bring that shit up?" he quizzed.

"As many times as I please or until you give a fuck," Farrah spat.

"How about, I don't give a fuck no more. I've said I was sorry a thousand times. I tried to show you that I was on some different shit, but nothing is ever good enough for you."

"It's not about nothing ever being good enough for me: It's about the level of respect that you have for me. When are you gonna stop and realize what you did to me was fucked up? I wish you could take your head out of your ass long enough to smell your own shit. You don't care about me, Corey. All you do is diss me and disrespect me." Farrah's hand trembled as she picked up her fork and ate a piece of her steak.

"Then why are you here, Farrah? If you're being *soooooo* disrespected, then why don't you get up out of your seat and move on wit' your life," Mills barked. "But you ain't doing that, though. You ain't going nowhere. You gon' continue to sit yo' little black ass right there and eat that good-ass piece of steak I'm paying for!"

"You know what? You're right about one thing. I don't know what the fuck I was thinkin'. This was a horrible idea." Farrah blinked away the tears that stung her eyes.

"You steady talkin' shit but I don't see you moving, though," Mills dared her.

"You know what? Fuck this." Farrah threw her fork on the table and stormed out of the restaurant.

"Yeah, go ahead. Run away like you did earlier today. So mature of you to run away from your problems. At least I handle mines!" Mills yelled out for her and the entire restaurant to hear.

For the second time in one day, Farrah took a cab. She was disappointed that she'd put herself in that predicament. She felt like such an idiot and couldn't wait to get home so she could cry out her emotions. She didn't want to start hysterically crying in the car and have the driver look at her like she was crazy. Every second that passed she felt suffocated. One more minute in that taxi and she was sure to explode. She hated that every time she was around Mills he brought out the absolute worst in her. He was annoying and self-centered as hell. Farrah was over him and his shenanigans.

All she wanted was to be happily married to him. But she'd attempted to make it work and failed. It was sad to face, but Farrah and Mills were done. She'd finally had enough. When they pulled up to her place, Farrah didn't even wait for the driver to tell her how much she had to pay. She took out a hundred-dollar bill, gave it to the man, and hurriedly got out of the cab.

"You forgot your change!" the driver screamed out of the passenger window.

"Keep the change!" Farrah screamed over her shoulder, as she entered her apartment.

"How was the date, girl?" London came out of her room, eating a bowl of ice cream.

"Fuck Mills!" Farrah stomped up the steps. "And fix me a bowl of ice cream! It's about to be a tears and a Ben and Jerry's kinda night!"

Chapter 18

Every little thing you do got me feelin'
some type of way.
—Sevyn Streeter, "It Won't Stop"

Going to the BET Hip Hop Awards in L.A. was a much-needed distraction from the turmoil Farrah had back at home. Working always took her mind off her troubles. It was 4:00 in the afternoon. The red carpet was in full effect. Hip-hop's elite was there. Everybody, including Lil Wayne, Nicki Minaj, Kendrick Lamar, Diddy, were working the carpet.

All of Farrah's clients were styled to perfection. She'd pulled the best of the best for each of them. 2 Chainz finally had a toned-down, fashion-forward ensemble that accentuated his height and physique. Farrah gave Meek Mill and Wale both a hard-edged, sleek and sexy look. The reporters and photographers were all over them, clamoring to get an interview and a picture. Farrah was over-the-moon proud.

She'd done it again. All the hard work she'd put in was a success. All three rap stars wanted to work with her again. As the men went down the press line, Farrah stood over to the side, ready to touch up their looks at a moment's notice. Out of nowhere the crowd of adoring fans in the pit went nuts. Farrah was deafened by ear-splitting screams. Someone huge had arrived.

Farrah wondered if it was Jay-Z. If it was she was sure to faint. He was her favorite rapper but it wasn't Hov. It was none other than the West Coast rapper himself, J.R. Farrah's mouth immediately went dry and her palms began to sweat. A rush of heat washed over her body as she watched him from afar. She'd thought she saw him at his best before, but that night J.R. took simple sexiness to a whole other level.

For the first time he didn't don his usual all–black-and-white attire. This time he opted for a deep purple Salvatore Ferragamo V-neck sweater. The sweater had a black-lined pocket on the top right area of the chest. The sleeves were slightly rolled up and three platinum bracelets hung off of his wrist. The rest of his outfit consisted of a crisp new pair of gray-fitted jeans and white, gray, and black Gucci high tops. A gray-and-white Gucci print scarf wrapped around his neck and Gucci silver-rimmed glasses completed the Godlike look. His nappy box was freshly cut with three parts on the side of his temple.

J.R. looked so good that Farrah wanted to run over and lick his face. *Maybe I should've gone to L.A. to see him,* she thought. That thought quickly went out the window when a hot and sexy woman stepped out of the SUV behind him. *Who the fuck is that?* Farrah wondered, screwing up her face. The chick was fuckin' gorgeous and had a body that killed. Her body reminded Farrah of the famous stripper and Drake's ex-girlfriend, Maliah.

The girl had small breasts, a slim waist, round hips, and a fat ass. The bitch was bad. Farrah instantly felt some type of way. J.R. wasn't her man, but deep down she felt like he was hers. She didn't want to see him with anyone else. Unfortunately, that wasn't the case because there he was, making his way down the carpet with the beautiful woman. As J.R. got closer, Farrah situated herself and made sure she was on point. She wouldn't be caught dead slipping in front of J.R. As Farrah adjusted her top, out of nowhere one of the reporters shouted her name.

"Farrah! How does it feel to be reunited with J.R.?"

Before she could even respond, all the other reporters recognized her and started yelling out questions as well. Farrah was mortified. She was there to work, not be on display. She wanted to run and hide, but she couldn't walk off and leave her clients behind. Farrah did what she thought best and pretended to be deaf. J.R. looked over his shoulder and spotted Farrah off to the side, cringing in embarrassment.

He felt sorry for her. This was all his fault. She hadn't asked to be kissed. If he hadn't ran on impulse and kissed her on stage, none of this would've ever happened. Every bit of him wanted to race over and comfort her, but he couldn't. Acknowledging her on any level would only make it worse for both of them, so he continued down the red carpet and acted as if she didn't exist.

He decided the best thing for him to do was get out of sight before reporters swarmed him and this whole scenario became any bigger than it was.

"J.R! How does it feel to see Farrah Mills again?" One reporter asked.

"Who is this mystery woman with you, J.R.?" another reporter yelled out.

"C'mon," J.R. said as he hurriedly grabbed his date and walked inside the arena. He was in no mood to answer any questions.

Lizzy was beaming from ear to ear. She was enjoying every minute of the event so far. She couldn't believe she was out with J.R. and in such a public way. Her moment had finally arrived for her to be recognized as J.R.'s woman. She was especially relishing the fact that Farrah had finally seen them together. She had read all about what had happened between her and J.R. in Paris, so she knew exactly who Farrah Mills was. And she also knew if Farrah ever tried to come at her man she'd be ready for it. There was no way she was gonna just sit around and let some bitch walk in on her territory.

The official after party for the Hip Hop Awards was hosted by the Game at club Dream and was in full swing. The club was filled to capacity. People were shoulder to shoulder and turned up, except for Farrah. All she wanted was to go back to the hotel and go to sleep, but her clients insisted that she come out with them. She couldn't turn them down because it would be bad for business, so she put on her business face and went. Just because she attended the party didn't mean she was enjoyng herself, though.

Farrah couldn't escape the shitty mood she was in. She been alone in L.A. for a few days and loneliness was starting to seep in. She missed her friends and calling Mills wasn't an option since they weren't speaking. Farrah missed having a man by her side. She missed the masculine touch and their hypnotic smell. Being alone was rough. Fuck that, it was unbearable.

It was bad enough she had to sit through the entire award show and watch J.R. laugh and smile in another bitch face. Farrah wished she could crawl under a rock and die. Her life was in shambles and the second J.R. walked into the building with the big booty bandit, Farrah's life got worse. J.R. and his whole crew mobbed Club Dream and instantly created a movie. They all headed up to VIP and ordered bottles of Ace of Spades, Cîroc, and Moët.

Farrah sat at the bar and took another shot of tequila. *This night is a wrap,* she thought. She would not torture herself and add to her misery by staying a second longer. Nope, it was time for her to go. Farrah picked up her clutch purse and walked up to the VIP section to say good-bye to her clients, but when she approached the steps who else but J.R. was standing at the top. She looked up and their eyes locked. As she looked into his eyes something strange took her over. She suddenly became tired of pretending that she didn't want him, that she didn't want to savor the sweet taste of his tongue or hear the tone of his deep, raspy voice in her ear.

Every part of her craved him. She no longer gave a single fuck about how Mills would feel or what the gossip rags would say. *Just make sure whatever you decide, you're happy*, resonated in her mind. That was what J.R. had said to her the last time they spoke and he was absolutely right. It was time for Farrah to live for herself and make herself happy. With all of the confidence and liquid courage running through her body, Farrah ran up the stairs toward J.R., grabbed him by the collar, and planted her lips on his. She didn't care that his date was standing right next to him or that all eyes were on them.

J.R. was hers and everybody would know it. J.R. was completely caught off guard by Farrah's forward behavior, but welcomed her soft lips. As soon as their lips met any awkward feeling was erased. When the two of them came together it was like fireworks on the Fourth of July.

She had no idea that the entire day she had been the only person on his mind. Every time he laughed or looked at Lizzy he secretly envisioned that it was Farrah he was sharing those moments with. He felt bad for dragging Lizzy into this, but Farrah was his baby and he didn't give a damn if anyone had a problem with it. After what seemed like an eternity, Farrah came up for air, took him by the hand and said, "Let's go." J.R. didn't hesitate to follow.

Lizzy could not beleive Farrah had the nerve to just walk up to J.R. and kiss him like that. She wanted to react, but it was like the shock of it all had her frozen in place. When she finally reacted, it was too late and J.R. was already down the stairs walking hand in hand with Farrah. Never in a million years did she think he would ever dog her out like that. Even though they had never discussed what their status was, what they had between them was special. She felt like the biggest idiot just standing there alone. Her bewilderment quickly turned into anger the more she thought of how J.R. played her like that in front of everybody. But if he wanted to play games like that, she was gonna give him the best game of his life.

A while later Farrah and J.R. were at his house. Rapid, thunderous rain had begun to pour from the sky. By the time they made it inside they both were drenched. Farrah didn't care. She felt alive. She felt free for the first time in months. She wanted to dance. She wanted to run wild in the streets. If she could she would've stayed outside in the rain and let God's blessing pour down upon her.

But this wasn't a movie: This was real life and her ass wasn't trying to catch a cold. Instead,

she stood shivering inside J.R.'s massive living
area while he grabbed them both towels and dry
clothes. Now that they were alone and her buzz
had somewhat subsided, Farrah was a nervous
wreck. All of the gumption she'd mustered back
at the club had fallen to the wayside. *What you
are going to do if he tries to have sex with you?*
she wondered. *Are you ready to give him some?
If you take it there you can't take it back. You
and Mills will be over for good. Okay, bitch stop
it. Just go with the flow,* she convinced herself. If
Farrah kept on questioning herself she was sure
to throw up.

"Here you go," J.R. tossed her a warm towel.

"Thank you." Farrah patted her face dry.

"Your place is beautiful," she said, admiring
his view.

Upon entry, Farrah was in awe of J.R's private
estate. He had a beachfront home in Laguna
Beach, California. The home was surrounded
by lush green gardens. It possessed a resort-
style pool and spa and had its very own private
staircase leading down to a beautiful secluded
beach and cove. J.R. had six spacious bedrooms
and seven and a half bathrooms. Endless walls
of glass, generously scaled rooms, and correlated
indoor-outdoor living were highlights of the
impeccable hideaway. Additional features of

the home included a gourmet chef kitchen, an executive office, a home gym, and elevator.

"Thank you. Here, you can put this on." J.R. handed her one of his Keith Haring OBEY T-shirts.

"It's raining hard as hell," he said, taking off his shirt and jeans in one fell swoop.

Farrah was mesmerized. Her mouth was wide open and she couldn't think straight. She thought J.R's chest and abs were on point, but to see the full package in 3-D had her body feeling things it'd never felt before. J.R. had nice, strong legs and the bulge inside his boxer briefs made her want to lie down and allow him to have his way with her.

"Good lord, is that real?" she said underneath her breath, staring at his crotch.

"You just gon' stand there wet?" J.R. asked, noticing the look of lust in her eyes.

"You have no idea how wet I am," Farrah blurted out unintentionally.

"Oh word? That box hot?" J.R. smirked.

"How rude." Farrah blushed.

"I'm rude, but you staring at *my* package," J.R. laughed, still in nothing but his boxer briefs.

"Whateva," Farrah waved him off.

"You wanna listen to some music?" J.R. walked over to his surround-sound system.

"Yeah, what you got?"

"I'll bump that new Drake." J.R. turned the CD on.

"Is Drake a rapper or an R and B singer?" Farrah questioned, thoroughly confused.

"Duh, an R and B singer," J.R. chuckled.

"Look," Farrah said, covering her eyes. "Can you please put some clothes on? I already know you're built like Zeus and shit. You don't have to put it all up in my face," Farrah joked.

"I'm sorry my sexiness is bothering you." J.R. grinned, throwing on a pair of basketball shorts. "You need me to help you outta that dress?" He asked, walking toward her.

"Hell no!" Farrah scooted back away from him. "You ain't coming near me. You ain't slick. You ain't gonna have me on my back calling out your name. Nope." She shook her head. "Ain't gonna happen Trey Songz," Farrah said, chuckling at her own joke. "Bathroom please?"

"Down the hall and to your right." J.R. laughed at her silliness.

"Thank you." Farrah skipped down the hallway.

After she'd washed her makeup off, washed up, and dressed in his T-shirt, Farrah returned to the living room to find the lights dimmed low, the fireplace lit, two glasses of wine, and J.R. on the floor.

"*Mmmmmm*, more liquor." She smiled glee-fully and ran over to where he was.

"I figured you would like that." J.R. lay on his back and looked at her.

With no makeup and nothing but his T-shirt on he'd never found Farrah more attractive. Flickers of light from the fireplace danced on her face. Farrah felt at peace and anxious all at the same time. It was taking everything in her not to lean over and devour him.

"So what now?" Farrah took a small sip of wine.

"What do you mean?"

"Is this how you do it when you woo the ladies? You throw on the fireplace, pour some wine, play some soft music, take your clothes off, and then get them into bed?"

"No." J.R. grinned, shaking his head.

"If you would've come home with Maliah two-point-oh would you have done this?" Farrah arched her brow.

"No, not at all. It's not even like that between me and her."

"Why not? She was gorgeous."

"Yeah, she's a looker, but I wasn't even trying to hit that tonight," J.R. confessed.

"Wow." Farrah cracked up, laughing at his bluntness.

"What makes you think I'd be sleeping with her tonight? I don't sleep around like that," J.R. declared. He wasn't lying about not sleeping with Lizzy. He hadn't slept with her in months. And he wasn't about to go and explain his and Lizzy's history either. Farrah didn't need to know all that.

"So let me guess. I'm special, huh?"

"If you don't know that by now, then you never will." J.R. massaged her thigh.

"Hmmm." Farrah nervously drank some more wine.

What was transpiring was all too much. The beautiful fireplace, delicious wine, and J.R.'s gorgeous face had her insides melting. Every time their eyes met and each time his fingertips touched a part of her skin it became harder and harder to control her feelings. She had to keep her emotions intact, though, because he had that kind of presence that would have her getting up in the morning fixing him breakfast. And Farrah did not cook, so the fact she was thinking about doing it said a lot in itself.

"I'm not fuckin' you," she said out loud, trying to convince herself more than anything.

"Who said you were?" J.R. furrowed his brow.

"Your penis did. I can hear it talkin' to me. It's sayin': *Come sit on me, Farrah. I won't hurt you*—but oh, it will." She licked her lips, staring at his crotch.

"You're drunk," J.R. chuckled.

"Mmm-hmm." Farrah nodded. "But I don't care."

"You can't fuck me anyway," he clarified.

"Excuse me?" Farrah said, appalled. "Chile, please. You better get yo' life. I could if I wanted to."

"No, you couldn't," J.R. laughed.

"Whatever," Farrah replied, sitting Indian-style.

For some reason, her feelings were hurt. Did J.R. not see her in a sexual way? Was he not attracted to her like she was to him?

"And yes, I find you extremely attractive." He spoke as if he was reading her mind. "But the first time we do anything it won't be me fuckin' you. I wanna make love to you."

Farrah sat speechless. Mills was the only other man she'd ever encountered that had ever spoken such sweet words to her. Except J.R. sounded like he actually meant it. There were no words to express how he made her feel in that moment. The only thing she could muster up to say was, "That was so sweet."

"Real talk and by the way, I like to see you less uptight. It suits you better."

"I am not uptight!" Farrah drew back her head.

"Yes, you are," J.R. disagreed.

"No, I am not." Farrah playfully hit him on the arm. "I am a ball of fun. I am everything." She drank some more.

"Okay, no more wine fore you." J.R. took her glass and finished the rest of her drink before she could.

"Look who's the party pooper now." Farrah poked out her bottom lip.

"Come here." J.R. pulled her onto him.

Farrah laid on top him and looked up at his face. There was nothing about him that she didn't admire. Even through her drunken haze she could still appreciate his undeniable good looks. J.R. had the creamiest cocoa skin she'd ever been blessed to see and touch. His eyebrows were silky and thick. She could look at his face for hours and never get bored.

"I want you to fuck me so hard," she blabbed.

"I told you we gon' make love," J.R. said, kissing her lips softly.

"I cannot fall in love with you," Farrah whispered.

"You already are in love with me." J.R. ran his hands through her hair as their tongues danced.

"*Noooooo*, I can't. When I fall in love, everything turns to shit." She relished the sweet taste of his tongue.

"Maybe because you loved the wrong people." J.R. gripped both of her thighs.

"If we fuck, is it gon' hurt?" Farrah asked, lost.

His lips and tongue were seducing the hell out of her neck.

"Maybe a little," J.R. whispered seductively.

"Dammit. Why it gotta be so big?" Farrah massaged his dick through his shorts. "You gon' fuck around and get me pregnant."

"Ain't nothing wrong wit' that. I want kids. Two boys and a girl," J.R. replied, between her moans of pleasure.

"Oooooh!" Farrah abruptly stopped kissing him. "We can name them Dolce, Gabbana, and Chanel."

"You're cute but you're crazy." J.R. cracked up laughing.

"You know what would be so good right now?" Farrah cupped his cheeks with her hands.

"What, baby?"

"Some Popeyes chicken," Farrah said, beaming.

"You serious?"

"Yeah." Farrah smiled, brightly.

A little over an hour later Farrah and J.R. sat Indian-style on the floor, eating mashed potatoes and gravy, corn, red beans and rice, and spicy chicken wings, all from Popeyes.

"This is the best night ever!" Farrah closed her eyes and savored the wonderful food in her mouth.

"This was a good idea." J.R. took a bite of chicken.

"How did you get this here anyway?"

"I called my peoples and had them open up a Popeyes just so we could eat."

"You didn't have to do that," Farrah said, sincerely.

"You said you wanted Popeyes so you got it. It was nothing."

"Give me a kiss." Farrah leaned forward.

J.R. met her halfway and kissed her sweetly.

"What am I gonna do with you?" She eyed him lovingly.

"Give me the chance to show you I'm the one you need," J.R. answered.

"Well, you keep on opening up Popeyes in the middle of the night and we might have something to talk about," Farrah joked.

Once they were full and done eating, J.R. and Farrah lay curled up in front of the fireplace wrapped up in each other's arms. For hours they lay talking. Then fatigue set in and before either of them knew it they both drifted off to sleep.

Chapter 19

You act so different around me.
  -Drake, "Hold On, We're Going Home"

By morning J.R. was still asleep but Farrah was wide awake and on the balcony staring at the ocean. It was a cloudy day, but it still felt warm out. There was a slight, cool breeze in the air as seagulls flew around in the sky and walked in the sand. Only a few people were on the beach. Farrah folded her arms and placed them on the rail. She was so relaxed. Being in California was blissful. The laid-back pace was what she needed.

What she hadn't realized she needed was J.R. He was all the therapy she needed. His spirit was beyond calming. When he looked at her she melted. All he cared about was making sure she was happy. He would do anything for her and she knew it. She only prayed she could give him all of her. He deserved the world and more.

He made her so utterly happy. She truly believed that it took her to be with him to see what love was truly like. Mills made her feel like this when they first started going out, but now, thinking back, she always had an unsettling feeling with Mills. It was like she never had his love to herself because Jade had always been in the picture. No matter how good Mills made her feel, she never felt like she truly had all of him. Not the way J.R. made her feel last night. He was with another woman and he didn't hesitate to leave with her. He showed her on the spot that she had him and no woman could keep him from her. Mills had never done that for her.

She knew she had to make a final decision on her marriage once and for all. She couldn't keep playing this back-and-forth game with Mills and she didn't want J.R. to get caught up in a mess either. She wished she could stay in the moment of being with him forever, but her real life and the drama that came with it was back in St. Louis waiting on her. But as she looked back out into the ocean, she closed her eyes and let the wind caress her face. Her life back in St. Louis was gonna have to take a backseat for a little bit, because these next few days she was going to thoroughly enjoy her time with J.R.

Wanting to be near him, she tiptoed back inside the living room where they'd slept that night and she lay back down beside him. With her head propped up on her hands, she gazed at J.R. He was perfect. She hated that he had such a hold on her. He looked so adorable as he slept. He didn't snore or anything. Gently, she traced his lips with her index finger. Out of nowhere he snapped his teeth at her finger, scaring the shit out of her.

"Boy!" She jumped back, frightened.

"I got you, didn't I?" J.R. said as he tickled her sides. "You thought I was asleep, didn't you?"

"I'm gonna kill you." Farrah laughed uncontrollably, kicking her legs.

"You shouldn't have been watching me while I was asleep then, psycho." J.R. stopped tickling her.

"You're the crazy one for pretending like you were sleeping." Farrah caught her breath and calmed down.

"Shut up and give me a kiss," J.R. demanded.

"Good morning." Farrah smiled, then took his face into her hands and kissed him softly. "I missed you."

"I haven't been anywhere," J.R. chuckled, confused.

"You were asleep and I couldn't talk to you," she said, pouting.

"You're cute. You know that?"

"Uh-huh," she laughed. "But seriously, I'm sad."

"Why?" J.R. lay beside her.

"'Cause I gotta go. My flight leaves in a few hours."

"Stay." J.R. held her hands. "You ain't gotta leave." He kissed her palm.

"I have work tomorrow."

"You can miss one day. Plus, I'm having a barbecue this afternoon. You have to stay."

"Will you be serving barbecue chicken and hot dogs?" Farrah asked, intrigued.

"It wouldn't be a barbecue without it."

"Okay you twisted my arm," she said, smiling gleefully. "I'll stay."

By midday the barbecue was in full motion. It seemed like all of Compton came out to Laguna Beach. J.R's family and friends were there in full party mode. Farrah knew that his neighbors had to be mortified by all of the gangsters and thugs, but if they were, they never said a word. Despite where his family and friends came from, J.R's people couldn't have been more welcoming and polite. They treated Farrah as if she were a part of the family.

His mother was especially kind. The two women had an instant connection, which pleased J.R. greatly. Farrah even got in the kitchen and made her famous six-cheese macaroni and cheese, which was an automatic crowd pleaser. At first Farrah was overwhelmed by all of the colorful personalities who filled J.R.'s home, but after a game of spades broke out, she felt right at home. Everyone was on chill mode. There was no drama.

Everyone laughed, talked, debated, played dominoes, volleyball, swam, and ate. As the day went on and the sun began to set, a bonfire was set and the guests who were still there cozied up with jackets, blankets, liquor, and s'mores. Farrah wished London could've been there to enjoy all the festivities, 'cause she was having a ball and creating memories that she would cherish forever. As Sevyn Streeter's summer hit "It Won't Stop" played, Farrah found herself in a very romantic mood and missing the hell out of J.R.

They'd barely gotten a chance to speak all day long. They did, however, steal a few lustful glances and sinful touches here and there. Nothing, though, beat when he was there by her side, giving her his undivided attention. Little did Farrah know, but J.R. was feeling the exact same way. He'd asked her to stay so that he could spend more time with her. But between playing host and staying on the grill, time slipped away.

Farrah was leaving the next day, so he had to make the little time they had left worthwhile. With a blanket big enough for two in his hand, J.R. made his way down his private staircase to the beach. The flames from the bonfire roared as more sticks were thrown into it. J.R. thought he'd have a problem spotting Farrah, but Farrah always stood out in the crowd. Her long hair blew angelically in the wind as she laughed with one of his cousins.

"I know you made me one of those," he said to Farrah as she demolished a s'more.

"I'm sorry," she said with her mouth full.

"You ain't shit," J.R. sat behind her and covered them both with the blanket.

"You want me to make you one?" she asked.

"Naw, I'm good. You have fun today?" he replied, inhaling the scent of her skin.

"Seriously, this is one of the best days of my life. I haven't had this much fun in literally forever. Thank you for asking me to stay."

"No problem, I'm just glad you're happy."

"You make me happy." Farrah lovingly kissed the side of his face.

Then J.R's guitar player pulled out his acoustic guitar and began to play. One of J.R.'s label mates instantly started to sing Coldplay's "Yellow". The setting was perfect. The sun had gone down and nothing but light from the fire pit lit the sky. Farrah and J.R. couldn't help but turn to each other and sing along.

. . . *Turn into something beautiful,*
D'you know? For you I bleed myself dry.

J.R. gazed deep into Farrah's eyes and sang, "Look at the stars. Look how they shine for you."

Farrah blushed so hard she swore her cheeks would break. Nothing could ruin the moment, but as always, when God shows his favor the devil is never too far behind. Farrah heard her phone beep alerting her that she had a text message. It read:

Mills: Where u at and y u ain't been answering ur phone? I luv u. We can work this shit out. Hit me back.
Sent: 8:02PM

Farrah didn't even bother to respond, but whether she responded or not didn't matter. J.R. had glanced over her shoulder and read the message. He wished he never read it because it only reminded him that Farrah wasn't really his.

And it enraged him to think she was married to such a total asshole. J.R. knew he was falling in love with Farrah. She made it so easy for him to love her. She complemented him well, but the fact still remained that she was married to another man. She'd made it clear in the past that she respected her husband and their marriage, which he found admirable. But the time they'd spent together over the last two days seemed to change all of that. Maybe she was starting to see that better did exist, that she could be loved without constantly having to fight for it.

Love wasn't meant to be a battle. And yes, no relationship was perfect. There would always be hurdles to overcome. If the rumors he'd heard in the news and then straight from Rock that her husband had a baby on her were true, then she definitely needed to leave him. Nobody deserved that. She brought so much light and joy into the world. She was everything he ever wanted in a woman and more. As much as he wanted to force her to stay with him, he knew the decision was hers to make. In the meantime he decided he would just enjoy his time with her and make every second count, so Farrah could realize he was all she needed.

Only she could realize what she was worth, though. She had to come to the conclusion that she deserved all of the goodness the world had to offer. She had to realize that she had some control over the madness that was happenning in her life, because she was allowing it to happen to her. The longer she stayed in an unhealthy relationship, the longer she would be sad and miserable. Only she could make that change. She just had to get the courage to say she was finally done.

By midnight the last guest left. Farrah knew J.R. had to be exhausted. He'd been an excellent host and grill master. The house, however, was a wreck. There were still plastic cups and plates everywhere. The trash was full. J.R., being the neat freak he was, couldn't wait till the maid came the next morning. He had to clean up the mess before he dared go to bed.

After searching for him all over the house, Farrah found him in the kitchen straightening up. He had no idea she was watching him. Solange's song "Looks Good With Trouble" featuring Kendrick Lamar was on and he was rapping along. He was so in the zone that it brought a grin to Farrah's face. The more she was around him, the more she couldn't escape her feelings. Love had found its way into her heart. She'd fought it tooth and nail, but there it was, sitting firmly in the center of her chest.

J.R. was beautiful on the inside and out. There was no other way to describe him. He had a quiet presence, but was the same man who wouldn't hesitate to fuck a nigga up if need be. If you looked up the definition of a man, you would find him. Farrah desperately wanted to be the woman to make his circle complete. She couldn't chance another chick having him. And yes, she was married, but her marriage was dead from the moment they said "I do."

Farrah had nothing else to hold onto. She couldn't and wouldn't forgive Mills for cheating and all the lies he'd told. This was the life she wanted and she wanted it with J.R. He was hers and it was high time she made it official. Unable to resist being apart from him a second longer, Farrah walked in behind J.R. and reached out for his hand.

He quickly turned around upon her touch. No words had to be spoken. The look in her eyes told him what time it was. J.R. didn't hesitate to take her into his arms. As he kissed her collarbone the sound of rain falling outside intensified their encounter. Secure in his arms, J.R. carried Farrah over to the window and placed her on the windowsill. Opening the window up, he resumed kissing her body.

Overwhelmed with desire, Farrah let a subtle moan escape her lips. Loving the way her skin felt against his, J.R. caressed her back as raindrops fell from the sky. A trail of kisses was then planted from her neck to her navel. Stopping once he got to her hip bone, J.R. picked Farrah up to unzip her skirt. Watching as it fell to the floor, he then sat her back down on the windowsill. Skillfully he released the clasp on her bra and took it off. Now fully undressed, Farrah couldn't wait for her body to be satisfied.

Staring each other intensely in the eyes, J.R. grabbed her face and kissed her hungrily. Barely able to breathe, she tore his 150-dollar Purple Label button-up shirt off. Farrah ran her hands over his chiseled chest as she released her lips from his and placed loving kisses onto his body. Each and every tattoo that adorned his chest was given her undivided attention. Leaning his head back, J.R. enjoyed the feeling that her lips gave him.

Wanting to feel him inside of her she unbuckled his pants and let them fall to his feet. Sticking her hand into the slit of his boxer briefs she found that she was working with a well-endowed man. The feel of his thick, hard penis in her hand caused Farrah to go insane. She couldn't wait to feel J.R.'s big dick inside of her.

She almost begged for it. Stroking him from his shaft to his head, Farrah licked his neck and listened to J.R.'s moans as they grew louder. His moans aroused her even more. Her heart was racing a mile a minute, but Farrah's nervousness only drove her passion for J.R. to a higher level. Not able to take it anymore, he wrapped each of her legs around him and entered her slowly. The sound of thunder and rain playing in the background made his first time going inside of her even better.

Massaging raindrops into her skin with his hands, J.R. felt complete for the first time in years. Picking Farrah up while still stroking her, he placed her up against the wall. J.R. turned her around and reentered with caution so he could feel all of her.

"Damn, you feel good," he groaned.

"Ooh . . . J.R."

"Farrah."

"Ooh . . . J.R., I can't breathe."

"Your pussy feels so tight, babe. This shit feels so good," he moaned. He held her hands up to the wall with one hand and then slapped her ass while pumping hard. The tingling sensation made her crave his stroke even more.

"J.R., give it to me deeper."

With both of her hands in his, J.R. leaned in so that his dick could reach her stomach. Digging in deep he hit all four corners until he found her spot. Suddenly her thighs started shaking and her lips began to tremble as she tried to hold on. Taking his hand around, he began stimulating her clit while continuously hitting her spot.

"Ooh, baby, you're pushing it in so far," Farrah screamed.

"You want some more of it?"

"Yes, baby, give it to me hard and deep!"

Pushing in even deeper, J.R. hit her spot with no remorse. He had Farrah's entire body shaking.

"Baby, I'm about to bust," J.R. grunted.

"Ooh, J.R., fuck me! Fuck me hard!" she pleaded.

Nearing an orgasm herself, Farrah started throwing it back at him so that her orgasm would intensify. They both pumped hard against one another, then, in a paroxysm of pleasure, both climaxed at the same time.

"Ooh . . . J.R. . . . ohh . . . I never came this hard before. Ooh," Farrah cried out loud. She caught herself and wondered if she said that out loud.

"Me either."

Never before in her life had she acted in such a way. J.R. did something to her that no other man had been able to do: Make her feel free. It hadn't even been a good five minutes and she already longed for his touch.

Being snuggled up underneath the sheets on a rainy Monday morning never felt so good, especially after getting dicked down the night before. Farrah and J.R. made love the whole night through. Sleep hadn't set in until the sun came up. *This has to be what pure bliss feels like*, Farrah thought, lying on her back naked, tangled up in J.R.'s sheets. The cool breeze coming from the cracked window caressed her skin.

The feeling he gave her was the kind you couldn't wash away with soap. She was truly astonished that someone could be so compassionate and genuine. Their souls were heading in the same direction. J.R. was simply the truth. The things he'd done to her body and the positions he'd put her in were simply sinful. She wanted more of him. Wondering why she was awake and in bed alone Farrah, parted her lips to call out J.R.'s name. Before she could get the words out he magically appeared.

"Moring sleepyhead." He grinned, holding a tray of breakfast food.

"No, you didn't make me breakfast in bed." Farrah sat up and covered her breasts with the sheet. "You must know I'ma fat girl at heart," she joked.

"Shit, a nigga like to eat too." J.R. sat the tray down onto the bed in between them.

He'd prepared an array of food, from hash browns, to grits, bacon, waffles, eggs, and sliced strawberries. Farrah was in food heaven.

"Thank you, boo-boo," she said excitedly and kissed J.R. on the lips.

"Small thing to a giant," he replied.

"I know that's right. Go head on baby." Farrah danced, eating a strawberry. "So what you got going on after I leave?"

"I have to start rehearsals for my world tour. The first leg will be overseas, then I'll come to the United States," J.R. explained.

"That sounds exciting. I'm so happy for you. Your first world tour, wow."

"Yeah, you gon' have to come out on the road with me for a few dates."

"Mmm, let me think about it." Farrah placed her index finger up to her lips and looked up at the ceiling. "I guess I can fit you into my busy schedule." She toyed with him.

"Keep on fuckin' wit' me, I'ma fold yo' ass up," J.R. played back.

For a while the two basked in the essence of one another as the rain serenaded them. Farrah and J.R. sat in the middle of the bed feeding each other and in between eating, stealing kisses. If she could Farrah would've stayed trapped in J.R.'s bed for the rest of eternity. *This all has to be a dream. Life cannot be this perfect,* she thought.

"I don't wanna leave." She pretended to cry.

"I don't want you to leave, either, especially when you sitting here lookin' so delectable." He pulled the covers off of her, revealing her supple breasts. "You know I'm about to get me some more of that, right?"

"Just let me know when," Farrah challenged.

"I cannot get enough of you." He took one of her breasts in his mouth and licked her nipple.

"You gon' make me wet," Farrah moaned.

"That's the plan." He slapped her thigh.

"But seriously," J.R. stopped. "What's up wit' you and ol' boy, 'cause I have made it perfectly clear that I want you."

"You got me," Farrah confessed. "I'm all yours. When I get home I'm going to tell Mills that I want a divorce."

"A'ight then so this is official," J.R. said more as a confirmation then as a question.

"Yep, so you better get rid of all them raggedy hoes you fuck wit' 'cause I will cut a bitch," Farrah warned.

"Ain't no other bitch but you," J.R. joked.

"Really?" Farrah quickly grabbed a pillow and hit him on the head with it.

"Oh, you wanna fight?" J.R. grabbed a pillow and hit her back.

"No," Farrah said softly.

While gazing into J.R.'s tranquil eyes, Farrah draped her arms around his neck, then kissed his lips. Passionately, their tongues intertwined.

Farrah felt as if she were floating on clouds made of air. For months she'd secretly reminisced on the taste of his tongue. As his tongue circled hers it tasted like wine. Enthralled by his touch, she gladly allowed him to untie the back of her dress. Fully exposed to the elements, she let the top of the dress fall to her waist.

While J.R. placed sensual kisses from her neck down to her breasts, Farrah closed her eyes and listened to the roaring waves before her. She didn't know what was more captivating: the sound of the rain outside or the feel of J.R.'s tongue flickering on her hard nipples. Each flick sent jolts of electricity throughout her stomach. As she reeled from his kisses, J.R. held each of her breasts in his hand and sucked on her nipples mercilessly.

Her butter-colored skin felt like the finest silk against his tongue. He couldn't wait to explore every crevice of her body. Easing his way further south of the border, J.R. pulled the sheet from off her body. For a second he sat back on his knees and admired her goddess-like physique. Every square inch of her was perfect and further proved that she was the woman of his dreams.

Not wanting to waste another second, he swiftly undressed as well. Completely naked, he gently laid Farrah down on the bed. Finally his fantasy was about to come true. Farrah couldn't wait for him to taste her and J.R. couldn't wait, either. Once his tongue met with her clit they both were satisfied. Farrah was in heaven. J.R.'s tongue was wreaking havoc on her pussy.

"J.R.," she moaned, kneading with her nipples. "Baby . . . ooooooooh."

"Damn you taste good." J.R. thumbed her clit while sucking the lips of her pussy.

He was driving Farrah insane. She couldn't control herself. Moans of pleasure were escaping through her lips and into the afternoon air.

"Oooooh baby put it in me," she begged. "Baby, please . . . let me feel it. Oooooooooh I can't take it anymore J.R."

Happy to oblige her request, J.R. softly kissed her navel, breasts, and lips before smoothly sliding his rock-hard dick into her wet slit. The first thrust was mind-blowing. J.R. couldn't get enough of her. Her pussy was wet and tight. The harder and deeper he stroked the more he didn't want the moment to end. With every thrust, her pussy would hug his dick tighter.

"Shit," Farrah said as he flipped her over.

At that very second she knew she wouldn't be able to feel her legs the next day. She put her face into the pillow and she matched his thrust as she threw her ass back onto his shaft. Loving the way she worked it, J.R. slapped her ass.

"J.R.!" Farrah screamed, turned on.

"You like that?" he groaned, pulling her hair.

"Yes, don't stop!" Farrah panted as her thighs began to shake.

She knew that she was being loud, but Farrah didn't care. Whatever he wanted of her she'd happily give. She'd be his slave, his freak, whatever. Determined to make the most of the opportunity, she spun around and pushed him onto his back. His dick was standing at full attention. Obsessed by the sight, Farrah ran her tongue across her upper lip, hungrily.

Before J.R. knew it, she'd taken all of him in her mouth. His long rod slid in and out of her mouth with velvet ease. While her tongue manipulated J.R.'s dick to the point he was almost experiencing convulsions, Farrah played with her clit. She was so wet her fingers kept slipping.

"Let me taste it." J.R. pulled her onto him.

In the sixty-nine position Farrah resumed sucking his dick with reckless abandon. J.R. had been with a lot of women, but never in his life had any woman devoured his dick like Farrah. The further she pushed him into her mouth the further she wanted to go. The way J.R. was licking her clit didn't help much either. The sensation was sending her over the edge. The orgasm that was building inside of her was so explosive she couldn't think straight.

As she licked the tip of J.R.'s dick she could tell by the stiffness of his penis that at any moment he was about to nut. Farrah had never allowed a man to cum in her mouth, but for some reason she couldn't see J.R. cumming anywhere else.

"Baby I'm gettin' ready to come." He kissed her butt checks.

"Me too," Farrah said, coming up for air.

Taking all of him back into her mouth she eagerly bobbed her head up and down his shaft until J.R.'s love juices filled her mouth and slid down her throat. Massaging her butt cheeks, J.R. licked her pussy lips until every sweet drop of juice lathered his tongue. Spent, Farrah wiped her mouth and placed her head on J.R.'s chest. With one of his arms wrapped around her neck, J.R. stroked his hard dick with his free hand.

"What are you doing?" Farrah asked.

"Gettin' ready for round two."

Chapter 20

Now the sky is clearer, I can see the sun.
       -Beyoncé, "After All is Said and Done"

Farrah had been back in St. Louis for a few days. Ever since she stepped off the plane she'd dreaded this moment. She'd tried to psych herself up into thinking that she'd be tough and that she wouldn't give a fuck about telling Mills that she wanted a divorce. But as soon as he entered the coffeehouse a flood of fear washed over her. He looked like he hadn't slept in days. She could tell he was sad and hurt, but what was she supposed to do? He was the one that brought this all on himself.

"What's up?" he said, sitting across from her.

"Hey," Farrah spoke softly.

It took every ounce of restraint Mills had not to reach across the table and choke the shit out of Farrah. How dare she look like a million bucks when he felt like shit? She looked so smug in her official Tinhead snapback, camel cashmere coat with black leather sleeves, army fatigue T-shirt, Hermès belt, black skinny jeans, and Givenchy booties. She looked as if she didn't have a care in the world, all the while Mills sat miserable with a hangover from all the drinking he had been doing since the night they'd gone out to dinner.

He knew the whole time she was gone to L.A. that she was with that nigga. He could smell him on her. Mills wanted to kill them both. But before he made a murder plot up in his head, he decided he'd hear what she had to say first. Maybe by some miracle she called him to be there to tell him she loved him and wanted to give their marriage another try. He looked down at her hand and noticed she was still wearing her wedding set. As he looked at her he could see a glimpse of concern and fear in her eyes. All hope wasn't lost. She still cared for him.

"So what's up? Why did you want to meet me here?" Mills asked sharply, slumped back in his seat.

Farrah took a deep breath. This was going to be harder than she thought. At one point he was everything, *they* had everything. Now it seemed there was nothing left.

"Umm." She paused, afraid. "I'm not gonna beat around the bush. I'm just gonna say it." She cleared her throat. "Umm . . . I don't think we should be together anymore."

"Okay, you've said that." Mills rolled his eyes, annoyed.

"Okay, well, maybe I need to be more specific. What I'm trying to tell you is that I want a divorce," Farrah shot, caught off guard by his stank attitude. "Nothing we've tried has worked and I'm tired. I can't make you into the man I want you to be; that's a man you obviously can't be. You're you and I have to accept that and remove myself from the situation. Neither one of us is happy and you know it."

"You can't tell me how I feel," Mills rebutted. "I can be happy witt you. You're the one with the problem."

"And the issues I have with you are things that I can't get past," she declared.

"So just fuck everything? I've tried to tell you over and over and show you over and over that I'm sorry, but I guess that ain't good enough for you," Mills said, boiling with anger.

"No, it's not," Farrah agreed. "I want to be happy and with everything that's happened, you and I will never be happy together. Too much has been said and done. I will *never*"—she stressed the word *never* —"accept your baby or its mother so—"

"My daughter's name is Jaysin and her mother's name is Jade," Mills cut her off.

"Yeah, okay, whatever," Farrah waved her hand as if there was a fly bothering her. Her nostrils flared and she felt pissed at the mere mention of that woman's name. "Like I said, this shit is a wrap."

If Mills was going to be an ass she was going to be an even bigger ass.

"Wow." Mills nodded his head and sat up straight. "So all of this has nothing to do with the fact that you fuckin' that nigga?"

Farrah scoffed and shook her head.

"No, this has nothing to do with *J.R.*" She stressed his name for dramatic effect, the same way Mills mentioned his daughter and baby mama's name. "This is strictly about you and me."

"So you are admitting that you have been fuckin' him?" Mills ice grilled her.

"Unlike you, I have no reason to lie," Farrah responded, coldly.

"Wow." Mills licked his bottom lip.

"I just want us both to be happy. You deserve to be with somebody who will accept you for who you are. We both deserve a fresh start with someone new."

"Don't say *we*," Mills replied in a sarcastic tone. "You're the one who wants to be with someone new, not me. I want you."

"You don't want me, Mills. If you did, you would have never done what you did. You've brought this all on yourself. I cannot and will not allow you to hurt me again," Farrah stated.

Mills tried his damndest to choke back the tears, but no amount of resistance could restrain them. It felt like he was suffering a heart attack. They were in too deep to give up now. But it was clear by the tone of her voice and her stiff demeanor that Farrah was done for good. There would be no going back this time. Mills tried to drum up some words to say that could possibly make her want to stay, but there were none. The hold he had on her was gone.

Farrah sat across from him with tears in her eyes as well. Even though he'd hurt her repeatedly, she never wanted to see him in any kind of pain. At one point he was her best friend. She never wanted him to cry, but tears were inevitable in this case. What they both envisioned to be an ever-after love had now faded and here they were taking their final bow.

Farrah hadn't expected to cry, but flashbacks of the good things they shared in their relationship flooded her mind. She remembered their first kiss outside of her door. Mills was walking Farrah to her apartment after giving her a ride home. She had just bumped into Khalil at a club and he had embarrassed her in public, like usual. Luckily, Mills was there and he stepped up and gave her a ride home. He made her feel so safe. Standing outside of her door, he hesitated to kiss her, but their attraction was undeniable. His lips felt so soft and supple. It felt so good when they kissed. She remembered them making love on her steps. The way he took control and took her to ecstacy. She even remembered the night Mills first told her he loved her. Farrah gazed off into space, reminiscing about how Mills showed up at her door demanding they talk. With a few drinks in his system, Mills had the courage to profess his love for her and tell her he had broken up with Jade and wanted to make him and her an official couple. At the time, Farrah felt like she was the luckiest girl in the world because Corey Mills was in love with her. And she would never forget the way he proposed to her. It was one of the most magical moments of her life.

Farrah snapped back to reality and looked over at Mills. It all hadn't been bad. But no amount of good memories could erase the tears he'd caused to run down her face. The stab to her heart he caused would forever leave a scar. She knew she would heal, but the scar would never go away and it was all his fault. She had loved him with every fiber of her being the entire time they were together. All she ever wanted was for him to love her the way she loved him. But their relationship was tainted from the start. She should have known better than to get with Corey Mills. She should have known he wasn't any better than his friend Khalil. Now more than ever she was convinced that dogs stick together. And that's exactly what Mills was; a low-down dirty dog that took advantage of her and broke her heart.

As tears spilled out onto her cheeks, Farrah pulled her engagement and wedding band off and placed them onto the table.

"I don't want that." Mills looked at the rings as if they were the plague.

"I don't either." Farrah got up and wiped the tears from her face.

For a brief second she wondered if should she say good-bye, but the moment she placed her rings onto the table that was her final good-bye. Mills looked up at her with resentment and sorrow in his eyes. He wanted to run over and grab Farrah and make her stay. How could she not see that he was dead inside without her? Couldn't she see that underneath all of the bullshit lay a love for her so deep he'd move heaven and earth?

She was his baby. And yes, he could've loved her so much better. He'd fucked up. There was no way he could take back his mistakes, but lord knows if he could, he would've. If Farrah would just give him the chance he would spend the rest of their lives making it up to her. As Farrah turned her back and walked out of the coffee shop, it became apparent to Mills that she really was done with him and there were no more chances left.

Chapter 21

All my friends say I can do better than you.
    -Missy Elliott featuring 702, "Beep Me 911"

Jade was sound asleep in her bed when someone began to ring her doorbell repeatedly like a maniac. Startled, but afraid that whoever was at the door would wake up the baby, she quickly rolled out of bed to see who it was. Jade didn't even bother to cover up the fact that all she wore was a tank top and panties. She was so sleepy she was surprised that she hadn't stumbled and busted her ass on the way to the door.

"Who is it?" she asked, digging her panties out of her butt.

"Me," Mills said, drunkenly.

Since his early-morning meeting with Farrah he'd done nothing but drink himself to death. It wasn't like drinking wasn't a part of his everyday routine at this point anyway. He'd become a stone-cold drunk. He'd gone from bar to bar getting hammered. He didn't give a fuck. He was rich. He could do whatever the fuck he wanted. He'd rather be drunk on a cloud far, far away from his problems.

Mills would rather do anything but deal with his demons. The only time he wasn't hammered was when he came to visit his daughter. Mills always made sure to sober up for that. But the minute he would leave Jaysin, he would be right back to hitting the bottle. Vodka had become his best friend, confidant, and support system. It was reliable, always easy to reach, and always there when he needed it, unlike his wife.

"What are you doing here so late?" Jade asked, opening the door. "Is something wrong?"

"Nah," Mills shook his head and braced himself in the doorway.

He was so drunk he couldn't even stand up straight. Everything around him was spinning.

"I'm good. I came to see my daughter," he said, with a bottle of Ketel One vodka in his hand.

"You do realize it's going on four o'clock in the morning?" Jade replied, smelling the liquor on his breath. "She's asleep, what you should be doing right about now."

"Fuck that! Go wake her up!" Mills yelled, spilling vodka everywhere.

"If you don't shut the hell up!" Jade covered his mouth with her hand. "Get in here." She yanked him inside.

"Damn girl! Your hand tastes finer than a muthafucka!" Mills slured his words as he ran his tounge on Jade's hand, "And you ain't got to be pulling on me like that," Mills griped.

"Shut up!" She snatched the bottle of liquor from his hand. "I'm getting ready to go back to bed, 'cause unlike you I have to be up in a few hours."

"For what?" Mills burped. "You ain't got no job."

"Really nigga?" Jade spat back, placing her hand on her hip. "I have to get up and take care of your daughter. *Our* daughter; whom you see only once or twice a week now. Nigga don't do me like that."

"Aww, calm down." Mills waved her off, taking off his jacket. "Get ya' panties out ya' ass. It was a fuckin' joke."

"Whatever," Jade said, going back to her room.

"Wait on me!" Mills followed behind her.

"Uh-uh." Jade spun around and placed her hand on his chest, stopping him. "Where you think you going?"

"To bed wit' you." Mills pushed her hand away and bypassed her.

"This nigga done lost his damn mind," Jade said out loud to herself.

Not in the mood to argue with a drunk man, she allowed Mills to sleep in their old bed together. By the time she reached the room he'd already kicked his shoes off and was lying down. It had been almost two years since he last slept in that bed with her. The sight instantly brought back old feelings that she'd tried to bury. Jade couldn't pretend like she didn't still love Mills. They'd been together six years before they broke up and he got with Farrah. And now that she had a child by him, they had a bond for life.

At one point they were like two peas in a pod. They were best friends and inseperable. She would have never though things would turn out like they had. She was fully aware that it was her fault they broke up, though. They had grown apart and she was bored. She thought the grass would be greener on the other side—but boy, was she wrong. She stepped out on Mills and after her failed "relationship" with Rock, Jade quickly realized she'd made a huge mistake by toying with Mills's heart. She pushed him into Farrah's arms. But that was then and this was now. Here he was lying in their bed like he used to and it gave her hope that maybe—just maybe—they had a future together. In bed, Jade pulled the covers up and lay on her side.

"Good night," she spoke softly.

"Good night." Mills rolled over onto her side of the bed and wrapped her up into his arms.

Jade was so stunned by his sudden show of action that she didn't know whether to push him away or go with it. The warmth of his body and having a man hold her made her go with the flow. After not being touched, caressed or held for over a year, Jade genuinely forgot how important it was for a woman to have those things in her life. Nothing beat receiving that treatment from a man you loved and adored.

Jade tried her hardest to go back to sleep, but she was shook by Mills's display of affection. He was married and made it perfectly clear that he loved his wife, so what the hell had changed? Farrah would be pretty damn upset if she knew that her husband was lying in bed with his baby mama with his hard dick pressed up against her ass check. The feel of it had Jade's emotions spinning out of control. She wasn't that grimy girl she used to be. She wasn't trying to get caught up sleeping with somebody else's husband.

But on the other hand, though, there was no way she could lie there and act as if her panties weren't wet as hell. She wanted to feel it, taste it, sit on it, ride it. Jade closed her eyes and took a deep breath. It was now or never. Turning over, she looked at Mills's face. He was sound asleep, but his sexy lips were begging her to kiss them. Jade quietly leaned over and softly kissed him. The first time Mills didn't budge, but the second time he began to stir in his sleep.

By the third peck he'd started to kiss her back. Next thing either of them knew they were in a full-blown make-out session. His hands were all over her and hers were all over him. Eager to finally touch and feel the hard dick throbbing in his pants, Jade eased her way down his chest and unzipped his jeans. Mills's thick dick instantly sprung out of his boxer briefs. Jade's mouth immediately began to water upon sight.

It was like she was a hungry tiger ready to devour her prey. Jade took Mills's dick into her mouth with a vengeance. The girth consumed her, but she relished the taste and how long it was. If there was one thing Jade could do better than most chicks, it was suck a dick. Ironically, she used to hate doing it, but over the years she'd mastered it. It had become an art to her. She was expertly skillfull at giving head. There were many different techniques she could do with a man's penis. She knew how to stroke it with her hands and how to simultaneously use her tongue to enhance the pleasure. She loved to torture and tease the man when she was going down.

She learned to stay in full control. She bobbed her head up and down Mills's long shaft and watched with glee as he groaned.

"Goddamn," he uttered, watching her do her thing.

It turned him on to the fullest to see his dick appear and disappear in her mouth. He hadn't come over for sex, but he damn sure wasn't going to pass it up either. Mills closed his eyes and savored the slurping noises that filled the quiet room.

"You like that, baby?" Jade licked her lips, coming up for air.

"Fuck Farrah," Mills groaned, not even realizing he'd called out the wrong woman's name.

"What the fuck did you say?" Jade sat up on her knees. "Did you really just call me Farrah?"

"Huh?" Mills asked, still reeling from the sensation of her sucking his dick.

"You just called me your wife's name! Get the fuck out!" Jade snapped, hitting him in the face with a pillow.

"What I do?" Mills blocked her hits with his hands.

"You really gon' call me by another bitch name and then have the nerve to ask me what did you do? Get out! Get out! Get out before I catch a case!" Jade got out of bed and stood, awaiting his departure.

"C'mon, Jade, quit trippin'. My bad, I ain't mean to. I'm drunk."

"Okay and I don't mean to put yo' ass out, but I am. You got me all the way fucked up." She waved her hands in the air. "What I look like? If you wanna be wit' Farrah so bad then go be wit' her retarded ass, but you not about to use me in the process!"

"Nobody's tryin' to use you." Mills sat on the side of the bed and faced her. "Can you just calm down and stop yelling." He held his head, trying to steady his vision.

"No, I can't! I just sat there and sucked your li'l lousy ass, drunk dick and you called me your wife's fuckin' name!" Jade screeched.

"She's not my wife anymore!" Mills barked. "She told me she wants a divorce!" Mills hung his head low.

Jade stood speechless. She had no idea that things between Mills and Farrah had gotten that bad. For a while now she had secretly wished they would divorce so she could have Mills all to herself again. She knew they were having troubles, but not of that magnitude.

"Sorry to hear that," she uttered, not sure of what else to say. "But that still don't take away from what you did."

"Look, I ain't mean to call you by her name. I'm drunk and I'm trippin'. I just . . . really need you to be here right now for me. I can't go back home," Mills revealed.

Although Jade was still highly upset, in a strange, twisted way she felt sorry for him and joy for herself. She felt sorry for Mills because she could tell that he was in so much pain. He'd been in pain for weeks now and she never liked to see anyone she cared for in pain. Despite everything Mills had done, at the core of him was a good man. She felt joy for herself because this was the opportunity she'd longed for for so long. She wasn't trying to be a home wrecker and she respected Mills and Farrah's marriage regardless of her personal feelings about Farrah. But now that Farrah had asked Mills for the divorce, Jade could finally make moves and work on her happily-ever-after story.

"Don't ever do no shit like that again." Jade walked over and stood in between Mills's legs.

"I'm sorry." He wrapped his arms around her waist and rested his head on her stomach.

Jade rubbed the top of his head and smiled like a Cheshire cat. This was the moment she'd been praying for for months. *Thank you, God*, she thought. This was her opportunity to get her man back. They could finally try to be a real family. Deep down she believed with all her heart that she and Mills belonged together.

It was the middle of winter. A few months had gone by and Farrah sat firmly perched inside a sterile conference room waiting for her lawyer. This was the day she'd been working toward for months. It had been a struggle to get there, but here she was, seconds away from finalizing her divorce. In less than an hour, she would legally be freed from her unhappy marriage and she could close that chapter of her life.

It was funny because she'd never expected to feel any kind of anxiety. Her palms were sweaty and she couldn't sit still. She had never expected things would turn out like this between her and Mills. She had loved that man with every fiber of her being and she always thought their love would stand the test of time. She had prayed and prayed that they'd somehow be able to work it out, but life and God had a different plan for them. And now, here they were, about to end it all.

"Farrah?" Her lawyer entered the conference room.

"Hi, Sharon," Farrah stood and shook her hand. "How are you?"

"I'm doing fine. The question is, How are you? Are you ready for this?" Sharon took a seat at the table.

"Yes," Farrah said, inhaling deep.

Now that the moment was a reality she was struggling with her choice. Had she given up too fast? Had she allowed her emotions to cloud logical thinking? Despite Mills's transgressions, she did still care for him. Farrah had no time left to ponder over the *should've, could've, would've*s, though. It was time for her to sign the divorce papers. There was no turning back now.

After Farrah and her lawyer had reviewed all of the paperwork and the divorce was offically finalized, Farrah met up with London and Camden for lunch at Prime 1000 Steakhouse. Farrah had to treat herself to a fabulous meal after the strenuous morning she had. Prime was an award-winning restaurant that prided themselves on providing their guests with seasonally influenced food.

"So how did everything go?" London asked over drinks.

"It's done." Farrah forced a smile.

"Hallelujah." London waved her hands in the air like a woman in church. "Ding-dong the witch is dead."

"Really, London?" Farrah shot a stern look.

"Yes, ma'am. You should be praising God too. Fuck Mills. He is a pathological liar. Everything he does is on creep mode. Ugh!" London screwed up her face. "I'm glad you got rid of that nigga."

"Well, tell us how you really feel," Camden said, sarcastically.

"I'm just sayin' she should have never married his ass in the first place," London continued with her rant. "You were too good for him. He didn't deserve you."

"Have you talked to him?" Camden asked.

"Nope." Farrah shook her head. "I haven't seen or spoken to Mills since the day I met with him at the coffee place and told him I wanted a divorce. I have no idea what he's been up to."

"It don't matter what he got going on." London rolled her neck. "You have a great dude in your life, who loves your ass to pieces. I'm team J.R. all the way."

"He is pretty wonderful, isn't he?" Farrah blushed as her phone rang. "Speak of the devil. Let me take this y'all. I'll be right back and don't start eating without me," she yelled over her shoulder, walking outside.

"Hello?" she answered sweetly.

"What's up, pretty girl?" J.R. spoke in a raspy tone.

"Hi, my baby," Farrah said, beaming. "How are you?"

"Tired than a muthafucka," J.R. yawned. "This tour is kicking my ass."

"Where are you at tonight? What state?" she asked, feeling bad that he sounded so exhausted.

"We're on our way to Atlanta, Georgia. What you up to?" J.R. gazed out the tour bus window.

"Having lunch with my girls."

"That's what's up. How did everything go?" He referred to her divorce.

"It went well. Everything's done," Farrah said after a pause.

"How are you feeling? You a'ight?" he asked out of genuine concern.

"Yeah, I'm fine," she replied. "I'm just happy that the whole chapter of my life is behind me now."

"Me too," J.R. laughed.

"Shut up," Farrah laughed too. "I miss you," she said, seriously. "It's been forever since we last saw each other."

"I know," J.R. sighed. "But I'ma be there soon. You're all mine when I get there."

"I sure as hell am. I want you to fuck this pussy up baby! And I can't wait to taste your dick, boo. You gonna have that chocolate ready for me?" Farrah joked. She had never been the type to talk nasty to any man she'd ever been with, but with J.R. she could say and act any way she wanted. There was no holding back between them and she loved that about their relationship. He brought out sides to her she never even knew existed, including that extra- freaky side of her.

"You stupid, man," J.R. bugged up laughing. "But listen babe, I gotta go. I'ma let you get back wit' your girls. Have fun."

"Okay." Farrah pouted, not wanting to get off the phone.

"I love you," J.R. spoke.

Farrah's heart skipped a beat hearing him say this. For months she'd wondered why he never said it to her, so she'd been wondering if J.R. felt that way for her. To hear him say that he loved her sent her over the moon, but for some reason she hesitated to say it back. It was like she was too afraid to say it.

"Okay babe, the girls are calling me back to the table. I'll talk to you later." She rushed him off of the phone.

J.R. was really thrown off with the way Farrah rushed him off the phone. He had just said to her the three words that women are always dying to hear from a man. Telling somebody he loved them was no easy task for J.R. There had been only three women he had ever said that to in his life and that was his mother, his first love, and now Farrah.

He had really fucked up with his first love by cheating on her left and right. He was young, dumb, and horny so he was getting pussy from anybody who offered. When his girl found this out she left him and never looked back. J.R. was hurt by all this, but it helped him grow. He eventually realized he was dead wrong for treating her like that and he made a vow that the next woman to have his heart would be his last and he would love, honor, and respect her the way she deserved. And being that he had fallen in love with Farrah, he didn't have time to be playing games with her.

He wanted to call her back and ask her straight up if she loved him, but on the other hand he was struggling hard to give her the benefit of the doubt that she really did have to get back to her girlfriends. He decided to let it be for now. He'd give her another opportunity to tell him she loved him. For now, he was just gonna let it go and get some rest. He was gonna need it if he was gonna put on a helluva concert tonight.

Chapter 22

I told her baby you can spend the night.
        -Lil Twist, "By the End of the Night"

Dr. Keiffer's office was swarming with parents and their rambunctious children. Some kids were sick, others were playing on the floor with toys, some were crying or sleeping. Jade had a massive headache; Jaysin wouldn't stop crying. No amount of patting her on the back or bouncing her up and down soothed her. Jade's appointment time was at 1:00 and it was now a half an hour later and she hadn't been seen.

It didn't make it any better that Jaysin was there to get her shots, which would result in even more crying. It also didn't help that Mills was supposed to meet her there and hadn't shown up yet. He was late as usual. Jade was over it. For months he'd been playing a back-and-forth game of acting as if he was all in, to then distance himself from her.

She didn't understand him. She'd put it out there on several occasions that she loved and wanted him. He'd come over, spend time with her and the baby, take her out, have sex with her, and show affection, but wouldn't fully commit to a relationship. Whenever she pressed the issue he'd get mad and say he was going through a lot and needed some time. Jade tried to be understanding and patient because he was going through a divorce, but he couldn't continue to spoon-feed her doses of hope. She wanted all of him, not half. There was no way in hell she was going to go from being the main chick to being reduced to the side chick.

"Oh my god, Jaysin, will you please stop crying." She placed her up on her shoulder and massaged her back.

Jade needed an aspirin and a cocktail ASAP.

"Sorry I'm late." Mills rushed in.

Jade didn't even respond. Instead, she rolled her eyes.

"Here, get your daughter. She won't stop crying." Jade handed her to him.

"Why haven't you been seen yet? I thought your appointment was at one?"

"It was. Dr. Keiffer is runnin' behind," Jade responded with an attitude.

"What's wrong wit' you?" Mills whispered so no one else could hear their conversation.

"My head hurts." Jade massaged her temple. "And I can never rely on your ass," she snapped.

"What the fuck you talkin' about? I'm here ain't I?"

"Yeah, when you got good and damn ready. I'm sick of everything being on your time."

"You can't be this mad because I'm a few minutes late. What is this about? 'Cause after the day I've had I ain't got time for a bunch of back-and-forth shit with you today?" Mills shot back.

"You ain't got time?" Jade turned and looked at him angrily.

"I swear you are so fuckin' self-centered." Jade shook her head. "It's all about you and your feelings. Fuck everybody else, right? Where were you?"

"For your information, I was late 'cause I was at my lawyer's office finalizing my fuckin' divorce."

Jade paused and let his words seep in. Mills was a free man. He was all hers. Farrah was no longer standing between them being together. If she wouldn't look like a complete fool, Jade would jump for joy and do the running man right in the middle of the waiting room. She had to play it cool, though.

"Mmm . . ." Jade crossed her legs. "So what now?"

"I don't know. You tell me." Mills rocked Jaysin in his arms.

She had finally calmed down and stopped crying.

"Mills, I'm not doing this with you. Either you want to be with me or not. I'm not doing this . . ." She pointed her hand toward him, then back to her. ". . . anymore."

"I guess we can try to work this out."

"You guess?" Jade snarled. "Who do you think I am?"

"Will you calm your crazy ass down? I'm just messing with you," Mills laughed. "I want us to be a family.

"Jade Simmons," the nurse called out her name.

"Well, if you want us to be a family . . ." Jade stood up and looked back at Mills. "Act like it," she said, picking up the baby bag and her purse.

"Okay, that's a wrap everyone! Thank you!" yelled the photographer in charge. As soon as he said this, people were in a total frenzy. The makeup artist started putting her things away. The photographer's assistants were busy taking down the background drop and disassembling the lights. The photographer went back to his desk and started reviewing the pictures he took from today's shoot.

"Excuse me?" said a soft-spoken voice. "Mr. Campbell?" she asked.

"Yes, little lady?" he replied, looking up at the figure standing in his office doorway. "They told me you would have my check ready after the shoot was completed?" she asked.

"Oh yes, that's right. I have it right here for you," Mr. Campbell said, reaching out to give her the check. "The pictures came out great, by the way. Just wait until they hit the stores. This is gonna be great!" he exclaimed as he went back to scrolling through his camera.

"Yes, I'm sure it will," was all he heard. He was about to say something else, but when he looked up, she was gone.

Chapter 23

I will always want you.
        -Miley Cyrus, "Wrecking Ball"

"Oh lord. Kill me now," Farrah groaned, reaching over for a tissue.

She was sick as hell with the flu and had been for a week. Her nose was stuffed up, her throat hurt, and her chest was filled with phlegm. She'd tried numerous medications to shake it, but so far nothing worked. She was in absolute hell. One minute she was hot, the next she was freezing cold. At this moment she was as cold as a glacier. The heat was on, but no amount of heat, blankets, or extra clothes could make her feel warm. She wanted to die. If she coughed one more time she was going to throw something.

"Ugh." She blew her nose.

Then her cell phone rang. It was J.R.

"Hello?" she coughed.

"Hey baby. How are you feeling?" J.R. asked.

"Like death," she said in a hoarse tone.

"Damn, I'm sorry. I wish I could be there to take care of you."

"Me too. This shit is torture." She searched the bed for more medicine, but found that she'd run out.

"Goddamn!" She tossed the box across the room.

"What?" J.R. asked, alarmed.

"I don't have anymore Sudafed." Farrah threw her head back onto the pillow.

"Ask London to run out and get you some more."

"She's still at work," Farrah groaned. "I'ma have to go to the store myself."

"Ain't it like thirty below there?"

"Yeah, I'll be fine," Farrah replied in between coughs.

"You sure you don't want me to send you a nurse?"

"Nah, it's just the flu. I'll survive. Let me get up and run to the store. I'll call you as soon as I get back."

"A'ight be careful babe," he said. "I love you."

"I will. I love you too J.R.," she responded. Farrah felt happy that she had finally expressed her love to him out loud. On the other end of the line, J.R. felt a sense of relief that she had finally said it back.

Minutes later Farrah was at Walgreens. She'd grabbed her medicine and was now in the baby and feminine products aisle. It never made any sense to her why the baby items were always in the same aisle as the feminine products. In true Farrah logic, she thought it was idiotic to have the two in the same aisle, because if a woman was purchasing tampons or pads, that meant she wasn't pregnant. It made perfect sense to her. She walked slowly down the aisle in search of the Kotex overnight maxi pads. Her time of the month was due soon and so she had to make sure she was stocked up. She found the pads at the bottom row and was stooping down to get them when she heard a familiar voice say, "Babe, we gotta get Jaysin some more wipes."

"*No-no-no-no-no,*" Farrah repeated, turning her face in the opposite direction so Mills and Jade would not recognize her.

This cannot be happening, she thought. On all of the days she would run into Mills. She hadn't seen nor heard from him in months and when she did, not only was he with the bitch he cheated on her with, but she was looking a hot freakin' mess. Farrah assumed when she left the house that running into Walgreens would be an in-and-out thing. She didn't care that her hair was pulled up into a ratty ponytail or that she wore a black peacoat, tattered sweatshirt, oversized sweatpants, and rain boots.

She wasn't supposed to run into anyone she knew! Yet here she was with a red stuffy nose, medicine, and overnight maxi pads in her hand. Realizing she couldn't stay crouched down on the floor forever, Farrah rolled her eyes and stood up. Cursing her very existence on earth, she cleared her throat.

"Farrah?" Mills called out, unsure if it was her.

"Hi." She waved her hand awkwardly.

Farrah had never felt like a bigger idiot. She looked like a creature from the woods while Jade stood before her dressed to the nines in a southwestern print oversized cardigan, skintight light blue skinny jeans, and Alexander Wang heels. Mills looked as if he'd stepped straight out of a *GQ* magazine shoot. His sex appeal was at an ultimate high. He donned a black-hooded jacket unzipped, black slouchy T-shirt, black skinny jeans, and Air Yeezys.

But no amount of sex appeal could take away the fact that he was standing in front of her with Jade. She was a little taken aback by the discovery that they were back together. She wondered how long they'd been a couple again. *Had he been fuckin' with her the whole time he was begging me for forgiveness?* she wondered.

In all honesty the timing didn't matter at all. Whether he got with Jade before or after their divorce would not make a difference to her because it stung either way you sliced it.

She wondered if they could see the agony in her eyes. He had to know that he was killing her softly with this shit. How could he go back to the same chick that stepped out on him and made him cry? The same chick that kept his baby against his will and was the cause of them being divorced? Farrah was starting to wonder if she ever really knew Mills at all.

"Funny running into you here," she said, smiling.

"How are you?" Mills reached out for a hug.

"No," Farrah quickly backed up. "You don't wanna do that."

"Exactly," Jade agreed with an attitude.

"I have the flu. I wouldn't want to get you or the baby sick." Farrah looked down at Jaysin, who was in her stroller.

"Oh wow. She's a big girl now. I mean not in a fat kind of way. Just bigger in size," Farrah explained.

"We get it," Jade quipped.

"Jade, I see nothing's changed."

"I concur." Jade eyed her up and down and laughed.

Farrah was always a hot mess whenever Jade was around and now standing there looking like she just came off the unemployment line, she knew Jade would look at her like she was about nothing.

"You two are back together?" Farrah asked Mills, feeling as if her heart was about to explode.

"Yep, one big happy family," Jade responded before Mills could. "Ain't that right baby?"

"It was good seeing you, Farrah," Mills chimed in, unwilling to play Jade's game. "I hope you feel better," Mills said.

"Thanks. Let me go pay for my stuff." Farrah unknowingly held up the bag of pads.

Mortified, she whisked past Jade and Mills. After paying for her things Farrah rushed out of the store, hopped in her Jeep, and sped home. Thank God London was there. Farrah needed someone to talk to.

"London!" Farrah yelled.

"What?" London shouted from her room.

"Girl," Farrah walked briskly into her room. "Guess who I just ran into at Walgreens of all places?"

"Who? Lindsay Lohan? 'Cause I thought I saw her yesterday."

Farrah screwed up her face.

"No fool. Mills and Jade," Farrah said with disgust.

"*Whaaat?*" London's mouth flew open.

"Yes, them muthafuckas are back together."

"I ain't surprised. What you expect from that nigga?"

"Not that shit. He talked about her ass like a dog when we were together. He said he would never get back with her."

"Farrah . . . you know that's what niggas do. They talk mad shit about a bitch and be the main one fuckin' her. Let Mills's sorry ass do whatever it is he gon' do. If Jade dumb enough to go back to his ass then let her. Hell, it's a weight off of your shoulders. Let her deal with his trifling ass and all the drama that comes along with him. 'Cause trust and believe ain't shit about that nigga changed."

Farrah felt like an absolute idiot and low-key stalker for constantly creeping on Mills's Instagram page. She should've been working, but now here she was going through his pics like a crazy ass. Ever since she saw him she hadn't been able to get him off of her mind. Prior to their divorce she hadn't thought about him at all. Mills wasn't even on her radar.

She had tossed his ass up the deuce and kept it moving. J.R. was the only man she was checking for. He'd been nothing but perfect, but after seeing Mills and Jade together a spark was ignited inside of Farrah. She didn't understand why it bothered her or why she cared, but she did. Although he was no longer her husband and she no longer wanted him to be, it pissed her off that he could so easily go back to the same woman who was a part of their demise.

If he'd never slept with Jade they wouldn't be divorced. They'd still be together building a home and a family. But he did and it was obvious that he'd moved on, which made Farrah wonder if all of the tears and begging to be back with her was ever real. How long had he and Jade been back on romantic terms? It'd only been a few months since Farrah had given him the ring back.

From the look of his Instagram pictures Jade's words were true. They were one, big happy family. It also looked like Mills was back living with Jade. Not only was he back living with her, but he was living with her in the home he'd bought for them. Farrah swore she'd been sucker punched in the gut. The disrespect had reached an all-new level. If he was trying to hurt her, he was succeeding. Farrah had way too much respect for their marriage to even dare post pictures of her and J.R. so soon after her divorce.

Obviously Mills didn't share the same sentiments. Every bit of her yearned to pick up the phone and give him a piece of her mind for making her look like such a big fool. But cussing him out wouldn't solve anything. Hurt would still lay in the pit of her stomach.

"What are you doing?" London asked, walking past her door.

"Huh?" Farrah jumped, hiding her phone in her lap.

"Yo' ass is up to something." London walked into her office.

"I don't know what you're talking about." Farrah placed her phone facedown onto her desk. "I'm working on something. The same thing you should be doing instead of worrying about me, you nosy li'l girl." Farrah faced her computer and pretended to work.

"Girl bye. You ain't foolin' me." London swiftly picked up her phone and stepped back.

"Give me back my phone, London!" Farrah hopped up.

"No, ma'am." London swiped the phone to unlock and saw that she was on Mills's Instagram page. "Really bitch?"

"I know!" Farrah sat back down and buried her face into her hands. "I'm an idiot."

"You sure are. Girl, you need to stay off that man's page."

"I can't help it," Farrah confessed.

"Yes you can. How many times do I have to tell you? Fuck Mills!" London slammed her phone down. "I keep tellin' yo' hardheaded ass. So what is it?"

London took a seat at Farrah's desk.

"You call yourself missing him or something? You regret the divorce?"

Farrah swallowed hard.

"I don't know. All I know is I feel some type of way and I don't know why. I don't want him back, but to see him with Jade bothers me."

"But why? This is what you wanted. What? You expected him to stay single or something? This is Mills we're talkin' about here. That nigga can't stay alone for five minutes. Why do you think he keeps on bouncing back and forth between you two?"

"That's the thing, though. I don't think I would be that upset if it were some random chick, but it's Jade. This bitch has caused me so much hell. She's the reason why Mills and I are divorced now."

"Let's keep it all the way one hundred. You and Mills are not together for multiple reasons. Y'all niggas were doomed from the start. That shit was never gonna work. And I understand your feelings being hurt. After all he put you through I would expect you to feel hurt. But you have to remember, my dear friend, that you are better off without him. Not to mention, you have a good man in your life now. J.R. is two times the man Mills is. He's funny, fine with a capital f and he treats you like a queen. Don't let this shit with Mills fuck up what you have going on with J.R." London preached on.

"Yeah, you're right. My man is da bomb dot com," Farrah said snapping her fingers. "I need to stop trippin'."

"You sure in the fuck do!" London said, laughing.

"Thanks for putting me in check, babe. I knew I keep you around for something," Farrah said jokingly.

"Whatever bitch. Bye!" London snapped back as she walked out of Farrah's office.

Chapter 24

I just love when I'm wit' you. Yeah, this shit is on ten.
                    -Drake, "Wu-Tang Forever"

J.R's Compton Most Wanted tour had finally reached St. Louis and Farrah was overflowing with excitement. She hadn't seen him since he flew her out to Germany during the first leg of his tour. Between both of their hectic schedules it'd been damn near impossible for them to link up since. But God had finally shown his favor and brought them back together. Farrah couldn't exit her car and enter the Scottrade building quick enough.

Her heart hadn't truly beaten since she last saw his beautiful chocolate face. The walk to the stage where he was going over sound check seemed like an eternity. Farrah wished she had the speed of a cheetah so she could get to him faster. She didn't want to spend another second apart from J.R. Then she spotted him out of the crowd of people on the stage. There he was on stage talking to the band.

His drummer tapped him on the arm and pointed in Farrah's direction to let him know she was there. J.R. turned around and locked eyes with her. Nothing about her had changed. She was still the prettiest girl in the world. Her bright smile lit up the entire arena. J.R. didn't hesitate to hop down from the stage and greet her with a big hug.

"Promise me we'll never stay apart that long again." Farrah's eyes instantly welled up with tears, upon his touch.

"I promise," J.R. whispered, kissing her neck and ear.

Neither of them cared that they were surrounded by an area full people. To J.R. and Farrah they were the only ones in the room. All that mattered was them cherishing the fact that they were back in each other's arms again.

"You gon' fuck around and make me fall in love with you," J.R. said.

"I thought you already did." Farrah played along.

"Only on Thursdays."

"It must be my lucky day 'cause today is Thursday," she laughed.

"Would you look at that." J.R. smiled fondly at her.

He didn't want to, but J.R. had to end their cakin' session and return to the stage to finish his sound check. After that he was all hers.

"Baby, I gotta get back on stage. You mind sitting out here and watching my sound check?"

"No, I would love to."

"Now I remember why I love you." He kissed her. "You want something to drink or eat? 'Cause this is gonna take a minute."

"Oooh yes, nachos please." Farrah did a happy dance.

"You got it." J.R. winked.

For an hour and a half Farrah sat in the center of the audience and watched her man do this thing. J.R. was a beast on stage. He commanded the stage. Every word he spoke like it was his last. Seeing him in action turned Farrah on to the fullest extent. By the time sound check was over her panties were soaked. J.R. had no idea how riled up she was until they entered his dressing room and Farrah pushed him up against the wall and began to have her way with him.

Dropping her purse to the floor, she held onto his face and kissed him back.

"Damn, I missed you," J.R. whispered as he lifted her up.

"I missed you too," she moaned.

Lifting her skirt, he reached for her thong to push it aside. He realized that she had on a pair of crotchless panties. He looked up and smiled in a conspiratorial way at her, then he unzipped his jeans and let them fall around his ankles. Gliding his way in, he grabbed her waist and stroked. With their eyes focused on his dick, Farrah held onto J.R.'s neck while letting out moans of ecstasy. She knew in her heart that she couldn't continue to play with J.R.'s feelings, but at that moment she had to have one more night of his good loving.

Farrah's neck was so close to his mouth that J.R. had no other choice but to lick and suck it. His hands gripped her waist as he relished the feeling her pussy gave him. He already made up in his mind that no other chick's pussy could feel the same. He almost felt as if he acquired a drug habit messing with Farrah. Her pussy was that addictive. Slowing down a bit, he made sure that every stroke spoke what he was feeling. Intently, he gazed into her eyes while pumping slow and hard.

Staring back at him, Farrah bit into her bottom lip and moaned in delight. She wanted to say something back with her body, but her heart wouldn't allow her to. She pressed up against his chest and she rubbed his back and kissed his ear. Kicking his shoes and pants off, J.R. took her over to the rug by the door, laid her down, and took his shirt off. Now on top of her, he pushed her shirt up and kissed her stomach.

"Ooh!"

Pushing her bra up over her breasts, he began to nibble and suck her nipples while still stroking her.

"You want it deeper?"

"Yes!"

He grabbed her legs, held them in the air, then balanced himself on his knees and pumped faster.

"Ohh, J.R.! Baby, please, I can't take it," Farrah begged.

"I like it when you scream my name like that."

J.R. spread her legs open and slowed it down for her. Taking his thumb, he played with her clit. The combination of his thumb and his dick drove Farrah crazy.

"Ohh, J.R.! Baby, it's yours!"

"Goddamn, yo' pussy drippin' wet. It's drippin' wet for me, baby?" J.R. teased as he felt her nearing an orgasm.

"Yes! Ohh, yes! Yes—ahh, J.R.! Ohh," she squealed as she was about to cum.

"Baby, I'm cumming," J.R. grunted as he came inside of her.

Still cumming, Farrah lay on the floor and held her legs because they were shaking uncontrollably. Panting, she tried to steady her breath, but found it hard to since J.R. was standing above her naked. The sight of his dick alone caused her to cum again. Looking at her, he put his clothes back on. Pulling her bra and shirt back down, she attempted to stand up, but failed.

J.R. reached his hand out to help her and lifted her up off the floor. Standing up, she tried to walk to her office, but she still felt weak and her leg went out on her. Almost falling, she was grabbed by J.R. before she hit the floor.

"You a'ight?"

"I'm fine." Farrah pushed him away. "I can stand up on my own." Embarrassed, she got an attitude yet again.

J.R. laughed.

"Man, you don't' know how happy I am that the show is over and that I get to chill wit' you for the next couple of days." J.R. held Farrah's hand as they entered her home.

"Me too." Farrah unlocked the door and led him in. "So this is my house," she said as they walked into the kitchen and living room area. With their busy schedules, J.R. had never been able to make it to her place until now.

"It's dope." He looked around her decor. "Where is your room?"

"Upstairs." She pointed toward the staircase.

"You wanna put your stuff down and go out onto the balcony?"

"Yeah." J.R. sat his luggage down onto the floor and followed her outside.

A brisk, cold wind swept over them as Farrah leaned on the balcony and looked out over the city. J.R. stood behind her with his arms wrapped around her waist. It didn't even matter how cold it was outside anymore. J.R.'s body heat made her warm.

"Words can't even describe how happy I am that you're here. Like you being here puts everything back into perspective."

"Everything like what?" J.R. questioned.

Farrah knew better than to tell him she had bumped into Mills. Or that she had been questioning her decision to divorce him. It would kill him and crush any future that they could potentially have together.

"Like that God brought us together for a reason. You make my life worth living. No other man has ever made me feel so at peace. There's no drama or remorse with you. You just make loving you so easy."

"That's the way it's supposed to be. Loving someone shouldn't be hard."

Deep down somewhere in her subconscious Farrah knew that J.R.'s words were true, but how could she truly believe that when all she'd ever known was heartache and betrayal? Every man that she'd ever given her heart to used her up and then discarded her emotions like it was yesterday's trash. She always gave more than she got back in return. She always put her all on the line.

No man had ever really truly cherished her heart, so how was she to trust that what she shared with J.R. was true? She believed the best in every man she'd ever dated, only to get the absolute worse out of them. She had to give it to J.R., though. He'd shown her nothing but the best of him so far. She hadn't found one flaw in him yet, which scared the hell outta her.

He is what she'd cried and asked God to give her for so long. She'd asked God for a man who was a faithful, God-fearing man, who was trust-worthy, honest, loyal, supportive, loving, caring, emotionally available, knew how to communicate, not abusive, driven, smart, funny, successful, spontaneous, charismatic, a provider, respectful, not a cheater, and would love her unconditionally. J.R. possessed every one of those qualities and some she'd never even mentioned. It scared Farrah that she could be so close to eternal bliss. To think that it was so close that she could reach and touch it was unfathomable.

"What you thinkin' about?" J.R. rested his chin on her shoulder.

"I just remembered that I have this charity event tomorrow that I cannot miss," she half told the truth. "It's being thrown by Billie Christianson. She's an influential socialite here in St. Louis. Her opinion of you can make you or break you in this town, so it is a must that I attend. You're not mad, are you?" She looked over her shoulder at him.

"Nah, do you thing. I'll just chill here until you get back. I need to catch up on some rest anyway."

"I'll only be gone a few hours. As soon as it's over, I'll be right back here putting this hand down on you."

After spending the entire night, morning, and afternoon making love, laughing, and eating, Farrah was up getting dressed for the charity event. She stood in front of her full-length mir-

ror, putting the finishing touches on her outfit.
Farrah was simply divine with her hair pulled
back in a sleek top knot. The only makeup
she wore was a blood wine-color lipstick and
mascara. The dress she rocked was gold, silk,
spaghetti strapped, and backless. She wore no
earrings or necklace, just a gold Cartier love
bracelet gifted from J.R.

J.R. lay in bed, pretending to watch the basketball on TV, but really he was watching her.
She was something beautiful. Farrah had no idea
just how much he loved her. From the moment
they met he knew that she was the one for him.
No other woman on the planet made him feel the
way she did. In time, he wanted to marry her and
have kids. First he wanted to travel the world
with her and show her how much she was truly
loved by him. He'd swim across the ocean for
her. Anything she wanted he was willing to try
his best to provide.

"Okay baby," Farrah turned around and posed.
"How do I look?"

"Stunning as always."

"Really, you mean it?"

"Fuck yeah. You making me wanna get up and
go wit' you. Muthafuckas getting ready to be on
you."

"I ain't think about none of these fuck niggas out here. You got my heart." She leaned over for a kiss.

J.R. kissed her long and hard. He wanted to give her something to think about while she was gone.

"You sure you don't want to put that dick up in me before I go?" She pulled up her dress.

"If I fuck you yo' ass staying home," J.R. said bluntly.

"You ain't never lied. That dick be pulling me right to sleep."

"Right, so take yo' ass on before I change my mind." J.R. handed her purse to her.

"Okay, well I love you. I'll be back as soon as I can." Farrah sashayed out of the room.

Farrah was about to walk into the ballroom when she remembered she was supposed to buy breath mints on her way there. Luckily, there was a convenience store right across the street so she didn't have to get back in her car and drive anywhere. She made her way into the store and grabbed the breath mints. She was searching for some change in her purse to pay for them when out of the corner of her eye she saw a picture of J.R. and the woman he was with the night of the BET Awards. Next to that picture, there was another picture of the same girl smiling, wearing a pastel yellow baby-doll dress. Right under the breast area was a white ribbon that tied into a perfect bow to accentuate a plump, round pregnant belly. She picked up the *Us Weekly* magazine and her heart dropped when she read the headline: *Compton rapper J.R. is having his first child! Lizzette Perez says she couldn't be happier!*

Farrah felt like she had just had the wind knocked out of her. She grabbed the magazine and the mints, threw a twenty-dollar bill on the counter, and ran out of the store. She found a bench on the sidewalk and began to read the full article. According to the article, Lizzette—or Lizzy, as she preferred to be called—was carrying J.R.'s baby and was five months' pregnant. She claimed she had tried to contact J.R. numerous times, but he would not return her calls. She went on stating that the last time she had seen or spoken to him was at the BET Awards when he left the after party with Farrah Mills. In the article, Farrah was being made out to be a home wrecker, messing up Lizzy and J.R.'s happy relationship. What didn't help was the fact that the article pointed out she was married when all of this happened.

Farrah felt her world crumble before her eyes. It was like déjà vu. Here she was, happily in love with a man who was apparently having a baby with somebody else. Farrah and J.R. had never discussed who the woman was that was with him the night of the BET Awards. She remembered they had joked around about her, but J.R. gave her the impression that she was just there as arm candy that night. She never bothered to ask any more questions on it. Now she wished to God she had.

She took out her phone and tried calling him, but he didn't pick up. He told her he was going to sleep when she left, so he had probably turned his phone off or put it on silent. Farrah had two choices right about now. Go home and confront J.R. about everything or put her business first and still attend the gala. She decided it'd be best for her to go to the event. Her drama would be waiting for her when she got home, so it made no sense for her to skip an event that would be good for the Glam Squad.

The fifth annual Autism Speak Gala at the Coronado Ballroom was a gorgeous affair. The room was gorgeously lit. Forty tables with the finest china filled half the room. Flowers flown in from Africa were formed into the perfect centerpieces. St. Louis's elite was in the building. Everyone from Rams football player Cain Townsend to former Cardinal player Albert Pujols was there. Artists like John Legend and Tamar Braxton were slated to perform. A three-course meal would be served and the finest liquor was being guzzled by the minute.

Farrah hardly knew anyone there besides Billie and socialites Dylan Carter and Mina Gonzalez. She stood alone up against the wall nursing a glass of champagne, wondering when it would be a good time to dip. Her feet were sore from wearing six-inch heels and she had been in a zombie-like state almost the entire time she'd been there. She kept thinking about what she had read and she could not believe this was happening to her. She kept trying to convince herself she was having a nightmare and any second now, she'd wake up.

Farrah glanced down at her watch. It was only a little after 9:00. She'd only been there an hour and was already over it. She was parandoid that perhaps some people at the party had read the article or heard about the rumor and were now talking about her. Everytime someone said hello to her or tried to make small talk, she became nervous that they would ask her about the situation. She'd already cut a check for 5,000 dollars and shown her face. She figured she'd done enough and decided to leave. Farrah gulped down the rest of her drink and headed for the door. On her way out she surprisingly ran into Mills, who was on his way in.

"Mills," she said, shocked.

"Hey." He looked equally as stunned. "I didn't know you would be here," he said, dressed in a custom Tom Ford suit.

He looked as dapper as he did on their wedding day.

"Yeah, I'm about to leave, though." Farrah spoke nervously.

"It's wack in there?"

"As hell," she laughed. "I couldn't take it anymore."

"Shit, you making me not want to go in."

"It's up to you. Just don't say I didn't warn you."

"Where you heading?" he asked, wanting her to stay.

"Home. J.R. is there waiting on me."

"Oh," Mills said with a look of disappointment in his eyes.

"Where is the Wicked Witch of the West? Oops—I mean Jade." Farrah smirked. It felt good to ask about somebody else's business if it meant stepping away from hers for a second.

"She at home," Mills chuckled.

"I'm surprised she's not attached to your hip."

"To be real with you, me too," he joked.

"That chick is crazy, but that's what you like."

"You didn't leave me much of a choice. You didn't want me."

"Mills," Farrah became serious. "Let's not go there."

"I'm just being real. I've been through too much shit to be hiding the way I feel. I miss you and I know somewhere deep down inside you miss me too."

"It doesn't matter if I miss you or not. Us dealing with each other isn't healthy."

"Says who? What we had before I fucked up was pretty fuckin' special."

"It was," Farrah admitted.

"Look, I don't wanna go in there. Let's go grab something to eat and talk."

Farrah didn't know if all the air in her lungs had escaped or not, but it sure felt like she couldn't breathe. This entire day was surreal to her. She had gone from being happily in love with the man of her dreams, to finding out he was having a kid with somebody else, and now here she was talking to her ex-husband. She felt like she was losing her mind. Maybe a quick bite to eat with Mills would help her get her mind off of things. It couldn't hurt anything. They'd eat and catch up and that would be it. She agreed to leave with him and they strolled onto the street. Little did either of them know, but as they left together a random partygoer snapped a picture of them.

Chapter 25

Got my old dude callin' and my new dude waitin'.
-Iggy Azalea, "Down South"

The minute Farrah's back met with the Four Seasons Hotel sheets she realized she'd fucked up in a major way. It was midnight and she and Mills had eaten at Uncle Bill's in their black-tie attire. They'd laughed, reminisced, and caught up on each other's lives. It was as if time had erased all the ill feelings they harbored for one another. When she looked at him Farrah no longer saw hate. All she saw was a man whom she'd once adored and was making her laugh at the moment.

She felt like shit when the reality of what they had done sunk in. On the other hand, though, J.R. had cheated on her, so she had nothing to feel bad about. She was tired of having men dog her out while she just sat there being faithful by

herself. She turned her phone off on purpose just
in case J.R. saw her missed calls. She wasn't up
to getting into a confrontation about him and
his future baby mama. She'd already been down
that road and it was not a road she was willing
to ride on again. Besides, the more she and Mills
talked, the more she realized she still loved him.
As they sat across the table from each other at
the restaurant she realized that they still had
unfinished business that needed attending to.
She had to figure out and understand why she
still cared. Was it because she still loved him? Or
was this a rebound for her because of what she
found out about J.R.?

Did she unknowingly want him back? Whatever
the answer was, she had to figure it out. And no,
fucking Mills wasn't the way to get to the root
of her problems or take away the pain she was
feeling from J.R.'s betrayal, but when he placed
his lips upon her, she felt like she was home again.
This man knew all the kinky things she liked and
he knew exactly what her soft spots were. The
familiar feeling of his hands rubbing her body felt
so right. She couldn't get enough of him. All she
saw was him. All she wanted to think and feel was
how good it felt to have her body pleasured. As he
climbed on top of her and slid his dick inside of her
wetness, she became lost in the euphoric feeling
that overtook her.

***

Mid-morning the following day Farrah was on her way to her apartment. She'd dreaded going home because she wasn't sure what would happen with J.R. when she got there. She wasn't sure if she was ready to confront him about everything. After turning her phone back on, she checked her voice mail and to her surprise, there was no message from J.R. She did hear a few voice mail messages from London telling her to call her back as soon as possible. London had also sent her a bunch of texts. The first few were to tell her about the article and then the rest were just asking Farrah to let her know she was okay. She learned through her Google alert that a picture of her and Mills leaving the charity gala had hit the Net. Farrah didn't care, though. The pictures from the *Us Weekly* article had also hit the Web so J.R. had to have known his spot was blown too. She didn't know what to expect or to find once she walked into the house. J.R. had blown up her phone the entire night. He didn't stop calling her until around six o'clock that morning. Farrah felt like throwing up as she parked her car. Her stomach was turning and she felt like absolute shit as she climbed the steps heading to her apartment.

What would J.R. say to her when he saw her? Would he cuss her out, or yoke her up? Would he admit to his wrongdoing? Would he apologize to her or expect her to apologize to him? Farrah was really not prepared for what was about to happen, but she had to face the music at some point, so she took a deep breath and braced herself.

Farrah slowly stepped into her room and looked around. She didn't see J.R. She kicked her heels off and quietly walked around the room to see if he was hiding in a corner or something. For whatever reason she feared seeing his face. When she didn't spot him or his things, her heart began to beat out of her chest.

"J.R.?" she called out only to get no answer.

He was gone. She should have known better. J.R. wasn't the kind of man to stick around and deal with nonsense. He was not the kind to argue and yell. He simply had no time for it. For them to sit there and get into a back-and-forth on who did what to who would be pointless. It wouldn't even be worth the rage. Sitting on her chaise lounge, Farrah pulled out her cell phone and held it in her hand. She wanted to call J.R. and at least try to get him to have a civil conversation with her. She was hurting and she knew he was hurting too. She felt like the biggest asshole having slept with Mills, though. It was a rash decision in an attempt to cover up the pain she was feeling.

She knew he had to have learned everything by now. There was no way he could not know that she knew about him and Lizzy and she knew he knew about her and Mills. Farrah went into her call log and pressed *call* when she got to his number. Her body felt like a ball of fire as the phone rang. She'd begun to perspire under her arms and under her breasts. With each ring she felt dizzier and dizzier. After six rings and no answer J.R.'s voice mail clicked in. Unable to find the words to explain or express everything that had happened, Farrah hung up.

Unlike Farrah, Mills didn't know that a picture of them leaving the charity gala had hit the Internet. He had his phone on silent the entire night and morning. He figured Jade would be pissed when he walked through the door, but Mills was all prepared to lie and say he'd crashed at Teddy's crib afterwards 'cause he was too drunk. Mills was completely caught off guard by Jade's fury when he entered their home.

"You might as well turn your black ass around and walk right the fuck back out," she snapped.

"I know you're mad, but damn, let me explain."

"Explain what—that you stuck your dick back in that bitch's pussy? Nigga, save it! I don't give a fuck about your explanation. I am going to say this to you, though." Jade got into his face.

"I know I fucked up and did you wrong in the past." She had a sudden flashback of the nights she wouldn't come home and he would call her phone. She would stroll in the house without a care in the world and not bother to give any explanations. If she did ever try to explain, she would just lie and say she had stayed at a friend's house.

"But I can't take it back," she said as she came back to reality. "If I could, I would, but that does not give your ass carte blanche to fuck around with my heart every chance you get. You're not going to keep going back and forth between me and that bitch. Like I told you before if you want her, then go be with her. If you want me, get your shit together and act like it! In the meantime turn your black ass around and get the fuck outta my house!"

Mills wanted to check her and remind her that she was living in his crib, but now wasn't the time. He could see by the tremble in her bottom lip that she was hurt. She was right. She didn't deserve his half-assed, selfish bullshit. He had to figure out his feelings and quick.

Chapter 26

You're my downfall; you're my muse,
my worst distraction, my rhythm and blues.
                              -John Legend, "All of Me"

The media attention surrounding Farrah and the drama between her and Mills and the "love triangle" as the media had titled it between her, Lizzette, and J.R. was crazy. Farrah couldn't leave the house without some photographer in her face. They camped outside her house and her office. It had never been this bad before. Farrah hated all of the media attention especially since it was for a negative reason. All of the gossip surrounding her life was surreal.

To make matters worse, another article was released a few days ago stating that Lizzette Perez was not pregnant with J.R.'s baby. It said that Lizzette and J.R. used to mess around at one point, but that they had stopped long before she became pregnant so it was highly unlikely that the baby would be his. The article did not disclose who the source was that stated all this. They just said that it came from a very reliable source. To read that the rumors might not be true was a relief and a burden for Farrah. In a huge way it was like a weight lifted off of her shoulders to know that J.R. hadn't cheated and gotten someone pregnant after all. On the other hand, though, this left Farrah with a lot of explaining and apologizing to do, because now she was the only one in the relationship that had cheated. The guilt of her sleeping with Mills was eating her up and she still wanted to talk to J.R. about everything. She didn't feel right that he never gave her the chance to talk about any of this.

She had called him twice since her initial phone call and he still hadn't answered the phone or returned her calls. She wondered how long he'd continue to give her the silent treatment, because so far the silence had been excruciating. Parked in an alley, Farrah sat with a black snapback and oversized Chanel shades on. Deciding she'd try calling J.R. one more time, she picked up her phone and dialed his number.

This time instead of it ringing a million times, her call was forwarded straight to voice mail. Farrah didn't know how much she could take.

She felt like she'd been slapped in the face. She didn't understand why he wouldn't at least speak to her so they could disscuss everything. He had to understand that she was just as mad as he was at one point. She slept with Mills under false notions. She was under the impression that J.R. had betrayed her at the time it happened.

Instead of hanging up like she'd done each time before, Farrah decided to leave a message.

"Hey, it's me. Umm . . . call me back. I really want to talk to you about everything that's happened. I didn't mean to leave you sitting at my place like that. You gotta understand, I read the article about you and Lizzette on my way to the gala. I had a lot to drink and wasn't thinking when I bumped into Mills. Anyway, I miss you. Call me back," she spoke softly.

Ending the call, Farrah stared out the window. She hoped J.R. would call her back this time, but even if he did, how would she defend her actions? She just felt horrible. Farrah didn't even have time enough to ponder her message when she heard a tap on her window. Caught off guard by the sudden sound, she jumped. She had no reason to be afraid, though. It was only Mills. They'd agreed to sneak and meet up to talk. Farrah unlocked the door and let him in.

"It's cold as a muthafucka out here," he said, shivering.

"Hi," she said flatly.

"You know with that hat and glasses on you look even more noticeable."

"Whatever." She flicked her wrist.

"This shit is crazy, man. These muthafuckin' paparazzi just won't quit."

"I'm sick of their asses." Farrah rolled her eyes.

"So what's going on wit' you?" Mills settled back in the passenger seat.

"Well, J.R.'s done fuckin' with me. The night you and I hooked up he was at my house."

"Damn," Mills laughed.

"That shit ain't funny," Farrah snapped. "I should have never left with you. I should've taken my ass home and you should have too."

"I know. I just don't like that nigga." Mills sucked his teeth.

"Why? He's done nothing to you. You're the one who fucked his bitch."

"Well, you couldn't have been so much his if it was so easy for you to sleep with me," Mills countered.

"I am his!" Farrah shot back, trying to make her words true.

"You ain't got to convince me," Mills scoffed.

"Anyway," Farrah changed the subject. "What happened between you and Jade?"

"She put me out," Mills laughed.

"Explain to me what the fuck is so funny?" She looked at him like he was crazy.

"It's funny 'cause she put me out of a house that ain't hers."

"Yeah, it's mine, but let's not even get in to all that," Farrah said as she rolled her eyes.

"You mean it's mine. You didn't want the house when I offered it to you. Remember?" Mills countered.

"Whatever! Your ass was dead fucking wrong for moving her ass into a house you bought for me in the first place. She probably don't even know that you did that shit."

"You can't get mad, Farrah. What I do is none of your business anymore. You're the one who wanted the fuckin' divorce. Live with your damn decision," Mills spat back.

"It's hard to live with my decisions when I still have feelings for you. I don't get it. I love you, but I know we shouldn't be together. Why does everything have to be so complicated?" Farrah said as she put her head in her hands. You could hear the desperation in her voice.

"I agree. I still care about you, but I love my family."

To hear Mills say that he loved his family hurt Farrah to the core. Jade had always been a thorn in Farrah's side. Hearing Mills say he loved his family was the same as him saying he loved Jade.

"Why am I even here?" she mumbled under her breath.

"What? What you say?" Mills asked.

"Nothing, I gotta go." She turned the key, starting the ignition.

The vibe inside the studio was mellow. The lights weren't up too high. The temp on the track J.R. was laying down was at a hypnotic pace. Bottles of liquor flowed and the finest weed was being lit. J.R. didn't care for any of that stuff, though. For hours he tried to spit some of the illest verses he could come up with, but the voice mail message Farrah left him a week prior plagued his mind. He was pissed that she had the balls to leave him that bullshit.

She'd obviously fucked her ex-husband and didn't even think enough of him to admit the truth. She at least deserved to give him that. But Farrah was a coward. He should've realized that from the moment they met. She didn't have the guts to leave her idiotic husband after he'd cheated on her and bore a child with another woman. But J.R. had looked past all that in hopes that she'd become his girl and he could show her what true love was really like.

But it was obvious no matter how much he proved his love for her, she would never accept it or see it for what it was because of how messed up she was from her past. It was like subconsciously she thought she didn't deserve it. What hurt J.R. so much was that she was so quick to go back to her ex and sleep with him off of some stupid article she read in a lame-ass magazine like *Us Weekly*. J.R. had never given her a reason to doubt him or mistrust him. He kept it real with her from the start. Maybe he should have told Farrah a little more about him and Lizzy's past, but he didn't think it was necessary. The past didn't matter to him. The picture of Farrah and Mills didn't show them doing anything physical, but J.R. had a gut feeling something had gone down between the two of them the night of the gala event.

That night J.R. put his phone on vibrate as soon as Farrah was gone so he didn't hear his phone when Farrah tried calling him. When he woke up around four o'clock the next morning and checked his phone, his mailbox was full of messages from Farrah, the press, his publicist, and everybody else trying to talk to him about the article with Lizzette and the pictures of Farrah and Mills. Everything happened so fast, he had to leave her house and go somewhere to clear his mind. He knew better than to call Farrah back because he had to collect himself before talking with her. He wanted to get all his facts straight before speaking with her.

Once he came to grips with everything going on, he moved quickly to do some damage control. He confronted Lizzy and tried to straighten everything out. That conversation was still plaguing his thoughts. He never thought Lizzy would be the type to pull some grimy shit like that. Even though it had happened a little over a week ago, J.R. still remembered it.

He had pulled up to her apartment and banged on the door until she answered.

"J.R., what are you doing here?" she asked as if he was the last person she expected to see.

"Are you fucking kidding me, Lizzette? You claiming to be pregnant with my seed and pose for some pictures and you don't know why the fuck I'm here?" J.R. yelled, walking past her and into the living room.

"I'm sorry, J.R., but I didn't know what else to do," she said as she sat on the couch and put her head down.

"Da fuck you mean you ain't know what to do?" J.R. looked down at her round stomach. "You know damn well that ain't my baby you're carrying, so why are you dragging me into something I ain't got shit to do with?" he asked.

Lizzy looked up at him and started sobbing uncontrollably. At first J.R. didn't care that she was crying. She deserved for him to yell at her. If he was any other type of man, she might've even been hit. But the more she cried and he saw how vulnerable and fragile she looked sitting on the couch crying, his anger began to subside a little bit.

"Look, Lizzy. I don't know what's going on with you, but you know that's not my baby. Me and you haven't had sex in a long time." J.R. spoke to her as he joined her on the couch.

"I know, J.R. I'm sorry," she said turning toward him. "I let my emotions get the best of me. I felt so stupid when you left me standing in the club. I really liked you and you just walked out with her without even saying anything to me. You never even called me to say it was over, J.R. You broke my heart!" she said as she broke out crying again.

"Okay, I was wrong for that. I should have never led you on like that and I'm sorry. But where in there do you get off saying you're pregnant by me?" J.R. asked, still trying to make sense of things.

"After not hearing from you for a few weeks, I went out drinking and I had a one-night stand with some random guy. I didn't get his number or anything, because I wasn't trying to have any connections with him," she explained. "So a few weeks later when I didn't get my period I panicked. I didn't get an abortion because I couldn't live with myself if I did that, so I decided to keep it." She stopped to blow her nose. "But then my doctor bills started adding up and I was desperate. I had heard rumors that magazines pay money for information and stuff, so I went to *Us* magazine and I told them I'd sell them the story and pose for pictures if they paid me." She turned to J.R. and looked up at him. "I was mad at you for not calling me and I knew if I told them it was your baby they'd pay me more money. I didn't think I'd feel so dirty after I did it. I tried to take it back, but it was too late. I'm sorry, J.R.!" she exclaimed, breaking out into tears again.

J.R. didn't know what to make out of what she had just told him. He was still pretty upset over what she did, but when he looked at her, he saw a desperate girl, alone and confused and he felt sorry for her.

"Okay. Listen, I'm still pretty pissed about what you did, but I'm gonna help you out and in return I need you to help me out," he said to her.

"What is it? I'll do anything," Lizzy said in a hopeful tone.

"I'm gonna give you some money to help you get on your feet and get ready for this baby of yours. All I ask of you is that you call the magazine and have them retract your story. Fair enough?" he asked.

"Okay. J.R., thanks for helping and being understanding. You really are one of the few good guys left," she said to him.

"Nigga!" One of the producers snapped J.R. back to reality. He had gotten lost in his thoughts again.

"My bad, son. Just give me a few," J.R. said to the producer as he walked out of the studio.

J.R. decided it was time to call Farrah. He'd ignored her phone calls long enough. J.R. pressed her name on his phone and waited for her to pick up.

"Hi, this is Farrah. Leave a message at the beep."

"Ay, I got your message. I love you and I can't change that, but you're a selfish person. Like . . .

you're selfish. I've worked hard at getting over the in-love part and I'm not trying to regress. I'm not tryin' to double back to that. You say you miss me . . . I miss you too, but man . . . I'm done. Be good." With that, J.R. hung up and went back to the studio. J.R. was over giving his all to her. If she couldn't comprehend how much he cared for her, then oh, well. She could continue down the self-destructive path she was on without him.

Farrah turned off the hot water that trickled down her body like raindrops and got out of the shower. Her phone had rung and by the sound of the ringtone she knew it was J.R. She was elated and sick to her stomach that he'd finally called her back. There was no telling what he was going to say. To her surprise, Farrah saw that he left her a message. Farrah pressed the number one, dialing her voice mail and listened to what he had to say.

When the words *I'm done* met with her ears, tears flooded her eyes. For some strange reason she'd tricked herself into believing that he'd forgive her or maybe that was the lie she told herself to get through the night. She never deserved to have a man like J.R. in her life. She was damaged goods. Her heart had been broken too many times to believe that true love could really exist for her. All she knew were tear-filled nights and unkept promises.

No man she ever dated loved her enough to stay. They all took her love and devotion for granted. No man ever treated her like the precious stone she thought she was. Every time J.R. told her how beautiful she was and how much he loved her, she never truly believed it. Now because of her distrust in men she'd lost one of the great ones.

Chapter 27

Act like an adult, have an affair for once.
  -Mýa featuring Jay-Z, "Best of Me (Remix)"

"Oh my god," Farrah peeked out of the window at the paparazzi, who swarmed her house.

"They've been out there all day. You would think they would've found a better story to write about by now." She closed the blinds.

"They will," London said, drily.

She was on the living room couch, eating popcorn and watching *106 & Park*. She was hardly in the mood to hear Farrah whine about the drama she'd created.

"This shit is getting out of hand, though," Farrah replied, oblivious to her friend's attitude. "Everywhere I go, they're there. I can't stay cooped up in this house forever. I have to get back to work."

"You sure in the fuck do. I'm tired of picking up your slack," London shot.

"You act like me missing work is my fault." Farrah sat beside her on the couch.

"Umm . . . bitch, it is," London said, mad as hell.

"How? It's not my fault that some nosy mutha-fucka took a picture of me and Mills leaving the party together."

"That's the thing. You shouldn't have been leaving with his ass in the first place. I told you not to fuck with him, but *noooo*, yo' big-head ass is hardheaded. Now look, your ass can't even leave the house and our business—" London pointed her hand back and forth between them— "is suffering. Ain't nobody got time for that."

"London, it's easy for you to say *leave him alone and don't fuck with him*," Farrah mocked her voice. "'Cause you've never had a husband."

"And bitch, neither have you," London snapped. "When are you going to get that Mills is a grimy person and definitely not the person for you? I'm so tired of seeing women try to make shit work with fuckin' niggas that ain't even worthy enough to tie they shoes. Like I told you before, nothing about Mills has changed. Hell, he probably has got worse because now he sees how big of a dummy you are."

"Whoa-whoa-whoa! Flag on the field. " Farrah signaled her hands like an NFL referee. "Your ass is going too far. You just violated the friendship code, my nigga. I'm dumb now? That really hurt my feelings," Farrah said, genuinely hurt.

"I'm sorry friend." London reached over and patted her hand. "I didn't mean to hurt your feelings, but you are stupid, though." She cracked up laughing.

"Fuck you." Farrah threw up her middle finger. "Who knows, I probably am—"

"You are," London interjected.

"But I can't for the life of me escape these feelings I have," Farrah continued on. "I love J.R., I do and I would give anything to make it work, but he's made it crystal clear that he ain't fuckin' wit' me."

"And he shouldn't," London agreed.

"Make me feel worse, why don't you."

"I'm just saying, you lost one," London mimicked Chrisette Michele's voice.

"I know I did." Farrah stared off into space somberly. "I don't know . . . it's just something inside of me that's confused and fucked up. I want to be happy, but I don't know how to get there."

"Maybe this is why things didn't work out between you and J.R. Maybe you have to find your happy before you can truly be with him."

***

Mills had only been put of the house a little over a week, but for him that was a week too long. He didn't realize how much he'd grown to love his family until he was forced to be away from them. He hadn't been able to wake up and see his daughter's beautiful face or be able to roll over and sample some of Jade's sweet nectar. He couldn't say that he was madly in love with Jade anymore, but he did care for her greatly.

No matter how you cut it, she was permanent fixture in his life. At one point they had a solid relationship, then she cheated and everything turned to shit. Mills hadn't been the same since. He would never put himself in the position to be hurt again. After Jade played him to the left and treated him like shit, a piece—if not most—of his heart died.

Mills realized that the world was a cold, selfish muthafucka and that you could truly trust no one. He loved Farrah when they were together and really didn't want her to leave, but by the time they got married Mills had already spiraled down the rabbit hole of only giving a fuck about himself. It sucked that everyone around him had to be a causality of his selfish ways, but Mills wasn't here to pacify feelings anymore.

The only thing he cared about was securing his own happiness and if that meant he had to lie or cheat, then so be it. Mills knew that in order to get back into the house peacefully he had to tell Jade what she wanted to hear. On that cold night he escorted her out to a lovely, romantic dinner at Scape. Scape was his go-to spot when he was trying woo chicks. Jade pretended as if she wasn't going out, but secretly she was doing cartwheels inside.

The fact that she could put Mills out of his own house and he still came running back to her was a turn-on. Mills's constant attention made her feel special and wanted. But she could never let him see how weak she truly was. She had to continue to show him her poker face. For it to have been a Friday night the restaurant wasn't as packed as it normally was. Mills sat across from Jade and ordered a nice bottle of wine from the bar. While they waited he and Jade began to chat.

"I wonder, is Jaysin asleep yet?" Jade looked at her watch. "I should call the babysitter and see how she's doing." Jade reached for her phone.

"Naw, chill. She's a'ight. If she wasn't we would've received a phone call by now."

"Okay." She put her phone up. "I just get so nervous whenever I leave her."

"That's natural. You're her mother, but right now you're with her father and Daddy needs some attention."

"That's Daddy's problem. It's always about what Daddy wants, fuck everybody else."

"Not true. None of this tonight is about me. This is all about you."

"Who do you think you're fooling, Mills? My ass wasn't born yesterday. This is about your ass wanting to come home."

"You do realize that I can come home anytime I want. It is my house," Mills said, sarcastically.

"You love throwing that shit up in my face, don't you? We all know that's your raggedy-ass house." Jade curled her upper lip.

"I'm just stating facts so you can understand it's not about that. Me taking you out to dinner is about me trying to show you that I love you and that I care." Mills gazed deep into her eyes.

"What I did with Farrah wasn't cool. It was a one-time thing and I shouldn't have done it, but I can't take it back. What I can do is tell you that I'm sorry. I shouldn't have done you like that. You've been nothin' but good to me since we started back fuckin' around."

"You can say that again," Jade agreed.

"Straight up." Mills reached across the table and took her hand. "I love you and I choose you. I don't want anybody else. All I want is you and Jaysin. Y'all are my family. Farrah or no other broad can come between that."

Jade wanted to react joyfully about Mills choosing her, but what kind consolation prize was that? Sure, he wanted her 'cause being with her meant he'd have access to his daughter, in-house pussy, a clean house, and a home-cooked meal everyday. Jade was no fool. She knew Mills's MO. The sad part was she didn't care. At that stage in her life she was content with the bullshit.

She understood that men were incapable of being with only one woman. In Jade's eyes all men cheated. It was the nature of the beast. No matter how hard a woman tried, a man just couldn't be tamed. They only knew how to be savage beasts. Being a woman you had to learn how to adapt to their environment or be left behind. Jade chose to adapt.

She was the kind of chick who thoroughly enjoyed the perks of dating a rich and successful man. Motherhood hadn't curbed her appetite for the finer things in life. Balmain, Lanvin, and Jimmy Choo stayed calling her name. She loved living a lavish lifestyle. Being with Mills afforded her the ability to be a stay-at-home mom. She didn't have to lift a finger if she didn't want to. Jade could be pretty and fly at all times.

Besides, her life now was a far better cry then how it was when she first met Mills. Suddenly

Jade got a flashback of being in Atlanta at the infamous Magic City strip club. The year was 2002. Mills and his crew were seated right by the stage in brown leather chairs, getting fucked up. Mills was higher then a muthafucka. He'd just won his first race and he was out celebrating. All the ATL playas were out that night.

Usher, Jermaine Dupri, Ludacris, and T.I. were there showing him love. Mills had already wasted five grand buying out the bar and throwing money on stage. To him the night couldn't get any better. Then the in-house DJ got on the mic and announced that the feature dancer of the night was about to hit the stage.

"Yo, watch this bitch that's about to come out," his boy Buck said.

"Please welcome to the stage Xtacy!"

Then through the speakers the words, *"All the chronic in the world couldn't even mess wit' you, you're the ultimate high. Here what I'm saying baby, Now check this out."*

Focusing his eyes on the stage, Mills watched as Xtacy crawled to the middle of the stage like a feline. Jodeci's "Feenin'" was playing as she eyed the crowd through her piercing black, slanted eyes. Immediately Mills was drawn to her. Xtacy wasn't like most strippers. She didn't come out pussy poppin' and sticking bottles in her coochie. She had a sense of sensuality about her. All of her movements were slow and catlike.

Unlike the other strippers who performed in the usual stripper attire of nothing but leather and spandex, Xtacy wore an all-black lace halter baby-doll top with matching black G-string panties from Agent Provocateur. Her hair and makeup wasn't wild or crazy-looking either. Everything was tastefully done. Just a simple wrap, smoky eyes, and Chanel lip gloss for her. To complete the ensemble she wore bronze body butter and black five-inch stilettos. The men were awestruck, to say the least. She looked like a naughty angel sent from heaven.

While K-Ci sang the words, *"Take my money, my house and my cars"* Xtacy twirled around the pole wondering who would be her victim that night. The club was filled with ballas so she had a lot of men to choose from. Making eye contact with Mills, she smiled. He was the perfect prey, dripping with ice, high as hell, and drunk as a skunk. Rolling over onto her back all the while still holding her gaze, Xtacy parted her legs.

Mills was in the high-rollers' section so she made sure to give him all she had. With her head arched back she looked at him and ran her wet tongue across her glossy upper lip. Rotating her hips, she began to play with her pussy. Mills didn't know if he was high and trippin' or was it the yak taking its effect, but he could have sworn she was staring at him. He had to make sure what he was thinking was true so he winked at her. Sure enough, she winked back.

He couldn't believe it. The girl was actually getting off on stage just by looking at him. Rolling back over onto her stomach, Xtacy took both of her legs and placed them into a Chinese split. Now sitting up, she humped the floor while her booty bounced in the air, all the while still staring at Mills. Then, out of nowhere she stopped, flashed a wicked grin, and got up.

The song was over and Mills didn't even know it. He never wanted the moment to end. Xtacy didn't even pay him any mind as she collected the twenty, fifty, and one-hundred-dollar bills from off the stage and left. To her it was nothing but a job and her shift was over.

Mills, on the other hand, wasn't through yet. He had fallen right into her trap. Something inside of him had to have her right then and there so he got up from the table and headed toward the back. Just as he was entering the back, Xtacy was exiting the stage and heading for the dressing room. Clearing his throat, he stepped to her.

"Yo, can I holla at you for a second?"

"How did you get back here? Shank, come get this nigga!" Xtacy yelled, irritated with his presence.

"Ay, calm down shorty I ain't out to harm you. I'm just tryin' to talk to you, see what's up."

"Look, get yo' ass away from me! I don't know you like that! *Shank!*"

"It's cool Xtacy. This is Mills. He's a friend of Ted," the guard Shank assured.

"Oh." Xtacy calmed down and looked Mills up and down.

She liked what she saw. He was tall with braids and smoldering brown eyes, but his looks didn't faze her one bit. What was in his pocket was her main concern. Giving him one last look she flung her hair over her shoulder and walked away. *No, this bitch ain't tryin' to play me*, Mills thought, but that thought went out the window once he caught a glimpse of her ass again. Xtacy had a big ol' voluptuous ass. Looking at her butt jiggle as she walked made Mills's dick even harder.

"Slow down mommy. I know you ain't gon' do me like that!" he yelled as he ran to catch up with her.

The girl could walk fast in some heels.

"Look!" Xtacy quickly turned around, stopping him dead in his tracks. "What happened on stage was just an act. Don't take it seriously, homeboy."

"Trust me, I know how to put on an act too, but what you did up on that stage wasn't no act. Yo' ass was for real," Mills countered.

"You think so?" Jade said, smirking.

"I know so."

Giving him the once-over again, Xtacy knew that she could trick at least a grand out of him, maybe more, so she placed her finger up to his lip, winked, and motioned for him to follow. With a walk made for the catwalk, she escorted him to the champagne room. Mills couldn't take his eyes off her ass. He was sprung off sight.

Xtacy held the door open for him and told the other guard Boo to give them some privacy. Boo knew the drill. Xtacy was about to put her thang down. The room was dimly lit. One brown leather couch sat up against the wall and a silver pole was placed in the middle of the floor. Two glasses and a bottle of Hennessy were already in the room so she poured them both a drink. While Mills wasn't looking, she dropped two E pills into his drink. He wanted a show and a show was exactly what he was gonna get.

"Here you go." She smiled deviously while handing him his drink.

"Thanks, ma."

Mills drank the whole thing in one gulp. Xtacy was happy to see him drink it all up. Now all she had to do was stall until the pills took effect on him. Holding onto the pole, Xtacy bent over and shook her ass while looking at him through her legs. Then she took her hand and slid it down the crack of her ass. Still bent over, she began playing with her clit again. Mills was in a trance. The girl knew how to move her body. Swiftly, without taking her eyes off of him, she dropped to the floor, got back up, and made her booty clap.

With a look of lust in her eyes, she turned around and unsnapped the top of her top. As the top fell to her waist, she bit down into her lower lip and massaged her breasts. Mills was on cloud nine. For some strange reason, he wanted to touch her real bad. Xtacy continued to massage her breasts and lick her nipples as she wound her hips to the beat of R. Kelly's "Seems Like You're Ready."

"Come here, ma." Mills couldn't take it anymore.

Smiling from ear to ear, Xtacy strutted over and straddled him. Not wasting any time, Mills took her breasts into his hands.

"Uh, ahh nigga no hands," she ordered while slapping his hands away.

Not missing a beat, Xtacy continued to wind her hips. Grinning, she bit down into her lower lip. Mills's dick was rock-hard and she could feel every inch of it. Smiling at a job well done, she ran her hands through her silky hair and slid them down her body slowly while rolling her torso like a belly dancer. Xtacy was in absolute control and loved every minute of it.

Swinging her hair over to the side, she made sure that he had a good view of her caramel-colored breasts. "Fuck this," Mills thought. His dick couldn't take it anymore so he placed his strong hands onto her wanting breasts again. Her nipples reminded him of Hershey kisses. Gently, he took one into his mouth and licked. The feel of his tongue on her nipples was sensational. Xtacy herself couldn't even deny the feeling.

Flipping her over onto her back, Mills gazed into her eyes and said, "State your name?"

"What?" she asked, caught off guard.

"Tell me your name," he demanded.

"Xtacy."

Knowing she was lying, he ignored her and made his way down. Normally he wouldn't go down on someone he didn't know, but tonight was different. His body was commanding him to. With her legs pushed back, Xtacy's pink clit was staring him in the face, begging him to lick it. She had to have the prettiest, juiciest pussy he'd ever seen. Burying his face in between her thighs, Mills licked her clit until she creamed.

"Damn you taste good," he whispered into the lips of her pussy.

"I know," she moaned as he licked faster.

In a matter of seconds Xtacy's thighs began to shake.

"*Oooooooooooh* . . . shit! Goddamn muthafucka, I'm cumming!" she screamed, cumming all over his lips.

Wiping his mouth, Mills made his way back up and said, "Now answer me. What's your name?"

"Xtacy," she panted, still reeling from her orgasm.

"Stop with the games. What's your real name?"

"Xtacy, what I just—"

Mills had rammed his ten-inch dick inside her warm, wet slit, hitting bottom.

"Now tell the truth," he groaned pumping in and out.

"Okay, okay, it's Jade!"

Jade hadn't meant for things to go this far. She figured she would get him buzzed, dance a little bit, then rob him of his wallet, but somehow Mills had flipped the script on her. She wondered if the pills she had slipped in his drink were defective. Truth was, there was nothing wrong with the pills. They hadn't worked on him because Mills and his peoples at the time popped pills on the regular, so two little E pills had no effect on him.

"You wet than a muthafucka!" Mills roared.

Ready to bust his first nut, Mills came long and hard inside of her. They didn't even use a condom. Once they were done, Jade got up and placed her clothes back on. Mills wanted to see her again, but he didn't want to seem desperate, so he went into his pocket and handed her ten one-hundred-dollar bills. She didn't know it then, but a month later Jade would be using some of that very same money to get an abortion.

A part of her did want to keep the baby, but she was in no position to have to raise a kid. She was barely taking care of herself as it was and besides that, she never even got his name or number to tell him or take him for child support. There was no way in hell that Jade was going to raise a child on her own, so she did what was best for her at the time and aborted the fetus.

Now, years later, the two were sitting and having lunch with one another. Even after all that time, the chemistry was still there. When she wasn't with Mills for the brief period of time they were broke up, Jade hated the struggle of having to fend for herself again. She didn't like it one bit, so if it meant she had to put up with a side bitch or him coming home at all times of the night or not coming home at all, then so be it. *It was the nature of the beast, the call of the wild.* Jade would be damned if she was left behind.

Chapter 28

I know there was a reason that I had to walk out but now I can't remember what the fight was about.
                    -Ledisi, "I Miss You Now"

The aromatic scent of lavender and honey flowed through the room like a note from a song as Farrah, London, and Camden enjoyed their girls' day at the spa. They were getting the full treatment: massages, facials, body wraps, hair, makeup, nails, and feet done. The day would be filled with nothing but relaxation and fun. Farrah missed kicking it with her girls.

For the past few weeks she'd been hanging pretty tough with Mills. Surprisingly, they'd been getting along famously and hadn't argued once. It had been nothing but laughter and fun. Knowing that London felt some type of way about her rekindled romance, Farrah chose to keep the two separate. She didn't feel like hearing London talk about Mills or vice versa.

She was over their nonstop shit talking. She
didn't have the time nor the patience for it. They
both would have to learn to accept the other.
Besides, Farrah needed both of them in her life.
London kept her grounded and sane. She kept
Farrah's mind on point. Mills was there to fill
the void of missing the hell outta J.R., which had
suddenly become harder.

Farrah felt as if she was going through heroin
withdrawals. The fact that all communication
was ceased was unbearable. She thought about
J.R. constantly through her days. There wasn't
a day that didn't go by where she didn't call or
think of him. Unfortunately for Farrah, he never
picked up the phone. He was a man of his word
and when he said he was done dealing with her,
he meant it.

J.R. deading her completely only made her
want him even more. She regretted breaking his
heart. She wished that she had the power to turn
back time and take it all back. Every time she
heard his music or saw one of his videos tears
welled up in her eyes. She loved and cared for
J.R. so much and since she couldn't have him
she needed someone to fill the void of J.R.'s
absence. That was another reason why she was
hanging out with Mills so much. Farrah couldn't
stand to be alone. Farrah sat at the manicurist's

table getting a fill-in as Camden and London got their feet done.

"When are we going to go out again? I feel we haven't been out in forever," London said, as she got her feet scrubbed.

"Ooh, let's go out tonight," Camden replied, gleefully.

"I'm down. What about you, Farrah?" London asked.

"I can't." She looked over her shoulder and poked out her bottom lip. "I have a date tonight with Mills."

"Mmm," London rolled her eyes.

"Please don't start. Today is supposed to be drama-free, remember?" Farrah said, irritated.

"I ain't sayin' a muthafuckin' thing. That's on you." London closed her eyes and relished the hot water swooshing around her feet.

"What's all on me?" Farrah asked, unable to let her comment go.

"Let it go. It don't even matter. If you like it, I love it."

"Good," Farrah snapped. "Then quit saying smart shit."

"Don't be getting no attitude with me, li'l girl," London shot back.

"Whatever, London. Your opinion isn't always necessary."

"In this case it is because I'm tryin' to stop you from making the biggest mistake of you life—but oops, too late." London smirked.

"London, you act like you're the relationship guru. You make fucked-up choices too, but I don't judge you, do I? I try to be there for you. Why can't you do the same for me?"

"C'mon guys, can't we all just get along," Camden joked, trying to lighten the mood.

"No-no-no-no." London sat up. "She wants to take it there, I'ma go there. Yes, I've made some stupid decisions when it comes to men, but the thing is I've learned from mine, unlike you."

"If this doesn't end now somebody's going to get stabbed," Camden said, becoming nervous.

"Okay well, I'm hardheaded. Shit take a li'l longer to sink in for me," Farrah replied with a laugh.

"Obviously," London laughed too. "Look, I'm not trying to hurt you or anything. I just don't wanna see you go through the same bullshit you've been going through. I couldn't go through that over and over again. But I understand that everybody handles things differently."

"Thank you," Farrah said, nodding. "Now can we please put the subject of me and Mills to rest?" Farrah asked.

"My pleasure."

***

Checking her watch, Farrah saw that she had less than an hour to get dressed. She was late for a date with Mills. Racing back into her room, she hurried and took a shower, applied her makeup, then stood in front of her walk-in closet. Farrah's closet was magnificent. It held five hundred outfits and well over three hundred pairs of shoes. Everything was colored coordinated and was put together according to style and season. She even had a rotating rack installed. If she wanted a specific outfit, instead of digging for it, all she would have to do was press a single button located on her wall.

Since she didn't know where they were going or what he had planned, she chose a simple, deep V-neck pink spaghetti strap baby-doll dress. Since it was a little chilly out, she adorned her arms with a pink shrug. Matching the dress with a pair of silver Gucci heels, she adorned her ears with a pair of diamond hoop earrings by Harry Winston. Andre already styled her hair into a bun and the M.A.C makeup she applied was flawless. Grabbing her silver clutch purse and keys, she headed out the door.

Twenty minutes later Farrah was at the Shell station on Arsenal. She looked on as Mills stepped out of his Benz truck. Every time she saw him she was amazed at how well he dressed and how good he looked. Mills was undeniably sexy. His hair and goatee were freshly cut and perfectly lined. His kissable lips looked good enough to eat. Just the sight of him turned her on. His gray Sox baseball cap, crisp white T-shirt, jeans, leather jacket, Tims, and an iced-out chain brought out the thug in him that she loved. The way he dressed reminded her of J.R. Both men had such style and swag. Farrah couldn't understand how she managed to love two men who were so alike yet so different at the same time. It was as if both men had the same hold on her.

"You look nice," she said, collecting her thoughts.

"Thank you." Mills smiled as she got out of the car. "You're going to ride with me. My man is going to watch your car while we're gone." A little unsure but not wanting to seem like a punk, Farrah agreed. Walking over to his car, she wondered if he was going to tell her that she looked nice.

"I'm glad I wore this dress because it's hot out here." She fanned herself, trying to get him to acknowledge her outfit.

"Yeah, I'm glad too. I wouldn't want you to be uncomfortable." Rolling her eyes as he opened the door for her, she got in.

"So where you wanna go?"

"Excuse me? You asked me out, not the other way around." Farrah was confused.

"I know I did. I just figured you might want to go somewhere special."

"I thought you had something special planned."

"Nah, I changed my mind. So where you wanna go?"

"Wherever you want to is fine with me." She sucked her teeth.

"All right then. Let's go to the movies."

"*To the movies?* Do I look like I'm dressed for the movies?"

"You said you were cool with wherever I want to go. I want to go to the show. There's a new Martin Lawrence movie out I want to see."

"Whatever. Let's just go so we can hurry up and get this thing over with." Halfway to the theater, Mills made another suggestion.

"You know what, I don't feel like going to the show tonight after all. Let's go to the old crib and chill," he exhaled, smoking a blunt.

"You mean our old apartment?" Farrah said, fanning the air, mad that the weed smoke might get into her clothes.

"Yeah, let's just kick back, watch TV, and order a pizza."

"Are you fuckin' kidding me?" she asked, ready to go off.

"Do I have to remind you about what you said?"

"No!"

Farrah couldn't believe the outcome of their date. Mills never ceased to surprise her. This wouldn't be the first time he completely messed up their date. Mills was conceited, selfish, and inconsiderate. How she ever found him attractive, she would never know. She cursed herself for allowing herself to fall for him. Pulling up to their loft building, Farrah sat with her arms crossed. She was pissed.

"What's wrong? You mad?" Mills asked, trying his damndest not to laugh.

"Shut up. Stop talkin' to me," she snapped.

"My bad. You coming or what?"

"You're not going to open the door for me?"

"You got two hands, don't you?"

"Ughh!" Farrah hopped out of the car and stomped up the steps behind him. As she followed him, she contemplated pulling one of her old moves and calling a taxi to come pick her up. Opening up the front door, he grabbed Farrah's hand before he could grab her phone.

"Don't touch me," she yelled as he pulled her into the building. Stepping into the loft, Farrah found a completely empty living room filled with thousands of pink and red rose petals scattered across the floor and a candlelit table set for two. Over twenty tea candles were lit around the room as Anthony Hamilton's "Since I Seen't You" played in the background. The only thing Farrah could do was smile. She was so overwhelmed.

"You said whatever I wanted to do was fine with you, so I'm here to let you know that the only thing I want tonight is to be alone with you so we can spend some quality time together," he said sincerely.

"I can't believe you did all of this for me," she said, blushing.

"I told you that I wanted to take care of you. What, you thought I was bullshittin'?" Leading her over to the table, Mills took her purse and helped her into her chair. Sitting across from her, he called out for the chef that he hired for the night.

"Good evening. I am Patrick, your chef. Tonight I have prepared a three-course meal for you. First we will start off with grilled marinated shrimp, served on a bed of polenta with a spicy pepper sauce. For the main course we have shrimp and bay scallops sautéed with garlic, tomato, white wine, arugula, and basil served over spaghetti. And to top that off, for dessert, I have prepared for you my world-famous chocolate-caramel cheesecake."

"Wow, sounds good to me."

"Thank you, Patrick," Mills said.

"You're welcome, sir. Your appetizers will be out shortly."

"I don't know about the garlic, your breath gonna be stanking," Mills teased.

"Man, you eating the same thing," she laughed. "But anyway, my breath won't be stinking because I always carry a toothbrush with me."

"For what? I wasn't gonna kiss you," he laughed.

"Ahh, that's messed up. I still can't get over all of this." She glanced around the room at the candles, roses, and table.

"Your man has never done anything like this for you?"

"I don't want to talk about him," she answered, caught off guard by the mention of J.R.

"I got yo' ass, didn't I?"

"Yes, you did."

"You should've seen your face. You were pissed off." He laughed and Farrah remembered how much she liked the sound of his laugh. It was a deep baritone laugh that could fill up a room.

"I was 'cause you were getting on my nerves."

"See, I was just tryin' to surprise you. You feel stupid don't you?"

"You ain't got to rub it in."

"Yes, I do," Mills laughed as Patrick brought out their appetizers.

The two fed each other in silence as they gazed into each other's eyes. Farrah was having a great time. Mills had never done anything like this before and neither had J.R. It really seemed like Mills was finally taking notice of the things Farrah wanted a man to do for her and he was taking action. After dessert Farrah excused herself to the bathroom. Standing in front of the sink, after brushing her teeth, she examined her face in the mirror. Pleased with the way she looked, she rejoined Mills in the living room.

"So are you enjoying yourself?"

"Yes, I am."

"Lets act like we don't know each other. Tell me something about yourself that most people don't know about you."

"Um, let me think . . . I love kids. I want to have a big family. Family and friends mean the world to me."

"How many kids do you want to have?"

"Maybe three or four, it all depends."

"Depends on what?"

"If I find the right man or not, plus I heard labor pains are a muthafucker."

Laughing at her last statement, Mills asked, "And who is the right man for you?"

"He has to be smart, sexy, funny, a little thuggish, loving, caring, attentive, respectful, and honest. Oh, and it doesn't hurt if he's good in bed," she laughed.

"So let me guess: The man you're with don't have none of those qualities. Because if he did, you wouldn't be here with me." Looking away, she tried not to show how she really felt, but was unable to. All of the pent-up frustration she had felt over the past year began to spill out of her. Turning her head and wiping the tears from her eyes, she tried not to let Mills see her cry.

"It's okay ma, I got you," he said, hugging her.

"I'm cool." Farrah pushed him away. She hated that she was showing her weaknesses, especially in front of this man. Mills was doing and saying all the right things, but it was impossible for her to tell if he was being sincere this time. She didn't want to be made a fool of again.

"Come here." He took her hand, guiding her into the middle of the floor.

"What are you doing?"

"Shh, just chill." Wrapping his arms around her waist, they danced to Donny Hathaway's, "I Love You More Than You'll Ever Know".

"I'm sorry for pushing you away."

"It's cool." He stroked her hair.

"I hate that you're making me feel so calm right now."

"Why? That's a good thing."

"Nothing in my life has ever been calm. I don't know how to react when things are going good."

"Look, I ain't out to hurt or lie to you. If you haven't noticed, I love your ass like crazy."

She flashed him a smile of contentment and laid her head on his chest as they swayed together in sync.

"Ay, blow out those candles for me," Mills asked, letting her go as the song went off. At first she was about to throw another hissy fit, but after taking another glance around the room she thought different. Mills went through all the trouble to set up a private dinner for her in his house; the least she could do was blow out some candles.

"You know the words to this song mean a lot to me," he said as the song played again.

"They do?" she asked, surprised.

"Yeah, every time I listen to it, I think of you," he said as he lit the fireplace.

"I don't know what to say."

"You ain't got to say nothing ma, it's cool. I'm just letting you know that I never stopped loving you."

"I never stopped loving you either, Mills." Farrah turned around and smiled at him. She knew she was getting caught up in the moment, but she was saying the truth. A part of her never stopped loving him.

"To be honest with you, I have been thinking about you a lot lately. I just want to spend all my time with you."

"Oh, so you want to spend all your time with me, huh?" Farrah replied.

"Yeah. I told you I want to be your man again," he said, watching her stop to pick up a light blue box in front of one the candles.

"What's this?"

"Open it." Biting down on her lip, she opened up the Tiffany box to find a diamond and platinum tennis bracelet.

"Mills!" Farrah exclaimed with her mouth wide open.

"I know we're not officially back together, but I wanted to give you something special. I don't expect you to give an answer right this second, but I want us to be back together. I promise to do all I can to be the man you deserve."

Feeling like she was going to pass out, Farrah sat down on the floor to catch her breath. She didn't know what to do. Things were beginning to get out of control between her and Mills. She was so confused about how to interpret everything that was happening. She was just supposed to be spending time with Mills to keep her occupied—not to get back into a relationship with him. Thoughts of J.R. entered her mind, and her heart felt like it was about to burst. She felt torn between two lovers.

"*Whaaat?* Somebody shut up Farrah?" Mills teased, sitting down in front of her.

"This is moving too fast for me."

"I know; it's moving fast for me too, but I can't help the way I feel, Farrah. I see you sitting here trying to be strong, but you don't have to do that. I got you and the quicker you admit it the better off you'll be." He stroked her cheek.

"I guess . . ." She trembled at his touch.

"Nah, you know." Mills kissed her lips roughly as Alicia Keys's "Diary" echoed throughout the room.

Mills placed his body on top of hers as he ran his tongue in circles across her neck. Farrah moaned. Caressing her breasts with his hand, he used the other to pull the straps of her dress down. Farrah was all too ready to get dick downed. After removing her dress, Mills planted small kisses all over her body.

Once he stopped at her thong, he looked up at her and gently removed them from her curvaceous hips. Surprised but pleased to see that her clit was swollen and extremely wet, he smiled. Taking his hand, Mills massaged her clit with his thumb. Not able to control herself anymore, Farrah began rotating her hips to Mills's rhythm.

Removing his thumb, he began to flick her clit with his tongue. Shivering shots of electricity coursed through her body. In absolute heaven, Farrah screamed from sheer ecstasy. Mills sucked her throbbing clit like there was no tomorrow, swirling his tongue up, down, from side to side, and around. Nearing her first orgasm, Farrah grabbed his head, begging for mercy. Not letting up, he inserted two fingers inside while still sucking her clit. Cumming in his mouth, Mills enjoyed the taste of her sweet juices.

Whimpering and moaning, she sucked his bottom lip. She wanted to taste the rest of him, so she licked his neck while she rubbed his back. She felt eager to get reacquainted with his body. Once she released the tool that was made to please her, he was completely naked.

Positioning herself between his legs, Farrah laid on top of him. In her hand was the one thing that she craved the most. Lowering her head, she placed her lips around the tip of his mammoth dick. She ran her tongue around the tip; then, while holding the shaft, she bobbed up and down. Her hand was her guide as she sucked his dick until his body began to convulse.

Knowing what this meant, she eased up, looked at him with lust in her eyes, and kissed him. Mills kissed her back so passionately, he began to scare himself. Taking control again, he placed himself in between Farrah's thighs. With one swift move he was inside of her. He pushed deep inside her vaginal walls as he gripped her waist and slid all the way to her soul.

"Ahh!" Farrah yelled as her eyes rolled into the back of her head and she tried to jerk her hips away from him.

Grabbing her hips to keep her from moving, Mills said, "You gon' quit fighting me now?"

"No," she said, knowing her response would make Mills work harder at what he was trying to accomplish. Mills laughed and placed her feet on his shoulders. Lifting her ass off the floor, he thumbed Farrah's clit and began pounding harder and deeper into her pussy—a pussy that was a perfect fit for his dick.

"You gon' quit fighting me now?"

"Yes, baby, yes," Farrah moaned in ecstasy as Mills's movements became faster. She grabbed his ass, wanting to cum with him. Their bodies moved together as they both came. After the mind-blowing orgasms, they were both drenched in sweat.

"Good," Mills said as he kissed her lips.

Chapter 29

You don't love me like you used to.
                    -Brandy, "U Don't Know Me
                            (Like U Used To)"

"Where you going?" Jade asked, walking into Mills's private bathroom.

"Out," he answered, not even bothering to look in her direction.

"Out where?" Jade snapped back.

"Why?" He screwed up his face and brushed his hair.

"'Cause I wanna know, that's why. What, you got something to hide?" Jade folded her arms across her chest.

"Nope," Mills said, grinning.

"You think this shit is funny? It's a fuckin' Tuesday night. Where are you going?" Jade shot.

"Out wit' my homeboy Shawn. You don't know him," Mills answered, lying.

"Yeah, I don't know him 'cause Shawn's ass probably a girl and her name is probably Shawna. I keep on telling you I'm not new to this shit," Jade scoffed.

"Well, like always, you're wrong. I'm not fucking with no other woman but you."

"Yeah and I'm boo-boo the fool. I don't give a fuck what you do as long as you're not fuckin' with Farrah."

"Why not Farrah?" Mills questioned.

"'Cause I don't like that bitch and I know she got the potential to take you from me."

"Ain't nobody taking me away from you. I keep tellin' you that," Mills assured.

"Mmm-hmm," Jade yawned, knowing damn well he was lying.

"I'm dead serious." Mills placed his arms around her waist. "You my baby. You gon' always be my number one."

"Yeah, until the next bitch wit' a pretty face comes along."

"No true," Mills objected.

"Okay, if it's not true, then stay at home with me," Jade challenged.

"I can't. I got somewhere I need to be." Mills turned back around and began grooming his face.

"Let me find out you fuckin' with Farrah again and I swear to god it's a wrap. Me and Jaysin will be up outta here so fast it'll make your head spin. As a matter of fact, now I don't want you to go," she spat with an attitude.

"What?" Mills looked at her through the mirror like she was crazy.

"You heard me. Stay yo' ass at home."

"You buggin'." Mills chuckled, not taking her seriously.

"I'm not playin'." Jade grabbed his keys off the bathroom counter. "You not going."

"Give me back my keys, man. I ain't got time to be playin' wit' you." Mills held out his hand, not in the mood.

"No!" She held them even tighter.

Mills glared at Jade, highly annoyed. This was just like the time she'd held him up from meeting with Farrah almost two years before. Him and Jade were barely a couple anymore and it was obvious she had somebody on the side, but the second it seemed Mills had found somebody it was a problem for her. Mills didn't have time to stand there and argue with her tonight. He was tired of this crazy cycle. He wasn't trying to go through all of that again.

"Mills . . . Mills!" Jade yelled, bringing him out of his thoughts. "I know you hear me!"

"I'ma tell you one more time before I have to fuck you up. Give me back my goddamn keys!" Mills snatched them from her hand.

"Think it's a game? You're not going!" Jade shouted, trying to figure out her next move.

It was déjà vu. Farrah was dressed to the nines. Her hair was curled and expertly pinned up to cascade down the left side of her face. She wore a black jersey spaghetti-strap maxi-dress that clung to her breasts, hips, and thighs as if it were a second skin on her. The last thing she should have been doing was waiting on Mills to show up for their date. He was supposed to be there by 8:00 and it was now 9:30. Life could not be repeating itself again. She just hoped and prayed that she wasn't waiting on Mills while he was out somewhere with Jade. It would kill her to think she had put herself in the same predicament she was in before. Farrah remembered the night vividly. She remembered how dumb she felt sitting around waiting for Mills. And how when he got there he had the nerve to be upset with her for having an attitude about his lateness. That nostaligic feeling came over her as she thought back to that night.

Just like tonight, she had spent hours preparing for their date. After waiting for what
seemed like days, he finally showed. Instead of
apologizing or even acknowledging his lateness,
he just strolled over the couch to sit. When
Farrah contronted him about how late he was,
it turned into a huge argument. After a long
and frustrating throw down between the two, it
ended up in a long night of passionate lovemak-
ing and dirty sex.

Sitting on her couch reminiscing on her and
Mills's past battles, Farrah unknowing fell asleep.
It was almost 6:00 in the morning when she woke
up still on her couch. Flabbergasted that it was
the next day and she was still home dressed in
her clothes, she checked her phone to see if Mills
had called. To her dismay he hadn't called or
texted. Farrah's heart sank to her feet. Mills had
completely stood her up.

Mills had a history of picking her up late or
canceling last minute, but he had never just not
shown up without giving so much as a phone
call or text to at least tell he couldn't make it. *I
am so fuckin' stupid,* she thought. Farrah had
somehow tricked herself into believing that
Mills had changed. She almost believed him
when he said he wouldn't hurt her anymore. But
maybe something had happened. Maybe he or

his daughter got sick and he couldn't call. *Yeah, that's it,* Farrah told herself.

Later on that day Farrah and London strolled through Forever 21. Farrah was a fashionista. She loved all of the big-name designers, but she was also a girl who loved nice clothes that didn't break the bank. She'd found multiple cute pieces to add to her closet, but Farrah couldn't fully concentrate on shopping. Her mind kept going back to Mills standing her up. Although she was mad at first, now she wanted to make sure he was okay.

All morning and early afternoon she'd been blowing up his phone. Like J.R., he wouldn't answer. She didn't know if he was hurt or if something bad had happened. She did know that she was worried sick. While London was in the dressing room trying on clothes, she tried calling him again.

After what seemed like a million rings, Mills's voice mail clicked in. Farrah didn't even bother to leave a message. She just wished he'd let her know he was okay. London came out of the dressing room and instantly knew something was wrong with Farrah. She looked like she was about to puke.

"Okay." London wrapped her arm around Farrah's shoulder. "What's wrong wit' you? Mama's here."

"I'm good. What you talking about?" Farrah tried to switch her attitude up.

"Farrah, don't lie to me. You know you can't hide shit. You wear your emotions on your face."

"Look, if I tell you, don't get to doing a bunch of extra shit, okay?" Farrah groaned.

"Scout's honor, as long as you ain't pregnant by that nigga."

"No, I'm not pregnant. We've only smashed once. Me and Mills had plans last night and he stood me up," Farrah said, looking down at the ground. She really didn't feel like looking at London's face because she knew she'd see disappointment all over it.

"Have you talked to him?" London quizzed.

"No, he won't answer the phone."

"Well, you haven't heard shit, so his ass ain't in the hospital or dead, so his ass okay. If some-thing had happened, we would have heard it on the radio or seen it on the news. He's just on some bullshit. He probably with another chick," London revealed, not knowing how much her words stabbed Farrah in the heart.

"You think he was with Jade?"

"What, you don't?" London asked, mockingly. Farrah sighed.

"I know you don't actually believe that he's stopped fuckin' with other bitches, especially Jade?"

"I mean, we never discussed it. I just assumed."

"Well, you know what they say about assuming. You make an ass outta yourself. Girl, yes, he's still fuckin' with her and they still stay together. You have officially been reduced from being the wife to the mistress," London stated bluntly.

"Damn," was all Farrah could reply.

Chapter 30

Know I love you more.
                    -Miley Cyrus, "Adore You"

Rihanna's "Photographs" played softly. Farrah sat solemnly on her living room floor looking at pictures. She had called out of work and had been sitting there for the most part of the morning. Pictures were scattered all over the carpet and she sat Indian-style at the center of it. A million tears flooded her face. Each tear felt like scorching hot lava sliding on her cheeks. She felt as if her heart had been torn in half. In one hand she held a picture of her and J.R. all hugged up. It was taken the night they shared their first kiss during his concert. She had just finished dressing him for his performance and he told her he wanted to take a picture to capture them looking young, so they could show their grandkids. Farrah found it amusing that he was talking about them having grandkids considering they weren't even together, but agreed to take the picture anyway.

She missed him with every fiber of her being. It had been weeks since they'd talked and she wished to God that she could just hear his voice again. But he had made it clear in his voice mail that he was completely done with her and she had no choice but to respect that. She had messed up in the worst way possible and that was something she could never take back.

In the other hand, she held a picture of her and Mills the night he proposed. She had her backside leaning up against him and he had his arms wrapped around her as he tenderly kissed her cheek. That night was one of the most unforgettable nights of her life. Mills finally proposing was supposed to be the beginning to their happily-ever-after. The second she put that ring on her finger, her life felt complete. She was officialy engaged to the man she loved. The man she would lovingly spend the rest of her life with. Everything was falling into place for her. Her business was in high gear, she had finally cut all the drama out of her life, and now she had a wedding to plan for. But that blissful feeling was short-lived when Mills's indiscretions came to light and her world was turned upside down. Now here she sat, crying in her living room; alone and heartbroken. Two days had gone by since Mills stood her up and he still hadn't called or so much as texted.

A loud knock coming from her front door startled her out of her trance. She forgot she had ordered Chinese food half an hour ago. She stuffed the pictures back inside the box they had come out of and walked toward her computer to turn the music down. Afterwards, she grabbed her purse and opened the door.

She was surprised to see Mills standing outside of her door.

"What are you doing here? How'd you know I was home?" she asked as she turned and walked back to her living room.

"I went by your office and London told me you decided to stay home," he explained. He pulled the door behind him and followed Farrah into the living room. "She didn't want to talk to me at first, but I got it out of her."

"Oh, okay. What is it? What do you want?" she asked nonchalantly.

"My bad about the other night. I got caught up," he answered.

"Caught up with who, exactly?" Farrah quizzed with an attitude.

"Who said I was with somebody?" Mills questioned.

"Just tell me, Was it Jade? Were you with her?" Farrah asked, not in the mood for a bunch of games.

"Yeah," Mills answered, tired of lying.

"Thanks for telling me the truth. Now you can turn around and get out."

"What?" Mills furrowed his brow.

"You heard me. Leave."

"A'ight." Mills shrugged and started to walk away.

"Wait," Farrah exclaimed. "I can't do this anymore!" she said as she burst out in tears.

"I can't either, Farrah," Mills said. He walked over to her and she buried her face in his chest. "I'm sorry," Mills whispered at her.

"I never meant to hurt you like this," was all he could say. Too much had happened between them and after all was said and done, he was out of words. He took her head in his hands and lifted her face toward his. He wiped her tears and leaned down to kiss her forehead.

"*Da fuck?* So you leave me all these messages about how you miss me and you fucked up, but you still hugged up on this chump-ass nigga?"

Farrah jumped back at the sound of J.R.'s voice. For a split second Farrah thought she was hearing things. *Lord, please don't let me lose my mind. I've lost too much already,* she thought to herself. But when she turned her head she felt relieved and scared to see J.R. standing in by the door. She was overcome with emotions.

"J.R.!" she exclaimed. "It's not what you think. It's not what it looks like." She tried to explain.

"Nah Farrah, it's cool. You ain't need to explain shit to me. I'ma just walk away from this. I can't be dealing with a fucked-up bitch like you," he spat.

J.R. had let himself in when he saw that her door wasn't closed all the way. He had never expected to walk in and find Farrah with Mills cuddled up and in her own apartment. He was disapointed and his heart felt heavy. For weeks he had tortured himself thinking about this woman and it was obvious he wasn't a thought in her mind. He had tried to just walk away from her after the stunt she pulled by running off with Corey Mills, but as much as he fought against his feelings, he couldn't stop caring for her. From the day he saw her at the club he had felt something for her that he had never felt for any other woman. The last few weeks not seeing or talking to her had been torture for him. Everything reminded him of her. He missed hearing her laugh and flirting with him over the phone. He missed the way she would joke around with him and the silly faces she made. He especially missed how good it felt when she nestled her head on his chest after they made love; and the way she'd scream his name when she was about to cum. After realizing how much he missed and loved her, he took the first flight out of L.A. and decided he'd give her another chance. Now, all he wanted was to leave and never see her again. It hurt him to see her with Mills, but he wasn't about to stand there and show it.

"Who da fuck are you calling a chump moth-afucka?" Mills asked as he shoved J.R. from behind.

J.R. lost his balance and stumbled forward. He put his hands out in front to stop from hitting the wall. J.R. crouched down and positioned himself to jerk up and land a perfect uppercut on Mills. It happened so fast Mills never saw it coming. Mills's body flew and crashed onto Farrah's living room coffee table. Glass shattered everywhere as Mills got right back up and tackled J.R. to the floor.

Farrah was frozen in place. It was like everything was happening in slow motion. The shock of what was happening was holding her hostage. She wanted to yell out for them to stop, but she couldn't move. She just stood there watching two guys beating each other up and it was all her fault. *How did I let it get to this?* she questioned herself. She had to put a stop to this madness. Then from deep within, she heard a stern voice saying, *This has gone on long enough, Farrah.*

It's time for you to be strong. And just like that, she found her courage and her body snapped out of its paralyzed state.

"*Stop it!*" she yelled out. "*Please! Stop fighting!*" Both men stopped mid-punch and she quickly jumped in between the two and split them apart. Now Farrah found herself standing in the middle of both men and she knew she had to make a final decision. She knew that with her decision, one of these men would walk out of her life forever.

"Farrah, let this nigga know you love me and he ain't got no business being here!" Mills spat. His left eye was swollen and blood poured from his mouth.

"Look Farrah, I need to know if we gon' make this work or not," J.R. said as his hands went back and forth between him and Farrah.

Farrah looked at J.R., then at Mills, then back at J.R. Both men had eager expressions on their faces. She closed her eyes and said a silent prayer asking God to help her make a choice. She could hear both men breathing heavily, trying to catch their breaths. *Just make sure whatever you decide, you're happy. Don't ever sell yourself short* were the words that came to mind. With that, Farrah knew what she had to do. She knew who her heart belonged to.

Keisha Ervin

She needed this man as bad as she needed air to breathe. He was the man of her dreams. He was the man who God had sent to her from up above. And even though she didn't think she deserved him, she damn sure wanted to win the honor of being called his lady. She wanted to prove that she was worthy of his love. He was her king and he deserved to be treated as such.

This was the man she could not live without. The man she wanted to give her heart, body, and soul to. She opened her eyes, turned her head, and looked at him.

"I choose you," she said the moment their eyes met.

Epilogue

Once I figured it out,
you were right here all along.
    —Justin Timberlake, "Mirrors"

"And that's the story of how me and your Paw-Paw met." Farrah closed the photo book.

"Dang, Granny. You was what y'all call it back in the day . . . ratchet," Ross joked, laughing.

"Hush up John Ross." Farrah couldn't help but laugh too.

"But seriously, Granny, everything gon' be straight. Paw-Paw wouldn't want you to be sad."

"I know. I just miss him so much. J.R. was my heart." Farrah gazed down lovingly at her wedding ring.

"He's here wit' you though, 'cause guess what? He's right here in your heart." John Ross pointed to his grandmother's chest.

"You're a sweet boy." Farrah pinched her grandson's cheek. "You look more and more like your Paw-Paw everyday."

"I'm tellin' you, they be on me, Granny." John Ross popped his collar.

"You so silly," Farrah giggled.

"Come on, Granny," John Ross said, standing up. "Let's finish packin'."